THE NEW FABER BOOK OF LOVE POEMS

James Fenton was born in Lincoln in 1949 and educated at Magdalene College, Oxford, where he won the Newdigate Prize for poetry. He has worked as political journalist, drama critic, book reviewer, war correspondent, foreign correspondent and columnist. He is a Fellow of the Royal Society of Literature and was Oxford Professor of Poetry for the period 1994–99. His *Selected Poems* was published in 2006.

The New Faber Book of
Love Poems

Edited by JAMES FENTON

faber and faber

First published in 2006
by Faber and Faber Limited
3 Queen Square London WC1N 3AU
This paperback edition first published in 2008

Photoset by RefineCatch Ltd, Bungay, Suffolk
Printed in England by Mackays of Chatham, plc

A CIP record for this book
is available from the British Library

ISBN 978-0-571-21815-8

10 9 8 7 6 5 4 3 2 1

CONTENTS

Love Poetry: An Introduction, xxv

[viii]

[xii]

[xviii]

'I have believed for a long time,' says Michael Longley in a note to his own recent gathering, 'that love poetry is at the core of the enterprise: if poetry is a wheel, then the hub of the wheel is love poetry. Poems that articulate all the other cares and attachments – children, family, friends, heroes, the dead, country, countryside, animals, art – radiate from the hub like spokes in a wheel.'[1] Another way of putting this: the short lyric that says 'I love you' is like the little black cocktail dress – no couture collection should be without such classics. No poetry collection either.

I love you. You love me. I used to love you. You don't love me. I want to sleep with you. Here we are in bed together. I hate you. You betrayed me. I've betrayed you. I want to kill you. Oh no! I *have* killed you. Such are the simple propositions on which these lyrics elaborate. Such are the situations they evoke. A lyric poem, typically, expresses an intense feeling of the moment, and the truth of the poem consists of its truth to that moment. It is all about the subjective, all about the here and now. It is not – alas for the loved one – a contract, or a prenuptial agreement.

Another thing about lyrical poetry: it has a close historical affinity with music. This does not mean that all or even the majority of the poems in this collection can be or have been set to music. But it does mean that they are not far from that possibility, and a few indeed are song lyrics which can only be fully appreciated with their musical settings in mind. A song has to be simple, both to be singable and to be understood in the course of performance. So a large number of these poems are simple too.

The period covered is that of the modern English language. This means I have not looked before Thomas Wyatt, in whose period the roughly comprehensible modern English language begins. Of course my cut-off point excludes many beauties, such as the anonymous early fourteenth-century quatrain:

Al night by the rosë, rosë,
Al night bi the rose I lay,
Dorst Ich nought the rosë stele,
And yet I bar the flour away.[2]

And it excludes such attractive poets as Charles of Orleans, a century later, the French poet captured at the Battle of Agincourt in 1415, and held prisoner in England until 1440, to whom such love poems as this are attributed:

My gostly fader, I me confesse,
    First to God and then to you,
        That at a window – wot ye how? –
I stale a cosse of grete sweetness,
Which don was out avisèness;
    But hit is doon not undoon now.
My gostly fader, I me confesse,
    First to God and then to you.

But I restore it shall doutless
    Agein, if so be that I mow;
        And that to Good I make a vow
And elles I axè foryefness.
My gostly fader, I me confesse,
    First to God and then to you.[3]

This is very nearly comprehensible, with a little guess-work. (The punctuation supplied by the editors helps.) But 'gostly fader' is some way from 'spiritual father', and 'I stale a cosse' from 'I stole a kiss.' By contrast, I think that most of the poetry in this book can be understood without notes.

A sort of discretion on the part of our broad-minded grammar allows us to use the words I and You without specifying the gender of either the first or the second person. This means that in many cases a love poem addressed by a man to a woman may serve as well to express the feelings of a woman for a man, or a man for a man, or a woman for a woman. Anyway, we have imaginations and we have the power of sympathy, so it seems that any of these situations can excite our interest. 'Don't ask, don't tell' is the motto under which much love poetry is written, or as Campion puts it:

You may do in the dark
What the day doth forbid.
Fear not the dogs that bark.
Night will have all hid.

Traditionally, love poetry is in favour of love's success, and unconcerned about the morality of the liaisons it promotes. Morality might indeed be seen as the enemy of the enterprise, unwelcome as the returning husband is unwelcome, or the sun at the window.

It is striking that at the heart of our tradition we have famous poems about which intrusive questions have been asked in vain. What precisely is the experience evoked by Shakespeare's sonnets? The passionate love of a man for a man is there at the centre of it, but what is meant by this love? Is it sexual? How far does it go? We know that around the end of the sixteenth and the beginning of the seventeenth century, these poems were in private circulation, and that they were published in 1609 without, as far as we can tell, causing any great scandal. Somehow, the way the poet was addressing a man appears to have been acceptable both in private and in public.

But by 1640 it seems that this was no longer the case, because in that year an edition of Shakespeare's poems had begun changing the sex of pronouns in order to imply that the addressee was always a woman. There followed centuries of neglect and disapproval, during which such authors as could bear to address themselves to the question of Shakespeare's feelings for the young man came up with ingenious solutions: Coleridge thought that the sonnets 'could only have come from a man deeply in love, and in love with a woman.' Where the evidence of the text made this construction impossible, Coleridge detected 'a purposed blind' – that is, a deliberate attempt to mislead the reader.[4]

Tennyson, who was much under the influence of Shakespeare's sonnets when he wrote *In Memoriam*, felt able to speak passionately of his feelings for his dead friend Arthur Hallam, to an extent that undoubtedly did seem to some of his contemporaries to verge on the unwise. But what an enviable freedom he allowed himself to express his overwhelming emotions, so that he can compare himself to a wife or widow, without letting himself be cramped by fear of misconstruction. He speaks to his friend's shade in a language which belongs to poetry, not to daily conversation, and of the line 'O, wast thou with me, dearest, then' he remarked 'If anybody thinks I ever called him "dearest" in his life they are much mistaken, for I never even called him "dear".'

Tennyson believed that, as he put it in a notebook jotting, 'Men should be androgynous and women gynandrous, but men should not be gynandrous nor women androgynous,' and in a poem entitled 'On One Who Affected an Effeminate Manner':

> While man and woman still are incomplete,
> I prize that soul where man and woman meet,
> Which types all Nature's male and female plan,
> But, friend, man-woman is not woman-man.

No doubt it was this clear sense of what was appropriate and what not, in the matter of male androgyny, that enabled Tennyson to write as he did, and to share Arthur Hallam's love of Shakespeare's sonnets. Benjamin Jowett said of Tennyson that

> . . . perhaps in his weaker moments, he had thought of Shakespeare as happier in having the power to draw himself for his fellow men, and used to think Shakespeare greater in his sonnets than in his plays. But he soon returned to the thought which is indeed the thought of all the world. He would have seemed to me to be reverting for a moment to the great sorrow of his own mind. It would not have been manly or natural to have lived in it always. But in that

peculiar phase of mind he found the sonnets a deeper expression of the never to be forgotten love which he felt more than any of the moods of many minds which appear among his dramas. The love of the sonnets which he so strikingly expressed was a sort of sympathy with Hellenism.[5]

Christopher Ricks points out that when the poet's son reproduced this passage in his memoir of his father, he cut out the last sentence and the one beginning 'It would not have been manly'.

What had happened, once again, was that a poetry which had been acceptable in 1850, when *In Memoriam* was published, had begun to seem perhaps a little vulnerable in 1897 when Hallam Tennyson published his memoir, while the word 'Hellenism' clearly set alarm bells ringing.

The case of Whitman may seem quite unmysterious: surely here if anywhere we find male homosexual love quite positively trumpeted, especially in the poems I have selected, which come mainly from 'Calamus', one of the more scandalous sections of *Leaves of Grass*. But Whitman was speaking in his role as Universal Man, or, as Auden put it, the Epic Bard of America. Auden said: '[Whitman] keeps using the first person singular and even his own name, but these stand for a *persona*, not an actual human being, even when he appears to be talking about his most intimate experiences.'[6] We may feel that he has revealed rather a lot about himself as a human being, more perhaps than he intended. But there is a difference of kind between the fraternalism of 'We Two Boys Together Clinging' and, say, Hart Crane's Cavafy-like 'Episode of Hands,' which in my judgment is pretty certainly to be understood as heading toward the bedroom.

Emily Dickinson has appeared in at least two anthologies of homosexual poetry, with lyrics such as the following:

Going – to – Her!
Happy – Letter! Tell Her –
Tell Her – the page I never wrote!

Tell Her, I only said – the Syntax –
And left the Verb and the Pronoun – out!
Tell Her just how the fingers – hurried –
Then – how they – stammered – slow – slow –
And then – you wished you had eyes – in your pages –
So you could see – what moved them – them – so –

Tell Her – it wasn't a practised writer –
You guessed –
From the way the sentence – toiled –
You could hear the Boddice – tug – behind you –
As if it held but the might of a child!
You almost pitied – it – you – it worked so –
Tell Her – No – you may quibble – there –
For it would split Her Heart – to know it –
And then – you and I – were silenter!

Tell Her – Day – finished – before we – finished –
And the old Clock kept neighing – 'Day'!
And you – got sleepy – and begged to be ended –
What could – it hinder so – to say?
Tell Her – just how she sealed – you – Cautious!
But – if she ask 'where you are hid' – until the evening –
Ah! Be bashful!
Gesture Coquette –
And shake your Head!

The idiom of this poem is that of the *envoi*, the traditional address of the poet to his poem or book before sending it out into the world, and at first sight it looks just as one might expect a discreet, even secretive, lesbian love poem of the nineteenth century to look. A part of this effect comes from the punctuation, which seems to suggest gasps of excitement, and then there is the reference to the tug of the bodice, which strikes one as very intimate and between-women.

Here is the same poem as it appears in R. W. Franklin's authoritative one-volume 'reading edition' of Dickinson's complete poems:

Going to Him! Happy letter!
Tell Him –
Tell Him the page I didn't write –
Tell Him – I only said the Syntax –
And left the Verb and the pronoun – out –
Tell him just how the fingers hurried –
Then – how they waded – slow – slow –
And then you wished you had eyes in your pages –
So you could see what moved them so –

Tell Him – it wasn't a Practised Writer –
You guessed – from the way the sentence toiled –
You could hear the Boddice tug, behind you –
As if it held but the might of a child –
You almost pitied it – you – it worked so –
Tell Him – No – you may quibble there –
For it would split His Heart, to know it –
And then you and I, were silenter.

Tell Him – Night finished – before we finished –
And the Old Clock kept neighing 'Day'!
And you – got sleepy –
And begged to be ended –
What would it hinder so – to – say?
Tell Him – just how she sealed you – Cautious!
But – if He ask where you are hid
Until tomorrow – Happy letter!
Gesture Coquette – and shake your Head!

This is very confusing, and to make matters worse it turns out that there were originally three manuscript versions of this poem, of which only two survive. The lost version began 'Going to them, happy letter!' and presumably spoke of 'them' throughout. The second, 'Going – to Her!', dates from early 1862, and is on embossed notepaper and signed Emily. The third is dated by Franklin, in his three-volume variorum edition, to 'about late summer' of the same year. Also on embossed paper, and also signed Emily, it is the version Franklin prefers for his one-volume edition, since it is the poet's last word on the matter, her last version. She had prepared it as if to be delivered to someone, but had never sent it, and it remained among her papers.

So what are we to say about the poem now? Was there a 'purposed blind', and if so in which direction? Did it begin as a poem about writing for the public, and wishing to explain how unsatisfactory one's attempts seem? Or did it begin as a poem with a female reader in mind, who then gets obliterated in favour of a more conventional male? Or is the poem, through the different versions, working its way towards expressing its true biographical impulse, that something had been written for a man, who must never be allowed to know the full history of its composition? Or is the whole situation of the poem imagined – a fiction?

Sometimes a poem is itself a riddle, and that is what Dickinson seems to have intended her poems to be. Sometimes a poem is in code, in the sense that a section, but only a section, of the readership is intended to get it. Here is Wilfred Owen, writing in the last year of his life:

I am the ghost of Shadwell Stair.
　　Along the wharves by the water-house,
　　And through the cavernous slaughter-house,
I am the shadow that walks there.

Yet I have flesh both firm and cool,
　　And eyes tumultuous as the gems
　　Of moons and lamps in the full Thames
When dusk sails wavering down the Pool.

Shuddering, a purple street-arc burns
　　Where I watch always. From the banks
　　Dolorously the shipping clanks.
And after me a strange tide turns.

> I walk till the stars of London wane,
>   And dawn creeps over Shadwell Stair.
>   But when the crowing sirens blare,
> I with another ghost am lain.

Scholars long ago noticed that Owen here was imitating the manner of Oscar Wilde in his 'Impression du Matin' and suggested that the 'ghost' of Owen's poem might be the same sort of street-walker as is found in that poem. Were this the intention, then perhaps the 'strange tide' that seems to follow the speaker of the poem might be her clients.

However, Owen's poem is one of several surviving works in which the poet is clearly trying to communicate a personal experience of the homosexual underworld of London and Edinburgh. We can tell this, not simply by asking what Owen was up to on his nocturnal wanderings around the East End of London, and 'putting two and two together,' but from a remarkable piece of surviving evidence, in a letter from C. K. Scott Moncrieff, an acquaintance of Owen's and later the biographer of Proust, to Edward Marsh.

Scott Moncrieff, during the influenza epic of 1918, had tried turning 'I am the ghost of Shadwell Stair' into French rhymed prose, and he quotes the first verse of his translation: 'Je suis le petit revenant du Bassin; le long de quai, par l'abreuvoir, et dans l'immonde abbatoir j'y piétine, ombre fantassin.' As Dominic Hibberd pointed out, the ghost is little, like Owen himself (he was five foot five), and in the last word 'fantassin' is revealed to be an infantryman. According to Scott Moncrieff (who could of course conceivably have been lying about this), Owen welcomed the French version 'rather as tho' it put the key in the lock of the whole.'[7] The evidence suggests that Owen was writing for a *coterie*, and that his friend had understood his meaning. The ghost of Shadwell Stair is Owen himself, looking for (and finding) someone with whom to spend the night. The 'strange tide' is composed of fellow members of the sexual underworld.

A biographical mystery of another kind is provided by Wordsworth's Lucy poems, which are exceptional in his oeuvre as being plain love lyrics, but which have never been neatly accounted for. 'A slumber did my spirit seal,' one of this group, puzzled Coleridge, who wrote to a friend: 'Some months ago Wordsworth transmitted to me a most sublime epitaph – whether it had any reality, I cannot say. – Most probably, in some gloomier moment he had fancied the moment in which his sister might die.' That is, in modern language, he *imagined* the moment in which his sister might die. Coleridge has been criticised for expressing this thought, but he knew Wordsworth well, and had as much insight as anyone into the way poetry gets written.

Why should it not be the case that Dorothy 'sat for' the Lucy poems, in the way an artist's model might sit for a scene out of fiction? And why should not Wordsworth make a poem out of a gloomy instant in which he imagined himself striking his brow and saying: 'I must have been dreaming, I thought she would live forever and now she's dead!'? Who has not been visited by such thoughts, such fears? Who has not woken from such dreams? It might have been a feeling that passed in an instant. Then again, it might have been a morbid fear, a recurrent nightmare that could only be exorcised by the writing of the poem.

The case of Wordsworth reminds us that the Romantic poets are not, generally speaking, the most prolific of the love poets. Byron addresses the subject with style, but anger and recrimination are his great theme. Coleridge comes across more as a friend than as a lover. I am not surprised to find his 'Christabel' reprinted in Terry Castle's *The Literature of Lesbianism*, but it is too long for inclusion here. The great love poets of the Romantic period are undoubtedly Blake and Burns – both, by the way, having a deep affinity for music.

Blake, as J. T. Smith records, wrote many songs 'to which he also composed tunes. These he would occasionally sing to his friends; and though, according to his confession, he was entirely unacquainted with the science of music, his ear was so good, that his tunes were sometimes most singularly beautiful, and were noted down by musical professors.'[8] In later life, on his visits to the painter John Linnell's Hampstead farmhouse, Blake 'liked sitting in the arbour, at the bottom of the long garden, or walking up and down the same at dusk, while the cows, munching their evening meal, were audible from the farmyard on the other side of the hedge. He was very fond of hearing Mrs Linnell sing Scottish songs, and would sit by the pianoforte, tears falling from his eyes, while he listened to the Border Melody, to which the song is set, commencing

> O Nancy's hair is yellow as gowd,
> And her een as the lift are blue.

'To simple national melodies,' Gilchrist continues, 'Blake was very impressionable, though not so to music of more complicated structure. He himself sang, in a voice tremulous with age, sometimes old ballads, sometimes his own songs, to melodies of his own.'[9]

Blake's melodies, which he lacked the skill to write down, are all lost, but his ballad 'William Bond' is reprinted here, and is no doubt the kind of thing he would sing on such occasions. You will see also that among the selections from Tennyson are poems that were set to music later in the nineteenth century. And in the twentieth I have tried to suggest at least some of the ways in which music and poetry have agreed, not least by including some of the blues lyrics which proved so influential throughout the world, bringing their own characteristic set of symptoms and problems to the expression of love. Just as, when the earliest poets of the anthology were writing, the influence of the Troubadours and of the Italians was pervasive throughout Europe, so it has been in our own era with blues and jazz.

Alphabetical order is as useful a way as any of jumbling the poets up, so that they seem to speak to each other, and hear each other sing; as Auden heard Campion; as Blake would have heard Burns; as Tennyson heard Shakespeare; as Yeats heard

Blake; and instantly understood, and loved the other's melody, within this half millennium of song.

NOTES

1 Michael Longley, *The Rope-Makers*, Enitharmon Press, 2005.
2 from Harley Lyrics, cited in Paul Keegan (ed.), *The New Penguin Book of English Verse*, Penguin, 2000.
3 text as in *Early English Lyrics*, chosen by E. K. Chambers and F. Sidgwick, Sidgwick & Jackson, 1926.
4 cited in Katherine Duncan-Jones (ed.), *Shakespeare's Sonnets*, the Arden Shakespeare, 1997.
5 cited in Christopher Ricks, *Tennyson*, Collier Books, New York, 1972.
6 cited in James Fenton, *The Strength of Poetry*, Oxford, 2001, p. 171.
7 Dominic Hibberd, *Owen the Poet*, Macmillan, 1986, p. 155. The French version retranslates as: 'I am the little ghost of the dock. I tread the ground alongside the quay, by the watering-place, and in the filthy abbatoir – a shadow infantryman.'
8 J. T. Smith, *Nollekens and his Times*, second edn., London, 1829, vol. 2, p. 465.
9 Alexander Gilchrist, *Life of William Blake, Pictor Ignotus*, Harper Perennial, 2005, p. 313.

THE NEW FABER BOOK OF LOVE POEMS

Coupling

On the wall above the bedside lamp
a large crane-fly is jump-starting
a smaller crane-fly – or vice versa.
They do it tail to tail, like Volkswagens:
their engines must be in their rears.

It looks easy enough. Let's try it.

Incident

When you were lying on the white sand,
a rock under your head, and smiling,
(circled by dead shells), I came to you
and you said, reaching to take my hand,
'Lie down.' So for a time we lay
warm on the sand, talking and smoking,
easy; while the grovelling sea behind
sucked at the rocks and measured the day.
Lightly I fell asleep then, and fell
into a cavernous dream of falling.
It was all the cave-myths, it was all
the myths of tunnel or tower or well –
Alice's rabbit-hole into the ground,
or the path of Orpheus: a spiral staircase
to hell, furnished with danger and doubt.
Stumbling, I suddenly woke; and found
water about me. My hair was wet,
and you were lying on the grey sand
waiting for the lapping tide to take me:
watching, and lighting a cigarette.

Happy Ending

After they had not made love
she pulled the sheet up over her eyes
until he was buttoning his shirt:
not shyness for their bodies – those
they had willingly displayed – but a frail
endeavour to apologise.

Later, though, drawn together by
a distaste for such 'untidy ends'
they agreed to meet again; whereupon
they giggled, reminisced, held hands
as though what they had made was love –
and not that happier outcome, friends.

Accidental

We awakened facing each other
across the white counterpane.
I prefer to be alone in the mornings.
The waiter offered us
melon, papaya, orange juice or fresh raspberries.
We did not discuss it.

All those years of looking but not touching:
at most a kiss in a taxi.
And now this accident,
this blind unstoppable robot walk
into a conspiracy of our bodies.
Had we ruined the whole thing?

The waiter waited:
it was his business to appear composed.
Perhaps we should make it ours also?
We moved an inch or two closer together.

Our toes touched. We looked. We had decided.
Papaya then; and coffee and rolls. Of course.

Send-off

Half an hour before my flight was called
he walked across the airport bar towards me
carrying what was left of our future
together: two drinks on a tray.

Cripple Creek

I got a gal at the head of the creek,
Go up to see her 'bout the middle of the week,
Kiss her on the mouth, just as sweet as any wine,
Wraps herself around me like a sweet pertater vine.

Goin' up Cripple Creek, goin' in a run,
Goin' up Cripple Creek to have a little fun.
Goin' up Cripple Creek, goin' in a whirl,
Goin' up Cripple Creek to see my girl.

Girls on the Cripple Creek 'bout half grown,
Jump on a boy like a dog on a bone.
Roll my britches up to my knees,
I'll wade old Cripple Creek when I please.

Cripple Creek's wide and Cripple Creek's deep,
I'll wade old Cripple Creek afore I sleep,
Roads are rocky and the hillside's muddy
And I'm so drunk that I can't stand study.

Down in the Valley

Down in the valley, valley so low,
Hang your head over, hear the wind blow.
   Hear the wind blow, love, hear the wind blow,
   Hang your head over, hear the wind blow.

If you don't love me, love whom you please,
But throw your arms round me, give me heart ease.
   Give my heart ease, dear, give my heart ease.
   Throw your arms round me, give my heart ease.

Down in the valley, walking between,
Telling our story, here's what it sings:
Here's what it sings, dear, here's what it sings,
Telling our story, here's what it sings:

Roses of sunshine, vi'lets of dew,
Angels in heaven knows I love you,
Knows I love you, dear, knows I love you,
Angels in heaven knows I love you.

Build me a castle forty feet high,
So I can see her as she goes by,
As she goes by, dear, as she goes by,
So I can see her as she goes by.

Bird in a cage, love, bird in a cage,
Dying for freedom, ever a slave;
Ever a slave, dear, ever a slave,
Dying for freedom, ever a slave.

Write me a letter, send it by mail,
And back it in care of the Birmingham jail.
Birmingham jail, love, Birmingham jail,
And back it in care of the Birmingham jail.

Frankie and Albert

Frankie was a good woman,
Ev'rybody knows,
She spent a hundred dollars
For to buy her man some clothes.
He was her man,
But he done her wrong.

Frankie went a-walkin'
Did not go for fun,
Underneath her little red petticoat

She had Albert's forty-one.
    Gonna kill her man
    For doin' her wrong.

Frankie went to the barroom
Ordered her a glass of beer,
Says to the bartender,
'Has my lovin' man been here?
    He's my man,
    But he's doin' me wrong.'

'I will not tell you no story,
I will not tell you no lie, –
Albert left here about an hour ago
With a gal named Alice Fly.
    He's your man,
    But he's doin' you wrong.'

Frankie went by the house,
She did not give no 'larm,
She looked in through the window glass
And saw Albert in the woman's arms.
    He was her man, Lawd,
    Doin' her wrong.

When Albert, he saw Frankie,
For the backdoor, he did scoot,
Frankie drew that forty-four,
Went – *rooty-toot-toot-toot-toot!*
    She shot her man,
    For doin' her wrong.

First time she shot him, he staggered,
Next time she shot him, he fell,
Third time she shot him, O Lawdy,
There was a new man's face in hell.
    She killed her man,
    For doin' her wrong.

When Frankie, she shot Albert,
He fell all in a knot,
Cryin', 'O Mrs. Johnson,
See where your son is shot.
    She's killed your son,
    The only one.

'O turn me over doctor,
Turn me over slow,
I got a bullet in my lef' han' side,
Great God, is hurtin' me so.
    I was her man,
    But I done her wrong.'

Frankie went to Mrs. Johnson,
Fell down on her knees,
Cryin' 'O Mrs. Johnson,
Will you forgive me please?
    I kilt your son,
    The onlies' one.'

'I will forgive you Frankie,
I will forgive you not,
You shot my lovin' Albert,
The only support I'm got.
    Kilt my son,
    The only one.'

   Poor boy, poor boy,
   Poor boy, poor boy.
   Done gone, done gone,
   Done gone, done gone.

Frankie went to the graveyard,
Fell down on her knees, –
'Speak one word, Albert,
And give my heart some ease.
    You was my man,
    But you done me wrong.'

A rubber tir'ed buggy,
A decorated hack
Took po' Albert to the graveyard
But it didn't bring him back.
   He was her man,
   But he done her wrong.

Poor boy, poor boy,
Poor boy, poor boy.
Done gone, done gone,
Done gone, done gone.

Frankie looked down Main street,
Far as she could see,
All she could hear was a two string bow,
Playin' *Nearer My God to Thee*,
   All over town,
   Po' Albert's dead.

Frankie said to the sheriff,
'What do you think it'll be?'
The sheriff said, 'It looks jest like
Murder in the first degree,
   He was your man,
   But you shot him down.'

It was not murder in the first degree,
Nor murder in the third,
A woman simply dropped her man,
Like a hunter dropped a bird.
   She shot her man,
   For doin' her wrong.

Last time I saw Frankie
She was sittin' in the 'lectric chair,
Waitin' for to go and meet her God
With the sweat drippin' outa her hair.
   He was her man
   But he done her wrong.

Poor gal, poor gal,
Poor gal, poor gal.
Done gone, done gone,
Done gone, done gone.

Shady Grove

Shady grove, my true love,
Shady grove I know,
Shady grove, my true love,
I'm bound for the shady grove.

Peaches in the summertime,
Apples in the fall,
If I can't get the girl I love,
Won't have none at all.

Once I was a little boy,
Playin' in the sand,
Now I am a great big boy,
I think myself a man.

When I wus a little boy,
I wanted a whittlin' knife;
Now I am a great big boy
An' I want a little wife.

Wish I had a banjo string,
Made of golden twine,
And every tune I'd pick on it –
Is 'I wish that girl were mine.'

Some come here to fiddle en dance,
Some come here to tarry,
Somes come here to fiddle en dance,
I come here to marry.

Ev'ry night when I go home,
My wife, I try to please her,
The more I try, the worse she gets,
Damned if I don't leave her.

Shady grove, my little love,
Shady grove, my darlin',
Shady grove, my little love
Goin' back to Harlan.

Fly around, my blue-eyed girl,
Fly around, my daisy,
Fly around, my blue-eyed girl,
Nearly drive me crazy.

The very next time I go that road
And it don't look so dark and grazy,
The very next time I come that road
I'll stop and see my daisy.

I once had a mulie cow,
Mulie when she's born,
Took a jay-bird forty year
To fly from horn to horn.

Shenandoah

Missouri, she's a mighty river.
  Away, you rolling river.
The redskins' camp lies on its borders
  Ah ha I'm bound away, 'cross the wide Missouri.

The white man loved the Indian maiden,
  Away, you rolling river.
With notions his canoe was laden.
  Ah ha I'm bound away, 'cross the wide Missouri.

'O, Shenandoah, I love your daughter,'
  Away, you rolling river.
'I'll take her 'cross yon rolling water.'
  Ah ha I'm bound away, 'cross the wide Missouri.

The chief disdained the trader's dollars;
  Away, you rolling river.
'My daughter never you shall follow.'
  Ah ha I'm bound away, 'cross the wide Missouri.

At last there came a Yankee skipper,
  Away, you rolling river.
He winked his eye, and he tipped his flipper.
  Ah ha I'm bound away, 'cross the wide Missouri.

He sold the chief that fire-water,
  Away, you rolling river.
And 'cross the river he stole his daughter.
  Ah ha I'm bound away, 'cross the wide Missouri.

'O, Shenandoah, I long to hear you,'
  Away, you rolling river.
'Across that wide and rolling river.'
  Ah ha I'm bound away, 'cross the wide Missouri.

An Ever-Fixed Mark

Years ago, at a private school
Run on traditional lines,
One fellow used to perform
Prodigious feats in the dorm;
His quite undevious designs
Found many a willing tool.

On the rugger field, in the gym,
Buck marked down at his leisure
The likeliest bits of stuff;
The notion, familiar enough,
Of 'using somebody for pleasure'
Seemed handy and harmless to him.

But another chap was above
The diversions of such a lout;
Seven years in the place
And he never got to first base
With the kid he followed about:
What interested Ralph was love.

He did the whole thing in style –
Letters three times a week,
Sonnet-sequences, Sunday walks;
Then, during one of their talks,
The youngster caressed his cheek,
And that made it all worth while.

These days, for a quid pro quo,
Ralph's chum does what, and with which;
Buck's playmates, family men,
Eye a Boy Scout now and then.
Sex is a momentary itch,
Love never lets you go.

ANONYMOUS

'Western wind, when wilt thou blow'

Western wind, when wilt thou blow
   The small rain down can rain?
Christ, if my love were in my arms
   And I in my bed again!

'Like to a ring without a finger'

Like to a ring without a finger,
Or a bell without a ringer,
Like a horse was never ridden,
Or a feast and no guest bidden,
Like a well without a bucket,
Or a rose if no man pluck it,
   Just such as these may she be said
    That lives, not loves, but dies a maid.

The ring, if worn, the finger decks;
The bell pulled by the ringer speaks;
The horse does ease if he be ridden;
The feast doth please if guest be bidden;
The bucket draws the water forth;
The rose, when plucked, is still most worth:
   Such is the virgin in my eyes
    That lives, loves, marries ere she dies.

Like a stock not grafted on,
Or like a lute not played upon,
Like a jack without a weight,
Or a bark without a freight,
Like a lock without a key,
Or like a candle in the day,

Just such as these may she be said
That lives, not loves, but dies a maid.

The graffed stock doth bear best fruit;
There's music in the fingered lute;
The weight doth make the clock go ready;
The freight doth make the bark go steady;
The key the lock doth open right;
A candle's useful in the night:
    Such is the virgin in mine eyes
    That lives, loves, marries ere she dies.

Like a call without a Non-sir,
Or a question and no answer,
Like a ship was never rigged,
Or a mine was never digged,
Like a wound without a tent,
Or a box without a scent,
    Just such as these may she be said
    That lives, not loves, but dies a maid.

The Non-sir doth obey the call;
The question answered pleaseth all;
Who rigs a ship sails with the wind;
Who digs a mine doth treasure find;
The wound by wholesome tent hath ease;
The box perfumed the senses please:
    Such is the virgin in mine eyes
    That lives, loves, marries ere she dies.

Like marrow-bone was never broken,
Or commendation and no token,
Like a fort and none to win it,
Or like the moon and no man in it,
Like a school without a teacher,
Or like a pulpit and no preacher,
    Just such as these may she be said
    That lives, not loves, but dies a maid.

The broken marrow-bone is sweet;
The token doth adorn the greet;
There's triumph in the fort being won;
The man rides glorious in the moon;
The school is by the teacher skilled;
The pulpit by the preacher filled:
    Such is the virgin in mine eyes
    That lives, loves, marries ere she dies.

Like a cage without a bird,
Or a thing too long deferred,
Like the gold was never tried,
Or the ground unoccupied,
Like a house that's not possessed,
Or the book was never pressed,
    Just such as these may she be said
    That lives, ne'er loves, but dies a maid.

The bird in cage doth sweetly sing;
Due season proffers everything;
The gold that's tried from dross is pured;
There's profit in the ground manured;
The house is by possession graced;
The book, when pressed, is then embraced:
    Such is the virgin in mine eyes
    That lives, loves, marries ere she dies.

'The man that hath a handsome wife'

The man that hath a handsome wife
    And keeps her as a treasure,
It is my chiefest joy of life
    To have her to my pleasure.

But if that man regardless were
    As though he cared not for her,

Though she were like to Venus fair,
  In faith I would abhor her.

If to do good I were restrained,
  And to do evil bidden,
I would be Puritan, I swear,
  For I love the thing forbidden.

It is the care that makes the theft;
  None loves the thing forsaken;
The bold and willing whore is left
  When the modest wench is taken.

She dull is that's too forwards bent;
  Not good, but want, is reason.
Fish at a feast, and flesh in Lent,
  Are never out of season.

The Unquiet Grave

'The wind doth blow to-day, my love,
  And a few small drops of rain;
I never had but one true-love;
  In cold grave she was lain.

'I'll do as much for my true-love
  As any young man may;
I'll sit and mourn all at her grave
  For a twelvemonth and a day.'

The twelvemonth and a day being up,
  The dead began to speak:
'Oh, who sits weeping on my grave,
  And will not let me sleep?'

' 'T is I, my love, sits on your grave,
  And will not let you sleep;

For I crave one kiss of your clay-cold lips,
    And that is all I seek.'

'You crave one kiss of my clay-cold lips;
    But my breath smells earthy strong;
If you have one kiss of my clay-cold lips,
    Your time will not be long.

' 'T is down in yonder garden green,
    Love, where we used to walk,
The finest flower that ere was seen
    Is wither'd to a stalk.

'The stalk is wither'd dry, my love,
    So will our hearts decay;
So make yourself content, my love,
    Till God calls you away.'

Somewhere Along the Line

You met me to apologise, you were saying
as we waited in the drizzle for the slow train.
When it focused in we said goodbye and we kissed
and from the window you were caught; teary and fixed.

You ran across the wooden bridge, I knew you would,
to get down on the other platform and to wave,
but as you did the eastbound Leeds train flickered past
and ran you like a movie through its window-frames.

I keep those animated moments of you as
our catalogue of chances rushed and chances missed.

MATTHEW ARNOLD 1822–88

The Forsaken Merman

Come, dear children, let us away;
Down and away below!
Now my brothers call from the bay,
Now the great winds shoreward blow,
Now the salt tides seaward flow;
Now the wild white horses play,
Champ and chafe and toss in the spray.
Children dear, let us away!
This way, this way!

Call her once before you go –
Call once yet!
In a voice that she will know:
'Margaret! Margaret!'
Children's voices should be dear
(Call once more) to a mother's ear;
Children's voices, wild with pain –
Surely she will come again!
Call her once and come away;
This way, this way!
'Mother dear, we cannot stay!
The wild white horses foam and fret.'
Margaret! Margaret!

Come, dear children, come away down;
Call no more!
One last look at the white-walled town,
And the little grey church on the windy shore,
Then come down!
She will not come though you call all day;
Come away, come away!

Children dear, was it yesterday
We heard the sweet bells over the bay?
In the caverns where we lay,
Through the surf and through the swell,
The far-off sound of a silver bell?
Sand-strewn caverns, cool and deep,
Where the winds are all asleep;
Where the spent lights quiver and gleam,
Where the salt weed sways in the stream,
Where the sea-beasts, ranged all round,
Feed in the ooze of their pasture-ground;
Where the sea-snakes coil and twine,
Dry their mail and bask in the brine;
Where great whales come sailing by,
Sail and sail, with unshut eye,
Round the world for ever and aye?
When did music come this way?
Children dear, was it yesterday?

Children dear, was it yesterday
(Call yet once) that she went away?
Once she sate with you and me,
On a red gold throne in the heart of the sea,
And the youngest sate on her knee.
She combed its bright hair, and she tended it well,
When down swung the sound of a far-off bell.
She sighed, she looked up through the clear green sea;
She said: 'I must go, for my kinsfolk pray
In the little grey church on the shore to-day.
'Twill be Easter-time in the world – ah me!
And I lose my poor soul, Merman! here with thee.'
I said: 'Go up, dear heart, through the waves;
Say thy prayer, and come back to the kind sea-caves!'
She smiled, she went up through the surf in the bay.
Children dear, was it yesterday?

Children dear, were we long alone?
'The sea grows stormy, the little ones moan;
Long prayers,' I said, 'in the world they say;
Come!' I said; and we rose through the surf in the bay.
We went up the beach, by the sandy down
Where the sea-stocks bloom, to the white-walled town;
Through the narrow paved streets, where all was still,
To the little grey church on the windy hill.
From the church came a murmur of folk at their prayers,
But we stood without in the cold blowing airs.
We climbed on the graves, on the stones worn with rains,
And we gazed up the aisle through the small leaded panes.
She sate by the pillar; we saw her clear:
'Margaret, hist! come quick, we are here!
Dear heart,' I said, 'we are long alone;
The sea grows stormy, the little ones moan.'
But, ah, she gave me never a look,
For her eyes were sealed to the holy book!
Loud prays the priest; shut stands the door.
Come away, children, call no more!
Come away, come down, call no more!

Down, down, down!
Down to the depths of the sea!
She sits at her wheel in the humming town,
Singing most joyfully.
Hark what she sings: 'O joy, O joy,
For the humming street, and the child with its toy!
For the priest, and the bell, and the holy well;
For the wheel where I spun,
And the blessed light of the sun!'
And so she sings her fill,
Singing most joyfully,
Till the spindle drops from her hand,
And the whizzing wheel stands still.
She steals to the window, and looks at the sand,

And over the sand at the sea;
And her eyes are set in a stare;
And anon there breaks a sigh,
And anon there drops a tear,
From a sorrow-clouded eye,
And a heart sorrow-laden,
A long, long sigh;
For the cold strange eyes of a little Mermaiden
And the gleam of her golden hair.

Come away, away children:
Come children, come down!
The hoarse wind blows coldly;
Lights shine in the town.
She will start from her slumber
When gusts shake the door;
She will hear the winds howling,
Will hear the waves roar.
We shall see, while above us
The waves roar and whirl,
A ceiling of amber,
A pavement of pearl.
Singing: 'Here came a mortal,
But faithless was she!
And alone dwell for ever
The kings of the sea.'

But, children, at midnight,
When soft the winds blow,
When clear falls the moonlight,
When spring-tides are low;
When sweet airs come seaward
From heaths starred with broom,
And high rocks throw mildly
On the blanched sands a gloom;
Up the still, glistening beaches,
Up the creeks we will hie,

Over banks of bright seaweed
The ebb-tide leaves dry.
We will gaze, from the sand-hills,
At the white, sleeping town;
At the church on the hill-side –
And then come back down.
Singing: 'There dwells a loved one,
But cruel is she!
She left lonely for ever
The kings of the sea.'

A Modern Sappho

They are gone – all is still! Foolish heart, dost thou quiver?
    Nothing stirs on the lawn but the quick lilac-shade.
Far up shines the house, and beneath flows the river –
    Here lean, my head, on this cold balustrade!

Ere he come – ere the boat by the shining-branched border
    Of dark elms shoot round, dropping down the proud
        stream,
Let me pause, let me strive, in myself make some order,
    Ere their boat-music sound, ere their broidered flags gleam.

Last night we stood earnestly talking together;
    She entered – that moment his eyes turned from me!
Fastened on her dark hair, and her wreath of white heather –
    As yesterday was, so to-morrow will be.

Their love, let me know, must grow strong and yet stronger,
    Their passion burn more, ere it ceases to burn.
They must love – while they must! but the hearts that love
        longer.
    Are rare – ah! most loves but flow once, and return.

I shall suffer – but they will outlive their affection;
    I shall weep – but their love will be cooling; and he,

As he drifts to fatigue, discontent, and dejection,
    Will be brought, thou poor heart, how much nearer to thee!

For cold is his eye to mere beauty, who, breaking
    The strong band which passion around him hath furled,
Disenchanted by habit, and newly awaking,
    Looks languidly round on a gloom-buried world.

Through that gloom he will see but a shadow appearing,
    Perceive but a voice as I come to his side –
But deeper their voice grows, and nobler their bearing,
    Whose youth in the fires of anguish hath died.

So, to wait! – But what notes down the wind, hark! are
        driving?
    'Tis he! 'tis their flag, shooting round by the trees!
– Let my turn, if it *will* come, be swift in arriving!
    Ah! hope cannot long lighten torments like these.

Hast thou yet dealt him, O life, thy full measure?
    World, have thy children yet bowed at his knee?
Hast thou with myrtle-leaf crowned him, O pleasure?
    – Crown, crown him quickly, and leave him for me!

Meeting

Again I see my bliss at hand,
The town, the lake are here;
My Marguerite smiles upon the strand,
Unaltered with the year.

I know that graceful figure fair,
That cheek of languid hue;
I know that soft, enkerchiefed hair,
And those sweet eyes of blue.

Again I spring to make my choice;
Again in tones of ire

I hear a God's tremendous voice:
'Be counselled, and retire.'

Ye guiding Powers who join and part,
What would ye have with me?
Ah, warn some more ambitious heart,
And let the peaceful be!

Dover Beach

The sea is calm to-night.
The tide is full, the moon lies fair
Upon the straits; on the French coast the light
Gleams and is gone; the cliffs of England stand,
Glimmering and vast, out in the tranquil bay.
Come to the window, sweet is the night-air!
Only, from the long line of spray

Where the sea meets the moon-blanched land,
Listen! you hear the grating roar
Of pebbles which the waves draw back, and fling,
At their return, up the high strand,
Begin, and cease, and then again begin,
With tremulous cadence slow, and bring
The eternal note of sadness in.

Sophocles long ago
Heard it on the Ægæan, and it brought
Into his mind the turbid ebb and flow
Of human misery; we
Find also in the sound a thought,
Hearing it by this distant northern sea.

The Sea of Faith
Was once, too, at the full, and round earth's shore
Lay like the folds of a bright girdle furled.
But now I only hear

Its melancholy, long, withdrawing roar,
Retreating, to the breath
Of the night-wind, down the vast edges drear
And naked shingles of the world.

Ah, love, let us be true
To one another! for the world, which seems
To lie before us like a land of dreams,
So various, so beautiful, so new,
Hath really neither joy, nor love, nor light,
Nor certitude, nor peace, nor help for pain;
And we are here as on a darkling plain
Swept with confused alarms of struggle and flight,
Where ignorant armies clash by night.

W. H. AUDEN 1907–73

'You were a great Cunarder, I'

You were a great Cunarder, I
Was only a fishing smack.
Once you passed across my bows
And of course you did not look back.

It was only a single moment yet
I watch the sea and sigh,
Because my heart can never forget
The day you passed me by.

'Seen when nights are silent'

Seen when nights are silent,
The bean-shaped island,
And our ugly comic servant,
Who was observant.

O the veranda and the fruit,
The tiny steamer in the bay
Startling summer with its hoot: –
You have gone away.

As I Walked Out One Evening

As I walked out one evening,
  Walking down Bristol Street,
The crowds upon the pavement
  Were fields of harvest wheat.

And down by the brimming river
  I heard a lover sing

Under an arch of the railway:
   'Love has no ending.

'I'll love you, dear, I'll love you
   Till China and Africa meet,
And the river jumps over the mountain
   And the salmon sing in the street,

'I'll love you till the ocean
   Is folded and hung up to dry
And the seven stars go squawking
   Like geese about the sky.

'The years shall run like rabbits,
   For in my arms I hold
The Flower of the Ages,
   And the first love of the world.'

But all the clocks in the city
   Began to whirr and chime:
'O let not Time deceive you,
   You cannot conquer Time.

'In the burrows of the Nightmare
   Where Justice naked is,
Time watches from the shadow
   And coughs when you would kiss.

'In headaches and in worry
   Vaguely life leaks away,
And Time will have his fancy
   To-morrow or to-day.

'Into many a green valley
   Drifts the appalling snow;
Time breaks the threaded dances
   And the diver's brilliant bow.

'O plunge your hands in water,
   Plunge them in up to the wrist;

Stare, stare in the basin
    And wonder what you've missed.

'The glacier knocks in the cupboard,
    The desert sighs in the bed,
And the crack in the tea-cup opens
    A lane to the land of the dead.

'Where the beggars raffle the banknotes
    And the Giant is enchanting to Jack,
And the Lily-white Boy is a Roarer,
    And Jill goes down on her back.

'O look, look in the mirror,
    O look in your distress;
Life remains a blessing
    Although you cannot bless.

'O stand, stand at the window
    As the tears scald and start;
You shall love your crooked neighbour
    With your crooked heart.'

It was late, late in the evening,
    The lovers they were gone;
The clocks had ceased their chiming,
    And the deep river ran on.

'O lurcher-loving collier, black as night'

O lurcher-loving collier, black as night,
Follow your love across the smokeless hill;
Your lamp is out, the cages all are still;
Course for her heart and do not miss,
For Sunday soon is past and, Kate, fly not so fast,
For Monday comes when none may kiss:
Be marble to his soot, and to his black be white.

'Dear, though the night is gone'

Dear, though the night is gone,
Its dream still haunts to-day,
That brought us to a room
Cavernous, lofty as
A railway terminus,
And crowded in that gloom
Were beds, and we in one
In a far corner lay.

Our whisper woke no clocks,
We kissed and I was glad
At everything you did,
Indifferent to those
Who sat with hostile eyes
In pairs on every bed,
Arms round each other's necks,
Inert and vaguely sad.

What hidden worm of guilt
Or what malignant doubt
Am I the victim of,
That you then, unabashed,
Did what I never wished,
Confessed another love;
And I, submissive, felt
Unwanted and went out.

'Underneath an abject willow'

Underneath an abject willow,
   Lover, sulk no more:
Act from thought should quickly follow.
   What is thinking for?
Your unique and moping station

Proves you cold;
   Stand up and fold
Your map of desolation.

Bells that toll across the meadows
   From the sombre spire
Toll for these unloving shadows
   Love does not require.
All that lives may love; why longer
   Bow to loss
   With arms across?
Strike and you shall conquer.

Geese in flocks above you flying,
   Their direction know,
Icy brooks beneath you flowing,
   To their ocean go.
Dark and dull is your distraction:
   Walk then, come,
   No longer numb
Into your satisfaction.

'Stop all the clocks, cut off the telephone'

Stop all the clocks, cut off the telephone,
Prevent the dog from barking with a juicy bone,
Silence the pianos and with muffled drum
Bring out the coffin, let the mourners come.

Let aeroplanes circle moaning overhead
Scribbling on the sky the message He Is Dead,
Put crêpe bows round the white necks of the public doves,
Let the traffic policemen wear black cotton gloves.

He was my North, my South, my East and West,
My working week and my Sunday rest,

My noon, my midnight, my talk, my song;
I thought that love would last for ever: I was wrong.

The stars are not wanted now: put out every one;
Pack up the moon and dismantle the sun;
Pour away the ocean and sweep up the wood;
For nothing now can ever come to any good.

'Some say that love's a little boy'

Some say that love's a little boy,
　　And some say it's a bird,
Some say it makes the world go round,
　　And some say that's absurd,
And when I asked the man next-door,
　　Who looked as if he knew,
His wife got very cross indeed,
　　And said it wouldn't do.

Does it look like a pair of pyjamas,
　　Or the ham in a temperance hotel?
Does its odour remind one of llamas,
　　Or has it a comforting smell?
Is it prickly to touch as a hedge is,
　　Or soft as eiderdown fluff?
Is it sharp or quite smooth at the edges?
　　O tell me the truth about love.

Our history books refer to it
　　In cryptic little notes,
It's quite a common topic on
　　The Transatlantic boats;
I've found the subject mentioned in
　　Accounts of suicides,
And even seen it scribbled on
　　The backs of railway-guides.

Does it howl like a hungry Alsatian,
    Or boom like a military band?
Could one give a first-rate imitation
    On a saw or a Steinway Grand?
Is its singing at parties a riot?
    Does it only like Classical stuff?
Will it stop when one wants to be quiet?
    O tell me the truth about love.

I looked inside the summer-house;
    It wasn't ever there:
I tried the Thames at Maidenhead,
    And Brighton's bracing air.
I don't know what the blackbird sang,
    Or what the tulip said;
But it wasn't in the chicken-run,
    Or underneath the bed.

Can it pull extraordinary faces?
    Is it usually sick on a swing?
Does it spend all its time at the races,
    Or fiddling with pieces of string?
Has it views of its own about money?
    Does it think Patriotism enough?
Are its stories vulgar but funny?
    O tell me the truth about love.

When it comes, will it come without warning
    Just as I'm picking my nose?
Will it knock on my door in the morning,
    Or tread in the bus on my toes?
Will it come like a change in the weather?
    Will its greeting be courteous or rough?
Will it alter my life altogether?
    O tell me the truth about love.

Lullaby

Lay your sleeping head, my love,
Human on my faithless arm;
Time and fevers burn away
Individual beauty from
Thoughtful children, and the grave
Proves the child ephemeral:
But in my arms till break of day
Let the living creature lie,
Mortal, guilty, but to me
The entirely beautiful.

Soul and body have no bounds:
To lovers as they lie upon
Her tolerant enchanted slope
In their ordinary swoon,
Grave the vision Venus sends
Of supernatural sympathy,
Universal love and hope;
While an abstract insight wakes
Among the glaciers and the rocks
The hermit's carnal ecstasy.

Certainty, fidelity
On the stroke of midnight pass
Like vibrations of a bell
And fashionable madmen raise
Their pedantic boring cry:
Every farthing of the cost,
All the dreaded cards foretell,
Shall be paid, but from this night
Not a whisper, not a thought,
Not a kiss nor look be lost.

Beauty, midnight, vision dies:
Let the winds of dawn that blow

Softly round your dreaming head
Such a day of welcome show
Eye and knocking heart may bless,
Find our mortal world enough;
Noons of dryness find you fed
By the involuntary powers,
Nights of insult let you pass
Watched by every human love.

Heavy Date

Sharp and silent in the
Clear October lighting
Of a Sunday morning
    The great city lies;
And I at a window
Looking over water
At the world of Business
    With a lover's eyes.

All mankind, I fancy,
When anticipating
Anything exciting
    Like a rendezvous,
Occupy the time in
Purely random thinking,
For when love is waiting
    Logic will not do.

Much as he would like to
Concentrate completely
On the precious Object,
    Love has not the power;
Goethe put it neatly:
No one cares to watch the

Loveliest sunset after
   Quarter of an hour.

Malinowski, Rivers,
Benedict and others
Show how common culture
   Shapes the separate lives:
Matrilineal races
Kill their mothers' brothers
In their dreams and turn their
   Sisters into wives.

Who when looking over
Faces in the subway,
Each with its uniqueness,
   Would not, did he dare,
Ask what forms exactly
Suited to their weakness
Love and desperation
   Take to govern there:

Would not like to know what
Influence occupation
Has on human vision
   Of the human fate:
Do all clerks for instance
Pigeon-hole creation,
Brokers see the Ding-an-
   -sich as Real Estate?

When a politician
Dreams about his sweetheart,
Does he multiply her
   Face into a crowd,
Are her fond responses
All-or-none reactions,
Does he try to buy her,
   Is the kissing loud?

Strange are love's mutations:
Thus, the early poem
Of the flesh sub rosa
   Has been known to grow
Now and then into the
Amor intellectu-
-alis of Spinoza;
   How we do not know.

Slowly we are learning,
We at least know this much,
That we have to unlearn
   Much that we were taught,
And are growing chary
Of emphatic dogmas;
Love like Matter is much
   Odder than we thought.

Love requires an Object,
But this varies so much,
Almost, I imagine,
   Anything will do:
When I was a child, I
Loved a pumping-engine,
Thought it every bit as
   Beautiful as you.

Love has no position,
Love's way of living,
One kind of relation
   Possible between
Any things or persons
Given one condition,
The one sine qua non
   Being mutual need.

Through it we discover
An essential secret

Called by some Salvation
  And by some Success;
Crying for the moon is
Naughtiness and envy,
We can only love what-
  -ever we possess.

I believed for years that
Love was the conjunction
Of two oppositions;
  That was all untrue;
Every young man fears that
He is not worth loving:
Bless you, darling, I have
  Found myself in you.

When two lovers meet, then
There's an end of writing
Thought and Analytics:
  Lovers, like the dead,
In their loves are equal;
Sophomores and peasants,
Poets and their critics
  Are the same in bed.

Law Like Love

Law, say the gardeners, is the sun,
Law is the one
All gardeners obey
To-morrow, yesterday, to-day.

Law is the wisdom of the old,
The impotent grandfathers feebly scold;
The grandchildren put out a treble tongue,
Law is the senses of the young.

Law, says the priest with a priestly look,
Expounding to an unpriestly people,
Law is the words in my priestly book,
Law is my pulpit and my steeple.
Law, says the judge as he looks down his nose,
Speaking clearly and most severely,
Law is as I've told you before,
Law is as you know I suppose,
Law is but let me explain it once more,
Law is The Law.

Yet law-abiding scholars write:
Law is neither wrong nor right,
Law is only crimes
Punished by places and by times,
Law is the clothes men wear
Anytime, anywhere,
Law is Good-morning and Good-night.

Others say, Law is our Fate;
Others say, Law is our State;
Others say, others say
Law is no more,
Law has gone away.

And always the loud angry crowd,
Very angry and very loud,
Law is We,
And always the soft idiot softly Me.

If we, dear, know we know no more
Than they about the Law,
If I no more than you
Know what we should and should not do
Except that all agree
Gladly or miserably
That the Law is
And that all know this,

If therefore thinking it absurd
To identify Law with some other word,
Unlike so many men
I cannot say Law is again,
No more than they can we suppress
The universal wish to guess
Or slip out of our own position
Into an unconcerned condition.
Although I can at least confine
Your vanity and mine
To stating timidly
A timid similarity,
We shall boast anyway:
Like love I say.

Like love we don't know where or why,
Like love we can't compel or fly,
Like love we often weep,
Like love we seldom keep.

Lady Weeping at the Crossroads

Lady, weeping at the crossroads,
Would you meet your love
In the twilight with his greyhounds,
And the hawk on his glove?

Bribe the birds then on the branches,
Bribe them to be dumb,
Stare the hot sun out of heaven
That the night may come.

Starless are the nights of travel,
Bleak the winter wind;
Run with terror all before you
And regret behind.

Run until you hear the ocean's
Everlasting cry;
Deep though it may be and bitter
You must drink it dry,

Wear out patience in the lowest
Dungeons of the sea,
Searching through the stranded shipwrecks
For the golden key,

Push on to the world's end, pay the
Dread guard with a kiss,
Cross the rotten bridge that totters
Over the abyss.

There stands the deserted castle
Ready to explore;
Enter, climb the marble staircase,
Open the locked door.

Cross the silent empty ballroom,
Doubt and danger past;
Blow the cobwebs from the mirror,
See yourself at last.

Put your hand behind the wainscot,
You have done your part;
Find the penknife there and plunge it
Into your false heart.

The More Loving One

Looking up at the stars, I know quite well
That, for all they care, I can go to hell,
But on earth indifference is the least
We have to dread from man or beast.

How should we like it were stars to burn
With a passion for us we could not return?
If equal affection cannot be,
Let the more loving one be me.

Admirer as I think I am
Of stars that do not give a damn,
I cannot, now I see them, say
I missed one terribly all day.

Were all stars to disappear or die,
I should learn to look at an empty sky
And feel its total dark sublime,
Though this might take me a little time.

To His Friend Master R. L., in Praise of Music and Poetry

If music and sweet poetry agree,
As they must needs, the sister and the brother,
Then must the love be great 'twixt thee and me,
Because thou lov'st the one, and I the other.
Dowland to thee is dear, whose heavenly touch
Upon the lute doth ravish human sense;
Spenser, to me, whose deep conceit is such
As, passing all conceit, needs no defence.
Thou lov'st to hear the sweet melodious sound
That Phoebus' lute, the queen of music, makes;
And I in deep delight am chiefly drowned
Whenas himself to singing he betakes:
   One god is god of both, as poets feign;
   One knight loves both, and both in thee remain.

APHRA BEHN 1640–89

The Defiance

By Heaven 'tis false, I am not vain;
  And rather would the subject be
Of your indifference, or disdain,
  Than wit or raillery.

Take back the trifling praise you give,
  And pass it on some other fool,
Who may the injuring wit believe,
  That turns her into ridicule.

Tell her, she's witty, fair, and gay,
  With all the charms that can subdue:
Perhaps she'll credit what you say;
  But curse me if I do.

If your diversion you design,
  On my good-nature you have prest:
Or if you do intend it mine,
  You have mistook the jest.

Juliet

How did the party go in Portman Square?
I cannot tell you; Juliet was not there.
And how did Lady Gaster's party go?
Juliet was next me and I do not know.

Pot Pourri from a Surrey Garden

Miles of pram in the wind and Pam in the gorse track,
   Coco-nut smell of the broom, and a packet of Weights
Press'd in the sand. The thud of a hoof on a horse-track –
     A horse-riding horse for a horse-track –
     Conifer county of Surrey approached
   Through remarkable wrought-iron gates.

Over your boundary now, I wash my face in a bird-bath,
   Then which path shall I take? that over there by the pram?
Down by the pond! or – yes, I will take the slippery third
       path,
     Trodden away with gym shoes,
     Beautiful fir-dry alley that leads
   To the bountiful body of Pam.

Pam, I adore you, Pam, you great big mountainous sports
       girl,
   Whizzing them over the net, full of the strength of five:
That old Malvernian brother, you zephyr and khaki shorts
       girl,
     Although he's playing for Woking,
     Can't stand up
   To your wonderful backhand drive.

See the strength of her arm, as firm and hairy as Hendren's;
   See the size of her thighs, the pout of her lips as, cross,
And full of a pent-up strength, she swipes at the
      rhododendrons,
     Lucky the rhododendrons,
     And flings her arrogant love-lock
   Back with a petulant toss.

Over the redolent pinewoods, in at the bathroom casement,
  One fine Saturday, Windlesham bells shall call:
Up the Butterfield aisle rich with Gothic enlacement,
    Licensed now for embracement,
    Pam and I, as the organ
  Thunders over you all.

Myfanwy

Kind o'er the *kinderbank* leans my Myfanwy,
  White o'er the play-pen the sheen of her dress,
Fresh from the bathroom and soft in the nursery
  Soap-scented fingers I long to caress.

Were you a prefect and head of your dormit'ry?
  Were you a hockey girl, tennis or gym?
Who was your favourite? Who had a crush on you?
  Which were the baths where they taught you to swim?

Smooth down the Avenue glitters the bicycle,
  Black-stockinged legs under navy-blue serge,
Home and Colonial, Star, International,
  Balancing bicycle leant on the verge.

Trace me your wheel-tracks, you fortunate bicycle,
  Out of the shopping and into the dark,
Back down the Avenue, back to the pottingshed,
  Back to the house on the fringe of the park.

Golden the light on the locks of Myfanwy,
  Golden the light on the book on her knee,
Finger-marked pages of Rackham's Hans Andersen,
  Time for the children to come down to tea.

Oh! Fuller's angel-cake, Robertson's marmalade,
  Liberty lampshade, come, shine on us all,
My! what a spread for the friends of Myfanwy
  Some in the alcove and some in the hall.

Then what sardines in the half-lighted passages!
    Locking of fingers in long hide-and-seek.
You will protect me, my silken Myfanwy,
    Ringleader, tom-boy, and chum to the weak.

A Subaltern's Love-Song

Miss J. Hunter Dunn, Miss J. Hunter Dunn,
Furnish'd and burnish'd by Aldershot sun,
What strenuous singles we played after tea,
We in the tournament – you against me!

Love-thirty, love-forty, oh! weakness of joy,
The speed of a swallow, the grace of a boy,
With carefullest carelessness, gaily you won,
I am weak from your loveliness, Joan Hunter Dunn.

Miss Joan Hunter Dunn, Miss Joan Hunter Dunn,
How mad I am, sad I am, glad that you won.
The warm-handled racket is back in its press,
But my shock-headed victor, she loves me no less.

Her father's euonymus shines as we walk,
And swing past the summer-house, buried in talk,
And cool the verandah that welcomes us in
To the six-o'clock news and a lime-juice and gin.

The scent of the conifers, sound of the bath,
The view from my bedroom of moss-dappled path,
As I struggle with double-end evening tie,
For we dance at the Golf Club, my victor and I.

On the floor of her bedroom lie blazer and shorts
And the cream-coloured walls are be-trophied with
    sports,
And westering, questioning settles the sun
On your low-leaded window, Miss Joan Hunter Dunn.

The Hillman is waiting, the light's in the hall,
The pictures of Egypt are bright on the wall,
My sweet, I am standing beside the oak stair
And there on the landing's the light on your hair.

By roads 'not adopted', by woodlanded ways,
She drove to the club in the late summer haze,
Into nine-o'clock Camberley, heavy with bells
And mushroomy, pine-woody, evergreen smells.

Miss Joan Hunter Dunn, Miss Joan Hunter Dunn,
I can hear from the car-park the dance has begun.
Oh! full Surrey twilight! importunate band!
Oh! strongly adorable tennis-girl's hand!

Around us are Rovers and Austins afar,
Above us, the intimate roof of the car,
And here on my right is the girl of my choice,
With the tilt of her nose and the chime of her voice,

And the scent of her wrap, and the words never said,
And the ominous, ominous dancing ahead.
We sat in the car park till twenty to one
And now I'm engaged to Miss Joan Hunter Dunn.

In a Bath Teashop

'Let us not speak, for the love we bear one another –
 Let us hold hands and look.'
She, such a very ordinary little woman;
 He, such a thumping crook;
But both, for a moment, little lower than the angels
 In the teashop's ingle-nook.

Indoor Games near Newbury

In among the silver birches winding ways of tarmac wander
 And the signs to Bussock Bottom, Tussock Wood and
  Windy Brake,
Gabled lodges, tile-hung churches, catch the lights of our
  Lagonda
 As we drive to Wendy's party, lemon curd and Christmas
  cake.
  Rich the makes of motor whirring,
  Past the pine-plantation purring
   Come up, Hupmobile, Delage!
  Short the way your chauffeurs travel,
  Crunching over private gravel
   Each from out his warm garáge.

Oh but Wendy, when the carpet yielded to my indoor pumps
 There you stood, your gold hair streaming,
 Handsome in the hall-light gleaming
There you looked and there you led me off into the game of
  clumps
 Then the new Victrola playing
 And your funny uncle saying
'Choose your partners for a fox-trot! Dance until its *tea*
  o'clock!
 'Come on, young'uns, foot it featly!'
 Was it chance that paired us neatly,
 I, who loved you so completely,
You, who pressed me closely to you, hard against your party
  frock?'

'Meet me when you've finished eating!' So we met and no
  one found us.
 Oh that dark and furry cupboard while the rest played
  hide and seek!
Holding hands our two hearts beating in the bedroom silence
  round us,

Holding hands and hardly hearing sudden footstep, thud
    and shriek.
    Love that lay too deep for kissing –
    'Where *is* Wendy? Wendy's missing!'
        Love so pure it *had* to end,
    Love so strong that I was frighten'd
    When you gripped my fingers tight and
Hugging, whispered 'I'm your friend.'

Goodbye Wendy! Send the fairies, pinewood elf and larch
    tree gnome,
    Spingle-spangled stars are peeping
    At the lush Lagonda creeping
Down the winding ways of tarmac to the leaded lights of
    home.
    There, among the silver birches,
    All the bells of all the churches
Sounded in the bath-waste running out into the frosty air.
    Wendy speeded my undressing,
    Wendy is the sheet's caressing
    Wendy bending gives a blessing,
Holds me as I drift to dreamland, safe inside my slumber
    wear.

The Licorice Fields at Pontefract

In the licorice fields at Pontefract
    My love and I did meet
And many a burdened licorice bush
    Was blooming round our feet;
Red hair she had and golden skin,
Her sulky lips were shaped for sin,
Her sturdy legs were flannel-slack'd,
The strongest legs in Pontefract.

The light and dangling licorice flowers
    Gave off the sweetest smells;
From various black Victorian towers
    The Sunday evening bells
Came pealing over dales and hills
And tanneries and silent mills
And lowly streets where country stops
And little shuttered corner shops.

She cast her blazing eyes on me
    And plucked a licorice leaf;
I was her captive slave and she
    My red-haired robber chief.
Oh love! for love I could not speak,
It left me winded, wilting, weak
And held in brown arms strong and bare
And wound with flaming ropes of hair.

ELIZABETH BISHOP 1911–79

from Songs for a Colored Singer

I

A washing hangs upon the line,
    but it's not mine.
None of the things that I can see
    belong to me.
The neighbors got a radio with an aerial;
    we got a little portable.
They got a lot of closet space;
    we got a suitcase.

I say, 'Le Roy, just how much are we owing?
Something I can't comprehend,
the more we got the more we spend. . . .'
He only answers, 'Let's get going.'
Le Roy, you're earning too much money now.

I sit and look at our backyard
    and find it very hard.
What have we got for all his dollars and cents?
    – A pile of bottles by the fence.
He's faithful and he's kind
    but he sure has an inquiring mind.
He's seen a lot; he's bound to see the rest,
    and if I protest

Le Roy answers with a frown,
'Darling, when I earns I spends.
The world is wide; it still extends. . . .
I'm going to get a job in the next town.'
Le Roy, you're earning too much money now.

The time has come to call a halt;
    and so it ends.
    He's gone off with his other friends.
    He needn't try to make amends,
this occasion's all his fault.
    Through rain and dark I see his face
    across the street at Flossie's place.
    He's drinking in the warm pink glow
    to th' accompaniment of the piccolo.*

The time has come to call a halt.
I met him walking with Varella
and hit him twice with my umbrella.
Perhaps that occasion was my fault,
but the time has come to call a halt.

Go drink your wine and go get tight.
    Let the piccolo play.
    I'm sick of all your fussing anyway.
    Now I'm pursuing my own way.
I'm leaving on the bus tonight.
    Far down the highway wet and black
    I'll ride and ride and not come back.
    I'm going to go and take the bus
    and find someone monogamous.

The time has come to call a halt.
I've borrowed fifteen dollars fare
and it will take me anywhere.
For this occasion's all his fault.
The time has come to call a halt.

* Jukebox.

Insomnia

The moon in the bureau mirror
looks out a million miles
(and perhaps with pride, at herself,
but she never, never smiles)
far and away beyond sleep, or
perhaps she's a daytime sleeper.

By the Universe deserted,
she'd tell it to go to hell,
and she'd find a body of water,
or a mirror, on which to dwell.
So wrap up care in a cobweb
and drop it down the well

into that world inverted
where left is always right,
where the shadows are really the body,
where we stay awake all night,
where the heavens are shallow as the sea
is now deep, and you love me.

Argument

Days that cannot bring you near
or will not,
Distance trying to appear
something more than obstinate,
argue argue argue with me
endlessly
neither proving you less wanted nor less dear.

Distance: Remember all that land
beneath the plane;
that coastline

of dim beaches deep in sand
stretching indistinguishably
all the way,
all the way to where my reasons end?

Days: And think
of all those cluttered instruments,
one to a fact,
canceling each other's experience;
how they were
like some hideous calendar
'Compliments of Never & Forever, Inc.'

The intimidating sound
of these voices
we must separately find
can and shall be vanquished:
Days and Distance disarrayed again
and gone
both for good and from the gentle battleground.

The Shampoo

The still explosions on the rocks,
the lichens, grow
by spreading, gray, concentric shocks.
They have arranged
to meet the rings around the moon, although
within our memories they have not changed.

And since the heavens will attend
as long on us,
you've been, dear friend,
precipitate and pragmatical;
and look what happens. For Time is
nothing if not amenable.

The shooting stars in your black hair
in bright formation
are flocking where,
so straight, so soon?
– Come, let me wash it in this big tin basin,
battered and shiny like the moon.

It is Marvellous

It is marvellous to wake up together
At the same minute; marvellous to hear
The rain begin suddenly all over the roof,
To feel the air suddenly clear
As if electricity had passed through it
From a black mesh of wires in the sky.
All over the roof rain hisses
And below, the light falling of kisses.

An electrical storm is coming or moving away;
It is the prickling air that wakes us up.
If lightning struck the house now, it would run
From the four blue china balls on top
Down the roof and down the rods all around us,
And we imagine dreamily
How the whole house caught in a bird-cage of lightning
Would be quite delightful rather than frightening;

And from the same simplified point of view
Of night and lying flat on one's back
All things might change equally easily,
Since always to warn us there must be these black
Electrical wires dangling. Without surprise
The world might change to something quite different,
As the air changes or the lightning comes without our blinking,
Change as our kisses are changing without our thinking.

Close, Close All Night

Close close all night
the lovers keep.
They turn together
in their sleep,

close as two pages
in a book
that read each other
in the dark.

Each knows all
the other knows,
learned by heart
From head to toes.

Breakfast Song

My love, my saving grace,
your eyes are awfully blue.
I kiss your funny face,
your coffee-flavored mouth.
Last night I slept with you.
Today I love you so
how can I bear to go
(as soon I must, I know)
to bed with ugly death
in that cold, filthy place,
to sleep there without you,
without the easy breath
and nightlong, limblong warmth
I've grown accustomed to?
– Nobody wants to die;
tell me it is a lie!
But no, I know it's true.

It's just the common case;
there's nothing one can do.
My love, my saving grace,
your eyes are awfully blue
early and instant blue.

WILLIAM BLAKE 1757–1827

Song

How sweet I roam'd from field to field,
    And tasted all the summer's pride,
'Till I the prince of love beheld,
    Who in the sunny beams did glide!

He shew'd me lilies for my hair,
    And blushing roses for my brow;
He led me through his gardens fair,
    Where all his golden pleasures grow.

With sweet May dews my wings were wet,
    And Phoebus fir'd my vocal rage;
He caught me in his silken net,
    And shut me in his golden cage.

He loves to sit and hear me sing,
    Then, laughing, sports and plays with me;
Then stretches out my golden wing,
    And mocks my loss of liberty.

Thel's Motto

Does the Eagle know what is in the pit?
Or wilt thou go ask the Mole:
Can Wisdom be put in a silver rod?
Or Love in a golden bowl?

The Little Black Boy

My mother bore me in the southern wild,
And I am black, but O! my soul is white;

White as an angel is the English child:
But I am black as if bereav'd of light.

My mother taught me underneath a tree
And sitting down before the heat of day,
She took me on her lap and kissed me,
And pointing to the east began to say.

Look on the rising sun: there God does live
And gives his light, and gives his heat away.
And flowers and trees and beasts and men recieve
Comfort in morning joy in the noon day.

And we are put on earth a little space,
That we may learn to bear the beams of love,
And these black bodies and this sun-burnt face
Is but a cloud, and like a shady grove.

For when our souls have learn'd the heat to bear
The cloud will vanish we shall hear his voice.
Saying: come out from the grove my love & care,
And round my golden tent like lambs rejoice.

Thus did my mother say and kissed me,
And thus I say to little English boy.
When I from black and he from white cloud free,
And round the tent of God like lambs we joy:

Ill shade him from the heat till he can bear,
To lean in joy upon our fathers knee.
And then I'll stand and stroke his silver hair,
And be like him and he will then love me.

The Clod & the Pebble

Love seeketh not Itself to please,
Nor for itself hath any care;

But for another gives its ease,
And builds a Heaven in Hells despair.

So sang a little Clod of Clay,
Trodden with the cattles feet:
But a Pebble of the brook,
Warbled out these metres meet.

Love seeketh only Self to please,
To bind another to its delight;
Joys in anothers loss of ease,
And builds a Hell in Heavens despite.

The Sick Rose

O Rose thou art sick.
The invisible worm,
That flies in the night
In the howling storm:

Has found out thy bed
Of crimson joy:
And his dark secret love
Does thy life destroy.

The Garden of Love

I went to the Garden of Love.
And saw what I never had seen:
A Chapel was built in the midst,
Where I used to play on the green.

And the gates of this Chapel were shut,
And Thou shalt not. writ over the door;
So I turn'd to the Garden of Love,
That so many sweet flowers bore.

And I saw it was filled with graves,
And tomb-stones where flowers should be:
And Priests in black gowns, were walking their rounds,
And binding with briars, my joys & desires.

[Fragments]

I laid me down upon a bank
Where love lay sleeping
I heard among the rushes dank
Weeping Weeping

Then I went to the heath & the wild
To the thistles & thorns of the waste
And they told me how they were beguild
Driven out & compeld to be chaste

*

I asked a thief to steal me a peach
He turned up his eyes
I askd a lithe lady to lie her down
Holy & meek she cries

As soon as I went An angel came
He winkd at the thief
And smild at the dame

And without one word said
Had a peach from the tree
And still as a maid
Enjoy'd the lady.

How to Know Love from Deceit

Love to faults is always blind
Always is to joy inclind

Lawless wingd & unconfind
And breaks all chains from every mind

Deceit to secresy confind
Lawful cautious & refind
To every thing but interest blind
And forges fetters for the mind

An Ancient Proverb

Remove away that blackning church
Remove away that marriage hearse
Remove away that man of blood
Youll quite remove the ancient curse

'Naught loves another as itself'

Naught loves another as itself
Nor venerates another so
Nor is it possible to Thought
A greater than itself to know

And father how can I love you
Or any of my brothers more
I love you like the little bird
That picks up crumbs around the door

The Priest sat by and heard the child
In trembling zeal he seizd his hair
He led him by the little coat
And all admird his priestly care

And standing on the altar high
Lo what a fiend is here said he
One who sets reason up for judge
Of our most holy mystery

The weeping child could not be heard
The weeping parents wept in vain
They strip'd him to his little shirt
& bound him in an iron chain

And burnd him in a holy place
Where many had been burnd before
The weeping parents wept in vain
Are Such things done on Albions shore

Merlins Prophecy

The harvest shall flourish in wintry weather
When two virginities meet together

The King & the Priest must be tied in a tether
Before two virgins can meet together

'Abstinence sows sand all over'

Abstinence sows sand all over
The ruddy limbs & flaming hair
But Desire Gratified
Plants fruits of life & beauty there

Several Questions Answerd

He who binds to himself a joy
Doth the winged life destroy
But he who kisses the joy as it flies
Lives in Eternitys sun rise

—

The look of love alarms
Because tis filld with fire

But the look of soft deceit
Shall Win the lovers hire

—

Soft deceit & Idleness
These are Beautys sweetest dress

—

What is it men in women do require
The lineaments of Gratified Desire
What is it women do in men require
The lineaments of Gratified Desire

[Fragments]

When a Man has Married a Wife
   he finds out whether
Her knees & elbows are only
   glued together

   *

Grown old in Love from Seven till Seven times Seven
I oft have wishd for Hell for Ease from Heaven

   *

A Woman Scaly & a Man all Hairy
Is such a Match as he who dares
Will find the Womans Scales scrape off the Mans Hairs

The Smile

There is a Smile of Love
And there is a Smile of Deceit
And there is a Smile of Smiles
In which these two Smiles meet

And there is a Frown of Hate
And there is a Frown of disdain
And there is a Frown of Frowns
Which you strive to forget in vain

For it sticks in the Hearts deep Core
And it sticks in the deep Back bone
And no Smile that ever was smild
But only one Smile alone

That betwixt the Cradle & Grave
It only once Smild can be
But when it once is Smild
Theres an end to all Misery

The Golden Net

Three Virgins at the break of day
Whither young Man whither away
Alas for woe! alas for woe!
They cry & tears for ever flow
The one was Clothd in flames of fire
The other Clothd in iron wire
The other Clothd in tears & sighs
Dazling bright before my Eyes
They bore a Net of Golden twine
To hang upon the Branches fine
Pitying I wept to see the woe
That Love & Beauty undergo
To be consumd in burning Fires
And in ungratified desires
And in tears clothd Night & day
Melted all my Soul away
When they saw my Tears a Smile
That did Heaven itself beguile
Bore the Golden Net aloft

As on downy Pinions soft
Over the Morning of my day
Underneath the Net I stray
Now intreating Burning Fire
Now intreating Iron Wire
Now intreating Tears & Sighs
O when will the morning rise

The Crystal Cabinet

The Maiden caught me in the Wild
Where I was dancing merrily
She put me into her Cabinet
And Lockd me up with a golden Key

This Cabinet is formd of Gold
And Pearl & Crystal shining bright
And within it opens into a World
And a little lovely Moony Night

Another England there I saw
Another London with its Tower
Another Thames & other Hills
And another pleasant Surrey Bower

Another Maiden like herself
Translucent lovely shining clear
Threefold each in the other closd
O what a pleasant trembling fear

O what a smile a threefold Smile
Filld me that like a flame I burnd
I bent to Kiss the lovely Maid
And found a Threefold Kiss returnd

I strove to sieze the inmost Form
With ardor fierce & hands of flame

But burst the Crystal Cabinet
And like a Weeping Babe became

A weeping Babe upon the wild
And Weeping Woman pale reclind
And in the outward air again
I filld with woes the passing Wind

William Bond

I wonder whether the Girls are mad
And I wonder whether they mean to kill
And I wonder if William Bond will die
For assuredly he is very ill

He went to Church in a May morning
Attended by Fairies one two & three
But the Angels of Providence drove them away
And he returnd home in Misery

He went not out to the Field nor Fold
He went not out to the Village nor Town
But he came home in a black black cloud
And took to his Bed & there lay down

And an Angel of Providence at his Feet
And an Angel of Providence at his Head
And in the midst a Black Black Cloud
And in the midst the Sick Man on his Bed

And on his Right hand was Mary Green
And on his Left hand was his Sister Jane
And their tears fell thro the black black Cloud
To drive away the sick mans pain

O William if thou dost another Love
Dost another Love better than poor Mary

Go & take that other to be thy Wife
And Mary Green shall her Servant be

Yes Mary I do another Love
Another I Love far better than thee
And Another I will have for my Wife
Then what have I to do with thee

For thou art Melancholy Pale
And on thy Head is the cold Moons shine
But she is ruddy & bright as day
And the sun beams dazzle from her eyne

Mary trembled & Mary chilld
And Mary fell down on the right hand floor
That William Bond & his Sister Jane
Scarce could recover Mary more

When Mary woke & found her Laid
On the Right hand of her William dear
On the Right hand of his loved Bed
And saw her William Bond so near

The Fairies that fled from William Bond
Danced around her Shining Head
They danced over the Pillow white
And the Angels of Providence left the Bed

I thought Love livd in the hot sun shine
But O he lives in the Moony light
I thought to find Love in the heat of day
But sweet Love is the Comforter of Night

Seek Love in the Pity of others Woe
In the gentle relief of anothers care
In the darkness of night & the winters snow
In the naked & outcast Seek Love there

'The Angel that presided oer my birth'

The Angel that presided oer my birth
Said Little creature formd of Joy & Mirth
Go love without the help of any King on Earth

To My Dear and Loving Husband

If ever two were one, then surely we.
If ever man were loved by wife, then thee.
If ever wife was happy in a man,
Compare with me, ye women, if you can.
I prize thy love more than whole mines of gold,
Or all the riches that the east doth hold.
My love is such that rivers cannot quench,
Nor ought but love from thee give recompence.
Thy love is such I can no way repay;
The heavens reward thee manifold, I pray.
Then while we live, in love let's so persever,
That when we live no more we may live ever.

Fiddler's Song

The storm is over, lady.
The sea makes no more sound.
What do you wait for, lady?
His yellow hair is drowned.

The waves go quiet, lady,
Like sheep into the fold.
What do you wait for, lady?
His kissing mouth is cold.

STERLING A. BROWN 1901–89

Long Gone

I laks yo' kin' of lovin',
  Ain't never caught you wrong,
But it jes' ain' nachal
  Fo' to stay here long;

It jes' ain' nachal
  Fo' a railroad man,
With a itch fo' travelin'
  He cain't understan'....

I looks at de rails,
  An' I looks at de ties,
An' I hears an ole freight
  Puffin' up de rise,

An' at nights on my pallet,
  When all is still,
I listens fo' de empties
  Bumpin' up de hill;

When I oughta be quiet,
  I is got a itch
Fo' to hear de whistle blow
  Fo' de crossin' or de switch,

An' I knows de time's a-nearin'
  When I got to ride,
Though it's homelike and happy
  At yo' side.

You is done all you could do
  To make me stay;
'Tain't no fault of yours I'se leavin' –
  I'se jes dataway.

I is got to see some people
    I ain't never seen,
Gotta highball thu some country
    Whah I never been.

I don't know which way I'm travelin' –
    Far or near,
All I knows fo' certain is
    I cain't stay here.

Ain't no call at all, sweet woman,
    Fo' to carry on –
Jes' my name and jes' my habit
    To be Long Gone. . . .

Georgie Grimes

Georgie Grimes, with a red suitcase,
    Sloshes onward through the rain,
Georgie Grimes, with a fear behind him,
    Will not come back again.

Georgie remembers hot words, lies,
    The knife, and a pool of blood,
And suddenly her staring eyes,
    With their light gone out for good.

Georgie mutters over and over,
    Stumbling through the soggy clay,
'No livin' woman got de right
    To do no man dat way.'

Rent Day Blues

I says to my baby
'Baby, but de rent is due;

Can't noways figger
What we ever gonna do.'

My baby says, 'Honey,
Dontcha worry 'bout de rent.
Looky here, daddy,
At de money what de good Lord sent.'

Says to my baby,
'Baby, I been all aroun';
Never knowed de good Lord
To send no greenbacks down.'

Baby says, 'Dontcha
Bother none about de Lord;
Thing what I'm figgerin'
Is how to get de next month's board.'

Says to my baby,
'I'd best get me on a spell;
Get your rent from heaven,
Maybe get your food from hell.'

Baby says, 'One old
Miracle I never see,
Dat a man lak you
Can ever get away from me.'

I says, 'Ain't no magician,
Baby, dat's a sho-Gawd fact;
But jest you watch me
Do de disappearin' act.'

'Ef you do, you're better
Dan de devil or de Lord on high';
An' I stayed wid my baby
Fo' a devilish good reason why.

'How do I love thee?'
(Sonnets from the Portuguese, XLIII)

How do I love thee? Let me count the ways.
I love thee to the depth and breadth and height
My soul can reach, when feeling out of sight
For the ends of Being and ideal Grace.
I love thee to the level of everyday's
Most quiet need, by sun and candle-light.
I love thee freely, as men strive for Right:
I love thee purely, as they turn from Praise.
I love thee with the passion put to use
In my old griefs, and with my childhood's faith.
I love thee with a love I seemed to lose
With my lost saints! – I love thee with the breath,
Smiles, tears, of all my life! – and, if God choose,
I shall but love thee better after death.

The Lost Mistress

I

All's over, then: does truth sound bitter
  As one at first believes?
Hark, 'tis the sparrows' good-night twitter
  About your cottage eaves!

II

And the leaf-buds on the vine are woolly,
  I noticed that, today;
One day more bursts them open fully
  – You know the red turns grey.

III

Tomorrow we meet the same then, dearest?
  May I take your hand in mine?
Mere friends are we, – well, friends the merest
  Keep much that I resign:

IV

For each glance of the eye so bright and black,
  Though I keep with heart's endeavour, –
Your voice, when you wish the snowdrops back,
  Though it stay in my soul for ever! –

V

Yet I will but say what mere friends say,
  Or only a thought stronger;
I will hold your hand but as long as all may,
  Or so very little longer!

Meeting at Night

I

The grey sea and the long black land;
And the yellow half-moon large and low;
And the startled little waves that leap
In fiery ringlets from their sleep,
As I gain the cove with pushing prow,
And quench its speed i' the slushy sand.

II

Then a mile of warm sea-scented beach;
Three fields to cross till a farm appears;
A tap at the pane, the quick sharp scratch
And blue spurt of a lighted match,
And a voice less loud, through its joys and fears,
Than the two hearts beating each to each!

Love Among the Ruins

I

Where the quiet-coloured end of evening smiles,
     Miles and miles
On the solitary pastures where our sheep
     Half-asleep
Tinkle homeward through the twilight, stray or stop
     As they crop –
Was the site once of a city great and gay,
     (So they say)
Of our country's very capital, its prince
     Ages since
Held his court in, gathered councils, wielding far
     Peace or war.

II

Now, – the country does not even boast a tree,
  As you see,
To distinguish slopes of verdure, certain rills
  From the hills
Intersect and give a name to, (else they run
  Into one)
Where the domed and daring palace shot its spires
  Up like fires
O'er the hundred-gated circuit of a wall
  Bounding all,
Made of marble, men might march on nor be pressed,
  Twelve abreast.

III

And such plenty and perfection, see, of grass
  Never was!
Such a carpet as, this summer-time, o'erspreads
  And embeds
Every vestige of the city, guessed alone,
  Stock or stone –
Where a multitude of men breathed joy and woe
  Long ago;
Lust of glory pricked their hearts up, dread of shame
  Struck them tame;
And that glory and that shame alike, the gold
  Bought and sold.

IV

Now, – the single little turret that remains
  On the plains,
By the caper over-rooted, by the gourd
  Overscored,
While the patching houseleek's head of blossom winks
  Through the chinks –

Marks the basement whence a tower in ancient time
 Sprang sublime,
And a burning ring, all round, the chariots traced
 As they raced,
And the monarch and his minions and his dames
 Viewed the games.

V

And I know, while thus the quiet-coloured eve
 Smiles to leave
To their folding, all our many-tinkling fleece
 In such peace,
And the slopes and rills in undistinguished grey
 Melt away –
That a girl with eager eyes and yellow hair
 Waits me there
In the turret whence the charioteers caught soul
 For the goal,
When the king looked, where she looks now, breathless,
 dumb
 Till I come.

VI

But he looked upon the city, every side,
 Far and wide,
All the mountains topped with temples, all the glades'
 Colonnades,
All the causeys, bridges, aqueducts, – and then,
 All the men!
When I do come, she will speak not, she will stand,
 Either hand
On my shoulder, give her eyes the first embrace
 Of my face,
Ere we rush, ere we extinguish sight and speech
 Each on each.

In one year they sent a million fighters forth
   South and North,
And they built their gods a brazen pillar high
   As the sky,
Yet reserved a thousand chariots in full force –
   Gold, of course.
Oh heart! oh blood that freezes, blood that burns!
   Earth's returns
For whole centuries of folly, noise and sin!
   Shut them in,
With their triumphs and their glories and the rest!
   Love is best.

Any Wife to Any Husband

I

My love, this is the bitterest, that thou –
Who art all truth, and who dost love me now
   As thine eyes say, as thy voice breaks to say –
Shouldst love so truly, and couldst love me still
A whole long life through, had but love its will,
   Would death that leads me from thee brook delay.

II

I have but to be by thee, and thy hand
Will never let mine go, nor heart withstand
   The beating of my heart to reach its place.
When shall I look for thee and feel thee gone?
When cry for the old comfort and find none?
   Never, I know! Thy soul is in thy face.

III

Oh, I should fade – 'tis willed so! Might I save,
Gladly I would, whatever beauty gave
   Joy to thy sense, for that was precious too.
It is not to be granted. But the soul
Whence the love comes, all ravage leaves that whole;
   Vainly the flesh fades; soul makes all things new.

IV

It would not be because my eye grew dim
Thou couldst not find the love there, thanks to Him
   Who never is dishonoured in the spark
He gave us from his fire of fires, and bade
Remember whence it sprang, nor be afraid
   While that burns on, though all the rest grow dark.

V

So, how thou wouldst be perfect, white and clean
Outside as inside, soul and soul's demesne
   Alike, this body given to show it by!
Oh, three-parts through the worst of life's abyss,
What plaudits from the next world after this,
   Couldst thou repeat a stroke and gain the sky!

VI

And is it not the bitterer to think
That, disengage our hands and thou wilt sink
   Although thy love was love in very deed?
I know that nature! Pass a festive day,
Thou dost not throw its relic-flower away
   Nor bid its music's loitering echo speed.

VII

Thou let'st the stranger's glove lie where it fell;
If old things remain old things all is well,

For thou art grateful as becomes man best:
And hadst thou only heard me play one tune,
Or viewed me from a window, not so soon
  With thee would such things fade as with the rest.

VIII

I seem to see! We meet and part; 'tis brief;
The book I opened keeps a folded leaf,
  The very chair I sat on, breaks the rank;
That is a portrait of me on the wall –
Three lines, my face comes at so slight a call:
  And for all this, one little hour to thank!

IX

But now, because the hour through years was fixed,
Because our inmost beings met and mixed,
  Because thou once hast loved me – wilt thou dare
Say to thy soul and Who may list beside,
'Therefore she is immortally my bride;
  Chance cannot change my love, nor time impair.

X

'So, what if in the dusk of life that's left,
I, a tired traveller of my sun bereft,
  Look from my path when, mimicking the same,
The fire-fly glimpses past me, come and gone?
– Where was it till the sunset? where anon
  It will be at the sunrise! What's to blame?'

XI

Is it so helpful to thee? Canst thou take
The mimic up, nor, for the true thing's sake,
  Put gently by such efforts at a beam?

Is the remainder of the way so long,
Thou need'st the little solace, thou the strong?
　　Watch out thy watch, let weak ones doze and dream!

XII

– Ah, but the fresher faces! 'Is it true,'
Thou'lt ask, 'some eyes are beautiful and new?
　　Some hair, – how can one choose but grasp such wealth?
And if a man would press his lips to lips
Fresh as the wilding hedge-rose-cup there slips
　　The dew-drop out of, must it be by stealth?

XIII

'It cannot change the love still kept for Her,
More than if such a picture I prefer
　　Passing a day with, to a room's bare side:
The painted form takes nothing she possessed,
Yet, while the Titian's Venus lies at rest,
　　A man looks. Once more, what is there to chide?'

XIV

So must I see, from where I sit and watch,
My own self sell myself, my hand attach
　　Its warrant to the very thefts from me –
Thy singleness of soul that made me proud.
Thy purity of heart I loved aloud,
　　Thy man's-truth I was bold to bid God see!

XV

Love so, then, if thou wilt! Give all thou canst
Away to the new faces – disentranced,
　　(Say it and think it) obdurate no more:
Re-issue looks and words from the old mint,

Pass them afresh, no matter whose the print
　　Image and superscription once they bore!

XVI

Re-coin thyself and give it them to spend, –
It all comes to the same thing at the end,
　　Since mine thou wast, mine art and mine shalt be,
Faithful or faithless, sealing up the sum
Or lavish of my treasure, thou must come
　　Back to the heart's place here I keep for thee!

XVII

Only, why should it be with stain at all?
Why must I, 'twixt the leaves of coronal,
　　Put any kiss of pardon on thy brow?
Why need the other women know so much,
And talk together, 'Such the look and such
　　The smile he used to love with, then as now!'

XVIII

Might I die last and show thee! Should I find
Such hardship in the few years left behind,
　　If free to take and light my lamp, and go
Into thy tomb, and shut the door and sit,
Seeing thy face on those four sides of it
　　The better that they are so blank, I know!

XIX

Why, time was what I wanted, to turn o'er
Within my mind each look, get more and more
　　By heart each word, too much to learn at first;
And join thee all the fitter for the pause
'Neath the low doorway's lintel. That were cause
　　For lingering, though thou called'st, if I durst!

XX

And yet thou art the nobler of us two:
What dare I dream of, that thou canst not do,
   Outstripping my ten small steps with one stride?
I'll say then, here's a trial and a task –
Is it to bear? – if easy, I'll not ask:
   Though love fail, I can trust on in thy pride.

XXI

Pride? – when those eyes forestall the life behind
The death I have to go through! – when I find,
   Now that I want thy help most, all of thee!
What did I fear? Thy love shall hold me fast
Until the little minute's sleep is past
   And I wake saved. – And yet it will not be!

Love in a Life

I

Room after room,
I hunt the house through
We inhabit together.
Heart, fear nothing, for, heart, thou shalt find her –
Next time, herself! – not the trouble behind her
Left in the curtain, the couch's perfume!
As she brushed it, the cornice-wreath blossomed anew:
Yon looking-glass gleamed at the wave of her feather.

II

Yet the day wears,
And door succeeds door;
I try the fresh fortune –
Range the wide house from the wing to the centre.

Still the same chance! she goes out as I enter.
Spend my whole day in the quest, – who cares?
But 'tis twilight, you see, – with such suites to explore,
Such closets to search, such alcoves to importune!

The Last Ride Together

I

I said – Then, dearest, since 'tis so,
Since now at length my fate I know,
Since nothing all my love avails,
Since all, my life seemed meant for, fails,
    Since this was written and needs must be –
My whole heart rises up to bless
Your name in pride and thankfulness!
Take back the hope you gave, – I claim
Only a memory of the same,
– And this beside, if you will not blame,
    Your leave for one more last ride with me.

II

My mistress bent that brow of hers;
Those deep dark eyes where pride demurs
When pity would be softening through,
Fixed me a breathing-while or two
    With life or death in the balance: right!
The blood replenished me again;
My last thought was at least not vain:
I and my mistress, side by side
Shall be together, breathe and ride,
So, one day more am I deified.
    Who knows but the world may end tonight?

III

Hush! if you saw some western cloud
All billowy-bosomed, over-bowed
By many benedictions – sun's
And moon's and evening-star's at once –
   And so, you, looking and loving best,
Conscious grew, your passion drew
Cloud, sunset, moonrise, star-shine too,
Down on you, near and yet more near,
Till flesh must fade for heaven was here! –
Thus leant she and lingered – joy and fear!
   Thus lay she a moment on my breast.

IV

Then we began to ride. My soul
Smoothed itself out, a long-cramped scroll
Freshening and fluttering in the wind.
Fast hopes already lay behind.
   What need to strive with a life awry?
Had I said that, had I done this,
So might I gain, so might I miss.
Might she have loved me? just as well
She might have hated, who can tell!
Where had I been now if the worst befell?
   And here we are riding, she and I.

V

Fail I alone, in words and deeds?
Why, all men strive and who succeeds?
We rode; it seemed my spirit flew,
Saw other regions, cities new,
   As the world rushed by on either side.
I thought, – All labour, yet no less
Bear up beneath their unsuccess.

Look at the end of work, contrast
The petty done, the undone vast,
This present of theirs with the hopeful past!
   I hoped she would love me; here we ride.

VI

What hand and brain went ever paired?
What heart alike conceived and dared?
What act proved all its thought had been?
What will but felt the fleshly screen?
   We ride and I see her bosom heave.
There's many a crown for who can reach.
Ten lines, a statesman's life in each!
The flag stuck on a heap of bones,
A soldier's doing! what atones?
They scratch his name on the Abbey-stones.
   My riding is better, by their leave.

VII

What does it all mean, poet? Well,
Your brains beat into rhythm, you tell
What we felt only; you expressed
You hold things beautiful the best,
   And pace them in rhyme so, side by side.
'Tis something, nay 'tis much: but then,
Have you yourself what's best for men?
Are you – poor, sick, old ere your time –
Nearer one whit your own sublime
Than we who never have turned a rhyme?
   Sing, riding's a joy! For me, I ride.

VIII

And you, great sculptor – so, you gave
A score of years to Art, her slave,

And that's your Venus, whence we turn
To yonder girl that fords the burn!
    You acquiesce, and shall I repine?
What, man of music, you grown grey
With notes and nothing else to say,
Is this your sole praise from a friend,
'Greatly his opera's strains intend,
But in music we know how fashions end!'
    I gave my youth; but we ride, in fine.

IX

Who knows what's fit for us? Had fate
Proposed bliss here should sublimate
My being – had I signed the bond –
Still one must lead some life beyond,
    Have a bliss to die with, dim-descried.
This foot once planted on the goal,
This glory-garland round my soul,
Could I descry such? Try and test!
I sink back shuddering from the quest.
Earth being so good, would heaven seem best?
    Now, heaven and she are beyond this ride.

X

And yet – she has not spoke so long!
What if heaven be that, fair and strong
At life's best, with our eyes upturned
Whither life's flower is first discerned,
    We, fixed so, ever should so abide?
What if we still ride on, we two
With life for ever old yet new,
Changed not in kind but in degree,
The instant made eternity, –
And heaven just prove that I and she
    Ride, ride together, for ever ride?

Two in the Campagna

I

I wonder do you feel today
   As I have felt since, hand in hand,
We sat down on the grass, to stray
   In spirit better through the land,
This morn of Rome and May?

II

For me, I touched a thought, I know,
   Has tantalized me many times,
(Like turns of thread the spiders throw
   Mocking across our path) for rhymes
To catch at and let go.

III

Help me to hold it! First it left
   The yellowing fennel, run to seed
There, branching from the brickwork's cleft,
   Some old tomb's ruin: yonder weed
Took up the floating weft,

IV

Where one small orange cup amassed
   Five beetles, – blind and green they grope
Among the honey-meal: and last,
   Everywhere on the grassy slope
I traced it. Hold it fast!

V

The champaign with its endless fleece
   Of feathery grasses everywhere!

Silence and passion, joy and peace,
 An everlasting wash of air –
Rome's ghost since her decease.

VI

Such life here, through such lengths of hours,
 Such miracles performed in play,
Such primal naked forms of flowers,
 Such letting nature have her way
While heaven looks from its towers!

VII

How say you? Let us, O my dove,
 Let us be unashamed of soul,
As earth lies bare to heaven above!
 How is it under our control
To love or not to love?

VIII

I would that you were all to me,
 You that are just so much, no more.
Nor yours nor mine, nor slave nor free!
 Where does the fault lie? What the core
O' the wound, since wound must be?

IX

I would I could adopt your will,
 See with your eyes, and set my heart
Beating by yours, and drink my fill
 At your soul's springs, – your part my part
In life, for good and ill.

No. I yearn upward, touch you close,
Then stand away. I kiss your cheek,
Catch your soul's warmth, – I pluck the rose
And love it more than tongue can speak –
Then the good minute goes.

XI

Already how am I so far
Out of that minute? Must I go
Still like the thistle-ball, no bar,
Onward, whenever light winds blow,
Fixed by no friendly star?

XII

Just when I seemed about to learn!
Where is the thread now? Off again!
The old trick! Only I discern –
Infinite passion, and the pain
Of finite hearts that yearn.

Bad Dreams I

Last night I saw you in my sleep:
And how your charm of face was changed!
I asked 'Some love, some faith you keep?'
You answered 'Faith gone, love estranged.'

Whereat I woke – a twofold bliss:
Waking was one, but next there came
This other: 'Though I felt, for this,
My heart break, I loved on the same.'

Inapprehensiveness

We two stood simply friend-like side by side,
Viewing a twilight country far and wide,
Till she at length broke silence. 'How it towers
Yonder, the ruin o'er this vale of ours!
The West's faint flare behind it so relieves
Its rugged outline – sight perhaps deceives,
Or I could almost fancy that I see
A branch wave plain – belike some wind-sown tree
Chance-rooted where a missing turret was.
What would I give for the perspective glass
At home, to make out if 'tis really so!
Has Ruskin noticed here at Asolo
That certain weed-growths on the ravaged wall
Seem' . . . something that I could not say at all,
My thought being rather – as absorbed she sent
Look onward after look from eyes distent
With longing to reach Heaven's gate left ajar –
'Oh, fancies that might be, oh, facts that are!
What of a wilding? By you stands, and may
So stand unnoticed till the Judgement Day,
One who, if once aware that your regard
Claimed what his heart holds, – woke, as from its sward
The flower, the dormant passion, so to speak –
Then what a rush of life would startling wreak
Revenge on your inapprehensive stare
While, from the ruin and the West's faint flare,
You let your eyes meet mine, touch what you term
Quietude – that's an universe in germ –
The dormant passion needing but a look
To burst into immense life!'

       'No, the book
Which noticed how the wall-growths wave' said she
'Was not by Ruskin.'

      I said 'Vernon Lee?'

ROBERT BURNS 1759–96

It Was Upon a Lammas Night
(Tune: Corn Rigs are Bonie)

It was upon a Lammas night,
    When corn rigs are bonie,
Beneath the moon's unclouded light,
    I held awa to Annie:
The time flew by, wi' tentless heed,
    Till 'tween the late and early;
Wi' sma' persuasion she agreed,
    To see me thro' the barley.

The sky was blue, the wind was still,
    The moon was shining clearly;
I set her down, wi' right good will,
    Amang the rigs o' barley:
I ken't her heart was a' my ain;
    I lov'd her most sincerely;
I kiss'd her owre and owre again,
    Amang the rigs o' barley.

I lock'd her in my fond embrace;
    Her heart was beating rarely:
My blessings on that happy place,
    Amang the rigs o' barley!
But by the moon and stars so bright,
    That shone that hour so clearly!
She ay shall bless that happy night,
    Amang the rigs o' barley.

I hae been blythe wi' comrades dear;
    I hae been merry drinking;
I hae been joyfu' gath'rin gear;
    I hae been happy thinking;

But a' the pleasures e'er I saw,
   Tho' three times doubl'd fairly,
That happy night was worth them a',
   Amang the rigs o' barley.

Corn rigs, an' barley rigs,
   An' corn rigs are bonie:
I'll ne'er forget that happy night
   Amang the rigs wi' Annie.

Green Grow the Rashes. A Fragment
(Tune: Green Grows the Rashes)

CHORUS

Green grow the rashes, O;
Green grow the rashes, O;
The sweetest hours that e'er I spend,
   Are spent amang the lasses, O.

There's nought but care on ev'ry han',
   In ev'ry hour that passes, O:
What signifies the life o' man,
   An' 'twere na for the lasses, O?
      Green grow, &c.

The warly race may riches chase,
   An' riches still may fly them, O;
An' tho' at last they catch them fast,
   Their hearts can ne'er enjoy them, O.
      Green grow, &c.

But gie me a canny hour at e'en,
   My arms about my Dearie, O;
An' warly cares, an' warly men,
   May a' gae tapsalteerie, O!
      Green grow, &c.

For you sae douse, ye sneer at this,
    Ye're nought but senseless asses, O:
The wisest Man the warl' saw,
    He dearly lov'd the lasses, O.
            Green grow, &c.

Auld Nature swears, the lovely Dears
    Her noblest work she classes, O:
Her prentice han' she try'd on man,
    An' then she made the lasses, O.
            Green grow, &c.

The Rantin Dog the Daddie O't
(Tune: Whare wad Bonie Annie Lie)

O wha my babie-clouts will buy,
O wha will tent me when I cry;
Wha will kiss me where I lie;
The rantin dog the daddie o't.

O wha will own he did the faut,
O wha will buy the groanin maut,
O wha will tell me how to ca't,
The rantin dog the daddie o't.

When I mount the Creepie-chair,
Wha will sit beside me there,
Gie me Rob, I'll seek nae mair,
The rantin dog the daddie o't.

Wha will crack to me my lane;
Wha will mak me fidgin fain;
Wha will kiss me o'er again;
The rantin dog the daddie o't.

Auld Lang Syne
(Tune: For Old Long Sine My Jo)

Should auld acquaintance be forgot
    And never brought to mind?
Should auld acquaintance be forgot,
    And auld lang syne!

    For auld lang syne my jo,
        For auld lang syne,
    We'll tak a cup o' kindness yet,
        For auld lang syne.

And surely ye'll be your pint stowp!
    And surely I'll be mine!
And we'll tak a cup o' kindness yet,
    For auld lang syne.
        For auld &c.

We twa hae run about the braes,
    And pou'd the gowans fine;
But we've wander'd mony a weary fitt,
    Sin auld lang syne.
        For auld &c.

We twa hae paidl'd in the burn,
    Frae morning sun till dine;
But seas between us braid hae roar'd,
    Sin auld lang syne.
        For auld &c.

And there's a hand, my trusty fiere!
    And gie's a hand o' thine!
And we'll tak a right gude-willie-waught,
    For auld lang syne.
        For auld &c.

Afton Water

Flow gently, sweet Afton, among thy green braes,
Flow gently, I'll sing thee a song in thy praise;
My Mary's asleep by thy murmuring stream,
Flow gently, sweet Afton, disturb not her dream.

Thou stock dove whose echo resounds thro' the glen,
Ye wild whistling blackbirds in yon thorny den,
Thou green crested lapwing thy screaming forbear,
I charge you disturb not my slumbering Fair.

How lofty, sweet Afton, thy neighbouring hills,
Far mark'd with the courses of clear, winding rills;
There daily I wander as noon rises high,
My flocks and my Mary's sweet cot in my eye.

How pleasant thy banks and green vallies below,
Where wild in the woodlands the primroses blow;
There oft as mild ev'ning weeps over the lea,
The sweet scented birk shades my Mary and me.

Thy chrystal stream, Afton, how lovely it glides,
And winds by the cot where my Mary resides;
How wanton thy waters her snowy feet lave,
As gath'ring sweet flow'rets she stems thy clear wave.

Flow gently, sweet Afton, among thy green braes,
Flow gently, sweet river, the theme of my lays;
My Mary's asleep by thy murmuring stream,
Flow gently, sweet Afton, disturb not her dream.

Tibbie Dunbar
(Tune: Johnny Mcgill)

O wilt thou go wi' me, sweet Tibbie Dunbar;
O wilt thou go wi' me, sweet Tibbie Dunbar;
Wilt thou ride on a horse, or be drawn in a car,
Or walk by my side, O sweet Tibbie Dunbar.

I care na thy daddie, his lands and his money,
I care na thy kin, sae high and sae lordly:
But say thou wilt hae me for better for waur,
And come in thy coatie, sweet Tibbie Dunbar.

The Taylor Fell Thro' the Bed
(Tune: Beware of the Rippels)

The Taylor fell thro' the bed, thimble an' a',
The Taylor fell thro' the bed, thimble an' a';
The blankets were thin and the sheets they were sma',
The Taylor fell thro' the bed, thimble an' a'.

The sleepy bit lassie she dreaded nae ill,
The sleepy bit lassie she dreaded nae ill;
The weather was cauld and the lassie lay still,
She thought that a Taylor could do her nae ill.

Gie me the groat again, cany young man,
Gie me the groat again, cany young man;
The day it is short and the night it is lang,
The dearest siller that ever I wan.

There's somebody weary wi' lying her lane,
There's somebody weary wi' lying her lane,
There's some that are dowie, I trow wad be fain
To see the bit Taylor come skippin again.

Lassie Lie Near Me

(Tune: Laddie Lie Near Me)

Lang hae we parted been,
Lassie my dearie;
Now we are met again,
Lassie lie near me.

> Near me, near me,
> Lassie lie near me
> Lang hast thou lien thy lane,
> Lassie lie near me.

A' that I hae endur'd,
Lassie, my dearie,
Here in thy arms is cur'd,
Lassie lie near me.
> Near me, &c.

My Love She's But a Lassie Yet

My love she's but a lassie yet,
My love she's but a lassie yet,
We'll let her stand a year or twa,
> She'll no be half sae saucy yet.

I rue the day I sought her O,
I rue the day I sought her O,
Wha gets her needs na say he's woo'd,
> But he may say he's bought her O.

Come draw a drap o' the best o't yet,
Come draw a drap o' the best o't yet:
Gae seek for pleasure where ye will,
> But here I never misst it yet.

We're a' dry wi' drinkin o't,
We're a' dry wi' drinkin o't:
The minister kisst the fidler's wife,
    He could na preach for thinkin o't.

Ae Fond Kiss
  (Tune: Rory Dall's Port)

Ae fond kiss, and then we sever;
Ae farewell and then forever!
Deep in heart-wrung tears I'll pledge thee,
Warring sighs and groans I'll wage thee.

Who shall say that fortune grieves him
While the star of hope she leaves him?
Me, nae cheerfu' twinkle lights me;
Dark despair around benights me.

I'll ne'er blame my partial fancy,
Naething could resist my Nancy:
But to see her, was to love her;
Love but her, and love for ever.

Had we never lov'd sae kindly,
Had we never lov'd sae blindly,
Never met – or never parted,
We had ne'er been broken-hearted.

Fare thee weel, thou first and fairest!
Fare thee weel, thou best and dearest!
Thine be ilka joy and treasure,
Peace, Enjoyment, Love and Pleasure!

Ae fond kiss, and then we sever;
Ae fareweel, Alas! for ever!
Deep in heart-wrung tears I'll pledge thee,
Warring sighs and groans I'll wage thee.

O, Whistle an' I'll Come to Ye, My Lad

O, whistle an' I'll come to ye, my lad!
O, whistle an' I'll come to ye, my lad!
Tho' father an' mother an' a' should gae mad,
O, whistle an' I'll come to ye, my lad!

But warily tent when ye come to court me,
And come nae unless the back-yett be a-jee;
Syne up the back-style, and let naebody see,
And come as ye were na comin to me.
And come as ye were na comin to me.

At kirk, or at market, whene'er ye meet me,
Gang by me as tho' that ye car'd na a flie;
But steal me a blink o' your bonie black e'e,
Yet look as ye were na looking to me.
Yet look as ye were na looking to me.

Ay vow and protest that ye care na for me,
And whiles ye may lightly my beauty awee;
But court na anither, tho' jokin ye be,
For fear that she wile your fancy frae me.
For fear that she wile your fancy frae me.

A Red, Red Rose
(Tune: Major Graham)

My luve is like a red, red rose,
    That's newly sprung in June:
My luve is like the melodie,
    That's sweetly play'd in tune.
As fair art thou, my bonie lass,
    So deep in luve am I,
And I will luve thee still, my dear,
    Till a' the seas gang dry.

Till a' the seas gang dry, my dear,
　　And the rocks melt wi' the sun!
And I will luve thee still, my dear,
　　While the sands o' life shall run.
And fare-thee-weel, my only luve,
　　And fare-thee-weel a while!
And I will come again, my luve,
　　Tho' it were ten-thousand mile.

Wantonness

Wantonness for ever mair,
Wantonness has been my ruin;
Yet for a' my dool and care,
It's wantonness for ever!

I hae lov'd the Black, the Brown,
I hae lov'd the Fair, the Gowden:
A' the colours in the town
I hae won their wanton favour.

To a Youthful Friend

1

Few years have pass'd since thou and I
   Were firmest friends, at least in name,
And childhood's gay sincerity
   Preserv'd our feelings long the same.

2

But now, like me, too well thou know'st
   What trifles oft the heart recall;
And those who once have lov'd the most
   Too soon forget they lov'd at all.

3

And such the change the heart displays,
   So frail is early friendship's reign,
A month's brief lapse, perhaps a day's,
   Will view thy mind estrang'd again.

4

If so, it never shall be mine
   To mourn the loss of such a heart;
The fault was Nature's fault not thine,
   Which made thee fickle as thou art.

5

As rolls the ocean's changing tide,
   So human feelings ebb and flow;
And who would in a breast confide
   Where stormy passions ever glow?

6

It boots not, that together bred,
    Our childish days were days of joy;
My spring of life has quickly fled;
    Thou, too, hast ceas'd to be a boy.

7

And when we bid adieu to youth,
    Slaves to the specious world's controul,
We sigh a long farewell to truth;
    That world corrupts the noblest soul.

8

Ah, joyous season! when the mind
    Dares all things boldly but to lie;
When thought ere spoke is unconfin'd,
    And sparkles in the placid eye.

9

Not so in Man's maturer years,
    When Man himself is but a tool,
When interest sways our hopes and fears,
    And all must love and hate by rule.

10

With fools in kindred vice the same,
    We learn at length our faults to blend,
And those, and those alone may claim
    The prostituted name of friend.

11

Such is the common lot of man:
    Can we then 'scape from folly free?

Can we reverse the general plan,
    Nor be what all in turn must be?

12

No, for myself so dark my fate
    Through every turn of life hath been;
Man and the world I so much hate,
    I care not when I quit the scene.

13

But thou, with spirit frail and light,
    Wilt shine awhile and pass away,
As glow-worms sparkle through the night,
    But dare not stand the test of day.

14

Alas! whenever folly calls
    Where parasites and princes meet,
(For cherish'd first in royal halls,
    The welcome vices kindly greet)

15

Ev'n now thou'rt nightly seen to add
    One insect to the fluttering crowd;
And still thy trifling heart is glad,
    To join the vain, and court the proud.

16

There dost thou glide from fair to fair,
    Still simpering on with eager haste,
As flies along the gay parterre,
    That taint the flowers they scarcely taste.

17

But say, what nymph will prize the flame
  Which seems, as marshy vapours move,
To flit along from dame to dame,
  An ignis-fatuus gleam of love?

18

What friend for thee, howe'er inclin'd,
  Will deign to own a kindred care?
Who will debase his manly mind,
  For friendship every fool may share.

19

In time forbear; amidst the throng
  No more so base a thing be seen;
No more so idly pass along:
  Be something, any thing, but – mean.

Remember Thee, Remember Thee!

Remember thee, remember thee!
  Till Lethe quench life's burning stream,
Remorse and shame shall cling to thee,
  And haunt thee like a feverish dream!

Remember thee! Ay, doubt it not;
  Thy husband too shall think of thee;
By neither shalt thou be forgot,
  Thou *false* to him, thou *fiend* to me!

She Walks in Beauty

1

She walks in beauty, like the night
  Of cloudless climes and starry skies;
And all that's best of dark and bright
  Meet in her aspect and her eyes:
Thus mellow'd to that tender light
  Which heaven to gaudy day denies.

2

One shade the more, one ray the less,
  Had half impair'd the nameless grace
Which waves in every raven tress,
  Or softly lightens o'er her face;
Where thoughts serenely sweet express
  How pure, how dear their dwelling place.

3

And on that cheek, and o'er that brow,
  So soft, so calm, yet eloquent,
The smiles that win, the tints that glow,
  But tell of days in goodness spent,
A mind at peace with all below,
  A heart whose love is innocent!

Endorsement to the Deed of Separation, in the April of 1816

A year ago you swore, fond she!
  'To love, to honour', and so forth:
Such was the vow you pledged to me,
  And here's exactly what 'tis worth.

'So, we'll go no more a roving'

1

So, we'll go no more a roving
  So late into the night,
Though the heart be still as loving,
  And the moon be still as bright.

2

For the sword outwears its sheath,
  And the soul wears out the breast,
And the heart must pause to breathe,
  And love itself have rest.

3

Though the night was made for loving,
  And the day returns too soon,
Yet we'll go no more a roving
  By the light of the moon.

THOMAS CAMPION 1567–1620

'Follow thy fair sun, unhappy shadow'

Follow thy fair sun, unhappy shadow,
Though thou be black as night,
And she made all of light
Yet follow thy fair sun, unhappy shadow.

Follow her whose light thy light depriveth,
Though here thou liv'st disgraced,
And she in heaven is placed,
Yet follow her whose light the world reviveth.

Follow those pure beams whose beauty burneth,
That so have scorched thee,
As thou still black must be,
Till her kind beams thy black to brightness turneth.

Follow her while yet her glorie shineth:
There comes a luckless night,
That will dim all her light;
And this the black unhappy shade devineth.

Follow still since so thy fates ordained:
The Sun must have his shade,
Till both at once do fade,
The Sun still proud, the shadow still disdained.

'When to her lute Corrina sings'

When to her lute Corrina sings,
Her voice revives the leaden strings,
And doth in highest notes appear

As any challenged echo clear;
But when she doth of mourning speak,
E'en with her sighs the strings do break.

And, as her lute doth live or die,
Led by her passion, so must I:
For when of pleasure she doth sing,
My thoughts enjoy a sudden spring;
But if she doth of sorrow speak,
E'en from my heart the strings do break.

'Turn back, you wanton flyer'

Turn back, you wanton flyer,
And answer my desire
With mutual greeting;
Yet bend a little nearer,
True beauty still shines clearer
In closer meeting.
Hearts with hearts delighted
Should strive to be united,
Either others arms with arms enchaining:
Hearts with a thought, rosy lips
With a kiss still entertaining.

What harvest half so sweet is
As still to reap the kisses
Grown ripe in sowing,
And straight to be receiver
Of that which thou art giver,
Rich in bestowing?
There's no strict observing
Of times, or seasons changing,
There is ever one fresh spring abiding:
Then what we sow with our lips
Let us reap, loves gains dividing.

'It fell on a summers day'

It fell on a summers day,
While sweet Bessie sleeping lay
In her bower, on her bed,
Light with curtains shadowed;
Jamy came, she him spies,
Opening half her heavy eyes.

Jamy stole in through the door,
She lay slumbering as before;
Softly to her he drew near,
She heard him, yet would not hear;
Bessie vow'd not to speak,
He resolved that dump to break.

First a soft kiss he doth take,
She lay still, and would not wake;
Then his hands learned to woo,
She dreamt not what he would do,
But still slept, while he smiled
To see love by sleep beguiled.

Jamy then began to play,
Bessie as one buried lay,
Gladly still through this sleight
Deceived in her own deceit;
And, since this trance begoon,
She sleepes every afternoon.

'Your fair looks enflame my desire'

Your fair looks enflame my desire:
   Quench it again with love.
Stay, O strive not still to retire,
   Do not inhuman prove.

If love may persuade,
　　Loves pleasures, dear, deny not;
Hear is a silent grovie shade:
　　O tarry then, and flie not.

Have I seized my heavenly delight
　　In this unhaunted grove?
Time shall now her fury require
　　With the revenge of love.
Then come, sweetest, come,
　　My lips with kisses gracing:
Here let us harbour all alone,
　　Die, die in sweet embracing.

Will you now so timely depart,
　　And not return again?
Your sight lends such life to my heart
　　That to depart is pain.
Fear yields no delay,
　　Secureness helpeth pleasure:
Then, till the time gives safer stay,
　　O farewell, my lives treasure!

'Hark, all you ladies that do sleep'

Hark, all you ladies that do sleep:
　　the Fairy Queen Proserpina
Bids you awake and pity them that weep;
　　you may do in the dark
What the day doth forbid:
　　fear not the dogs that bark,
　　　　　　　Night will have all hid.

But if you let your lovers mone,
　　the Fairy Queen Proserpina
Will send abroad her Fairies every one,

that shall pinch black and blue
Your white hands, and fair arms,
    that did not kindly rue
            Your Paramours harms.

In myrtle arbours on the downs,
    the Fairy Queene Proserpina,
This night by moonshine leading merry rounds,
    holds a watch with sweet love;
Down the dale, up the hill,
    no plaints or groans may move
            Their holy vigil.

All you that will hold watch with love,
    the Fairy Queene Proserpina
Will make you fairer then Dione's dove;
    Roses red, Lillies white,
And the clear damask hue,
    shall on your cheeks alight:
            Love will adorne you.

All you that love, or loved before,
    the Fairy Queene Proserpina
Bids you encrease that loving humour more:
    they that yet have not fed
On delight amorous,
    she vows that they shall lead
            Apes in Avernus.

'Tune thy Music to thy heart'

Tune thy Music to thy heart,
Sing thy joy with thanks, and so thy sorrow:
    Though Devotion needs not Art,
Sometime of the poor the rich may borrow.

Strive not yet for curious ways:
Concord pleaseth more, the less 'tis strained;
   Zeal affects not outward praise,
Only strives to shew a love unfained.

   Love can wondrous things effect,
Sweetest Sacrifice, all wrath appeasing;
   Love the highest doth respect,
Love alone to him is ever pleasing.

'The peaceful western wind'

   The peaceful western wind
   The winter storms hath tamed,
   And nature in each kind
   The kind heat hath inflamed.
The forward buds so sweetly breathe
  Out of their earthy bowers,
That heaven, which views their pomp beneath,
  Would fain be decked with flowers.

   See how the morning smiles
   On her bright eastern hill,
   And with soft steps beguiles
   Them that lie slumbering still.
The music-loving birds are come
  From cliffs and rocks unknown,
To see the trees and briers bloom
  That late were overflown.

   What Saturn did destroy,
   Loves Queen revives again;
   And now her naked boy
   Doth in the fields remain:
Where he such pleasing change doth view
  In every living thing,

As if the world were born anew
  To gratify the Spring.

  If all things life present,
  Why die my comforts then?
  Why suffers my content?
  Am I the worst of men?
O beauty, be not thou accused
  Too justly in this case:
Unkindly if true love be used,
  'Twill yield thee little grace.

'A secret love or two, I must confess'

A secret love or two, I must confess,
  I kindly welcome for change in close playing:
Yet my dear husband I love nevertheless,
  His desires, whole or half, quickly allaying,
At all times ready to offer redress.
  His own he never wants, but hath it duly,
  Yet twits me, I keep not touch with him truly.

The more a spring is drawn, the more it flows;
  No Lamp less light retains by lighting others:
Is he a loser his loss that never knows?
  Or is he wealthy that wast treasure smothers?
My churl vows no man shall sent his sweet Rose:
  His own enough and more I give him duly,
  Yet still he twits me, I keep not touch truly.

Wise Archers bear more then one shaft to field,
  The Venturer loads not with one ware his shipping:
Should Warriors learn but one weapon to wield?
  Or thrive fair plants ere the worse for the slipping?
One dish cloys, many fresh appetite yield:
  Mine own I'll use, and his he shall have duly,
  Judge then what debter can keep touch more truly.

'Thrice toss these Oaken ashes in the air'

Thrice toss these Oaken ashes in the air,
Thrice sit thou mute in this inchanted chair;
Then thrice three times tie up this true loves knot,
And murmur soft, she will, or she will not.

Go burn these poisnous weeds in yon blue fire,
These Screech-owls feathers, and this prickling briar;
This Cypress gathered at a dead man's grave;
That all thy fears and cares an end may have.

Then come, you Fairies, dance with me a round;
Melt her hard heart with your melodious sound:
In vain are all the charms I can devise:
She hath an Art to break them with her eyes.

THOMAS CAREW 1594/5–1640

Song: Mediocrity in Love Rejected

Give me more love, or more disdain;
  The torrid or the frozen zone
Bring equal ease unto my pain,
  The temperate affords me none;
Either extreme, of love or hate,
Is sweeter than a calm estate.

Give me a storm; if it be love,
  Like Danaë in that golden shower,
I swim in pleasure; if it prove
  Disdain, that torrent will devour
My vulture-hopes; and he's possessed
Of heaven, that's but from hell released.
  Then crown my joys, or cure my pain;
  Give me more love, or more disdain.

Song: To My Inconstant Mistress

When thou, poor excommunicate
  From all the joys of love, shalt see
The full reward, and glorious fate,
  Which my strong faith shall purchase me,
  Then curse thine own inconstancy.

A fairer hand than thine shalt cure
  That heart which thy false oaths did wound;
And to my soul, a soul more pure
  Than thine shall by Love's hand be bound,
  And both with equal glory crowned.

Then shalt thou weep, entreat, complain
  To Love, as I did once to thee;

When all thy tears shall be as vain
    As mine were then, for thou shalt be
    Damned for thy false apostasy.

Disdain Returned

He that loves a rosy cheek,
    Or a coral lip admires,
Or from star-like eyes doth seek
    Fuel to maintain his fires;
As old Time makes these decay,
So his flames must waste away.

But a smooth and steadfast mind,
    Gentle thoughts, and calm desires,
Hearts with equal love combined,
    Kindle never-dying fires.
Where these are not, I despise
Lovely cheeks, or lips, or eyes.

No tears, Celia, now shall win
    My resolved heart to return;
I have searched thy soul within,
    And find nought but pride and scorn;
I have learned thy arts, and now
    Can disdain as much as thou.
Some power, in my revenge, convey
That love to her, I cast away.

To a Lady that Desired I Would Love Her

Now you have freely given me leave to love,
        What will you do?
Shall I your mirth or pastime move

When I begin to woo?
Will you torment, or scorn, or love me too?

Each petty beauty can disdain, and I,
     Spite of your hate,
Without your leave can see, and die;
     Dispense a nobler fate:
'Tis easy to destroy, you may create.

Then give me leave to love, and love me too,
     Not with design
To raise, as love's curst rebels do
     When puling poets whine,
Fame to their beauty from their blubbered eyne.

Grief is a puddle, and reflects not clear
     Your beauty's rays;
Joys are pure streams, your eyes appear
     Sullen in sadder lays;
In cheerful numbers they shine bright with praise,

Which shall not mention, to express you fair,
     Wounds, flames, and darts,
Storms in your brow, nets in your hair,
     Suborning all your parts,
Or to betray or torture captive hearts.

I'll make your eyes like morning suns appear,
     As mild and fair,
Your brow as crystal smooth and clear,
     And your disheveled hair
Shall flow like a calm region of the air.

Rich nature's store, which is the poet's treasure,
     I'll spend to dress
Your beauties; if your mine of pleasure
     In equal thankfulness
You but unlock, so we each other bless.

A Song

Ask me no more where Jove bestows,
When June is past, the fading rose;
For in your beauty's orient deep
These flowers, as in their causes, sleep.

Ask me no more whither doth stray
The golden atoms of the day;
For in pure love heaven did prepare
Those powders to enrich your hair.

Ask me no more whither doth haste
The nightingale, when May is past;
For in your sweet dividing throat
She winters, and keeps warm her note.

Ask me no more where those stars light,
That downwards fall in dead of night;
For in your eyes they sit, and there
Fixéd become, as in their sphere.

Ask me no more if east or west
The phoenix builds her spicy nest;
For unto you at last she flies,
And in your fragrant bosom dies.

No Platonique Love

Tell me no more of minds embracing minds,
 And hearts exchang'd for hearts;
That Spirits Spirits meet, as Winds do Winds,
 And mix their subt'lest parts;
That two unbodi'd Essences may kiss,
And then like Angels, twist and feel one Bliss.

I was that silly thing that once was wrought
 To practice this thin Love;
I climb'd from Sex to Soul, from Soul to Thought;
 But thinking there to move,
Headlong, I rowl'd from Thought to Soul, and then
From Soul I lighted at the Sex agen.

As some strict down-look'd men pretend to fast
 Who yet in Closets Eat;
So Lovers who profess they Spirits taste,
 Feed yet on grosser meat;
I know they boast they Soules to Soules Convey,
How e'r they meet, the Body is the Way.

Come, I will undeceive thee, they that tread
 Those vain Aeriall waies,
Are like young Heyrs, and Alchymists misled
 To waste their wealth and Daies,
For searching thus to be for ever Rich,
They only find a Med'cine for the Itch.

JOHN CLARE 1793–1864

The Milking Hour

The sun had grown on lessening day
A table large and round
And in the distant vapours grey
Seemed leaning on the ground
When Mary like a lingering flower
Did tenderly agree
To stay beyond her milking hour
And talk awhile with me

We wandered till the distant town
Had silenced nearly dumb
And lessened on the quiet ear
Small as a beetle's hum
She turned her buckets upside-down
And made us each a seat
And there we talked the evening brown
Beneath the rustling wheat

And while she milked her breathing cows
I sat beside the streams
In musing o'er our evening joys
Like one in pleasant dreams
The bats and owls to meet the night
From hollow trees had gone
And e'en the flowers had shut for sleep
And still she lingered on

We mused in rapture side by side
Our wishes seemed as one
We talked of time's retreating tide
And sighed to find it gone
And we had sighed more deeply still

O'er all our pleasures past
If we had known what now we know
That we had met the last

Song

I hid my love when young while I
Coudn't bear the buzzing of a flye
I hid my love to my despite
Till I could not bear to look at light
I dare not gaze upon her face
But left her memory in each place
Where e'er I saw a wild flower lye
I kissed and bade my love goodbye

I met her in the greenest dells
Where dew-drops pearl the wood bluebells
The lost breeze kissed her bright blue eye
The bee kissed and went singing bye
A sunbeam found a passage there
A gold chain round her neck so fair
As secret as the wild bee's song
She lay there all the summer long

I hid my love in field and town
Till e'en the breeze would knock me down
The bees seemed singing ballads o'er
The flye's buzz turned a lion's roar
And even silence found a tongue
To haunt me all the summer long
The riddle nature could not prove
Was nothing else but secret love

How Can I Forget

That farewell voice of love is never heard again,
Yet I remember it and think on it with pain:
I see the place she spoke when passing by,
The flowers were blooming as her form drew nigh,
That voice is gone, with every pleasing tone –
Loved but one moment and the next alone.
'Farewell' the winds repeated as she went
Walking in silence through the grassy bent;
The wild flowers – they ne'er looked so sweet before –
Bowed in farewells to her they'll see no more.
In this same spot the wild flowers bloom the same
In scent and hue and shape, ay, even name.
'Twas here she said farewell and no one yet
Has so sweet spoken – How can I forget?

'Tho' hid in spiral myrtle Wreath'

Tho' hid in spiral myrtle Wreath,
Love is a sword that cuts its Sheath:
And thro' the Slits, itself has made,
We spy the Glitter of the Blade.

But thro' the Slits, itself had made,
We spy no less too, that the Blade
Is eat away or snapt atwain,
And nought but Hilt and Stump remain.

She Moved Through the Fair

My young love said to me, 'My brothers won't mind,
And my parents won't slight you for your lack of kind.'
Then she stepped away from me, and this she did say,
'It will not be long, love, till our wedding day.'

She stepped away from me and she moved through the fair,
And fondly I watched her go here and go there,
Then she went her way homeward with one star awake,
As the swan in the evening moves over the lake.

The people were saying no two were e'er wed
But one had a sorrow that never was said,
And I smiled as she passed with her goods and her gear,
And that was the last that I saw of my dear.

I dreamt it last night that my young love came in,
So softly she entered, her feet made no din;
She came close beside me, and this she did say,
'It will not be long, love, till our wedding day.'

My Lover

For I will consider my lover, who shall remain nameless.

For at the age of 49 he can make the noise of five different
    kinds of lorry changing gear on a hill.

For he sometimes does this on the stairs at his place of work.

For he is embarrassed when people overhear him.

For he can also imitate at least three different kinds of train.

For these include the London tube train, the steam engine,
    and the Southern Rail electric.

For he supports Tottenham Hotspur with joyful and
    unswerving devotion.

For he abhors Arsenal, whose supporters are uncivilized and
    rough.

For he explains that Spurs are magic, whereas Arsenal are
    boring and defensive.

For I knew nothing of this six months ago, nor did I want to.

For now it all enchants me.

For this he performs in ten degrees.

For first he presents himself as a nice, serious, liberated
    person.

For secondly he sits through many lunches, discussing life
    and love and never mentioning football.

For thirdly he is careful not to reveal how much he dislikes
    losing an argument.

For fourthly he talks about the women in his past,
    acknowledging that some of it must have been his fault.

For fifthly he is so obviously reasonable that you are inclined
    to doubt this.

For sixthly he invites himself round for a drink one evening.

For seventhly you consume two bottles of wine between you.

For eighthly he stays the night.

For ninthly you cannot wait to see him again.

For tenthly he does not get in touch for several days.

For having achieved his object he turns again to his other interests.

For he will not miss his evening class or his choir practice for a woman.

For he is out nearly all the time.

For you cannot even get him on the telephone.

For he is the kind of man who has been driving women round the bend for generations.

For, sad to say, this thought does not bring you to your senses.

For he is charming.

For he is good with animals and children.

For his voice is both reassuring and sexy.

For he drives an A-registration Vauxhall Astra estate.

For he goes at 80 miles per hour on the motorways.

For when I plead with him he says, 'I'm not going any slower than *this*.'

For he is convinced he knows his way around better than anyone else on earth.

For he does not encourage suggestions from his passengers.

For if he ever got lost there would be hell to pay.

For he sometimes makes me sleep on the wrong side of my own bed.

For he cannot be bossed around.

For he has this grace, that he is happy to eat fish fingers or Chinese takeaway or to cook the supper himself.

For he knows about my cooking and is realistic.

For he makes me smooth cocoa with bubbles on the top.

For he drinks and smokes at least as much as I do.

For he is obsessed with sex.

For he would never say it is overrated.

For he grew up before the permissive society and remembers his adolescence.

For he does not insist it is healthy and natural, nor does he ask me what I would like him to do.

For he has a few ideas of his own.

For he has never been able to sleep much and talks with me
late into the night.

For we wear each other out with our wakefulness.

For he makes me feel like a light-bulb that cannot switch
itself off.

For he inspires poem after poem.

For he is clean and tidy but not too concerned with his
appearance.

For he lets the barber cut his hair too short and goes round
looking like a convict for a fortnight.

For when I ask if this necklace is all right he replies, 'Yes, if
no means looking at three others.'

For he was shocked when younger team-mates began using
talcum powder in the changing-room.

For his old-fashioned masculinity is the cause of continual
merriment on my part.

For this puzzles him.

Flowers

Some men never think of it.
You did. You'd come along
And say you'd nearly brought me flowers
But something had gone wrong.

The shop was closed. Or you had doubts –
The sort that minds like ours
Dream up incessantly. You thought
I might not want your flowers.

It made me smile and hug you then.
Now I can only smile.
But, look, the flowers you nearly brought
Have lasted all this while.

Defining the Problem

I can't forgive you. Even if I could,
You wouldn't pardon me for seeing through you.
And yet I cannot cure myself of love
For what I thought you were before I knew you.

The Aerial

The aerial on this radio broke
A long, long time ago,
When you were just a name to me –
Someone I didn't know.

The man before the man before
Had not yet set his cap
The day a clumsy gesture caused
That slender rod to snap.

Love came along. Love came along.
Then you. And now it's ended.
Tomorrow I shall tidy up
And get the radio mended.

The Orange

At lunchtime I bought a huge orange –
The size of it made us all laugh.
I peeled it and shared it with Robert and Dave –
They got quarters and I had a half.

And that orange, it made me so happy,
As ordinary things often do
Just lately. The shopping. A walk in the park.
This is peace and contentment. It's new.

The rest of the day was quite easy.
I did all the jobs on my list
And enjoyed them and had some time over.
I love you. I'm glad I exist.

As Sweet

It's all because we're so alike –
Twin souls, we two.
We smile at the expression, yes,
And know it's true.

I told the shrink. He gave our love
A different name.
But he can call it what he likes –
It's still the same.

I long to see you, hear your voice,
My narcissistic object-choice.

NOEL COWARD 1899–1973

I am No Good at Love

I am no good at love
My heart should be wise and free
I kill the unfortunate golden goose
Whoever it may be
With over-articulate tenderness
And too much intensity.

I am no good at love
I batter it out of shape
Suspicion tears at my sleepless mind
And, gibbering like an ape,
I lie alone in the endless dark
Knowing there's no escape

I am no good at love
When my easy heart I yield
Wild words come tumbling from my mouth
Which should have stayed concealed;
And my jealousy turns a bed of bliss
Into a battlefield.

I am no good at love
I betray it with little sins
For I feel the misery of the end
In the moment that it begins
And the bitterness of the last good-bye
Is the bitterness that wins.

Any Little Fish

I've fallen in love with you,
I'm taking it badly,
Freezing, burning,
Tossing, turning,
Never know when to laugh or cry,
Just look what our dumb friends do, they welcome it gladly.
Passion in a dromedary doesn't go so deep,
Camels when they're mating never sob themselves to sleep,
Buffaloes can revel in it, so can any sheep;
Why can't I?

   Any little fish can swim, any little bird can fly,
   Any little dog and any little cat
   Can do a bit of this and just a bit of that;
   Any little horse can neigh, and any little cow can moo,
   But I can't do anything at all
   But just love you.

   Any little cock can crow, any little fox can run,
   Any little crab on any little shore
   Can have a little dab and then a little more;
   Any little owl can hoot, and any little dove can coo,
   But I can't do anything at all but just love you.

You've pulled me across the brink,
You've chained me and bound me,
No escape now,
Buy the crêpe now,
When is the funeral going to be?
Whenever I stop to think,
See nature all around me,
Then I see how stupidly monogamous I am,
A lion in the circumstances wouldn't give a damn,
For if there was no lioness he'd lie down with a lamb;
Why can't I?

Any little bug can bite, any little bee can buzz,
Any little snail on any little oak
Can feel a little frail and have a little joke;
Any little frog can jump like any little kangaroo,
But I can't do anything at all but just love you.

Any little duck can quack, any little worm can crawl,
Any little mole can frolic in the sun
And make a little hole and have a little fun;
Any little snake can hiss in any little local zoo,
But I can't do anything at all but just love you.

Mad About the Boy

SOCIETY WOMAN

I met him at a party just a couple of years ago,
He was rather over-hearty and ridiculous
But as I'd seen him on the Screen
He cast a certain spell.
I basked in his attraction for a couple of hours or so,
His manners were a fraction too meticulous,
If he was real or not I couldn't tell
    But like a silly fool, I fell.

Mad about the boy,
I know it's stupid to be mad about the boy,
I'm so ashamed of it
But must admit
The sleepless nights I've had about the boy.
On the Silver Screen
He melts my foolish heart in every single scene.
Although I'm quite aware
That here and there
Are traces of the cad about the boy,
Lord knows I'm not a fool girl,

I really shouldn't care,
Lord knows I'm not a schoolgirl
In the flurry of her first affair.
Will it ever cloy?
This odd diversity of misery and joy,
I'm feeling quite insane
And young again
And all because I'm mad about the boy.

SCHOOLGIRL

Home work, home work,
Every night there's home work,
While Elsie practises the gas goes pop,
I wish, I wish she'd stop,
Oh dear, oh dear,
Here it's always 'No, dear,
You can't go out again, you must stay home,
You waste your money on that common Picturedrome,
Don't shirk – stay here and do your work.'
Yearning, yearning,
How my heart is burning.
I'll see him Saturday in *Strong Man's Pain*
And then on Monday and on Friday week again.
To me he is the sole man
Who can kiss as well as Colman,
I could faint whenever there's a close-up of his lips,
Though John Barrymore is larger
When my hero's on his charger
Even Douglas Fairbanks Junior hasn't smaller hips.
If only he could know
That I adore him so.

Mad about the boy,
It's simply scrumptious to be mad about the boy,
I know that quite sincerely
Housman really
Wrote *The Shropshire Lad* about the boy.

In my English Prose
I've done a tracing of his forehead and his nose
And there is, honour bright,
A certain slight
Effect of Galahad about the boy.
I've talked to Rosie Hooper,
She feels the same as me,
She says that Gary Cooper
Doesn't thrill her to the same degree.
In *Can Love Destroy?*
When he meets Garbo in a suit of corduroy,
He gives a little frown
And knocks her down.
Oh dear, oh dear, I'm mad about the boy.

COCKNEY

Every Wednesday afternoon
I get a little time off from three to eleven,
Then I go to the Picture House
And taste a little of my particular heaven.
He appears
In a little while,
Through a mist of tears
I can see him smiling
Above me.
Every picture I see him in,
Every lover's caress,
Makes my wonderful dreams begin,
Makes me long to confess
That if ever he looked at me
And thought perhaps it was worth the trouble to
Love me,
I'd give in and I wouldn't care
However far from the path of virtue he'd
Shove me,
Just supposing our love was brief,

If he treated me rough
I'd be happy beyond belief,
Once would be enough.

Mad about the boy,
I know I'm potty but I'm mad about the boy.
He sets me 'eart on fire
With love's desire,
In fact I've got it bad about the boy.
When I do the rooms
I see 'is face in all the brushes and the brooms.
Last week I strained me back
And got the sack
And 'ad a row with Dad about the boy.
I'm finished with Navarro,
I'm tired of Richard Dix,
I'm pierced by Cupid's arrow
Every Wednesday from four till six.
'Ow I should enjoy
To let 'im treat me like a plaything or a toy,
I'd give my all to him
And crawl to him,
So 'elp me Gawd I'm mad about the boy.

TART

It seems a little silly
For a girl of my age and weight
To walk down Piccadilly
In a haze of love.
It ought to take a good deal more to get a bad girl down,
I should have been exempt, for
My particular kind of Fate
Has taught me such contempt for
Every phase of love,
And now I've been and spent my last half-crown
To weep about a painted clown.

Mad about the boy,
It's pretty funny but I'm mad about the boy,
He has a gay appeal
That makes me feel
There's maybe something sad about the boy.
Walking down the street,
His eyes look out at me from people that I meet,
I can't believe it's true
But when I'm blue
In some strange way I'm glad about the boy.
I'm hardly sentimental,
Love isn't so sublime,
I have to pay my rental
And I can't afford to waste much time,
If I could employ
A little magic that would finally destroy
This dream that pains me
And enchains me,
But I can't because I'm mad about the boy.

Let's Do It
(With acknowledgements to Cole Porter)

Mr Irving Berlin
Often emphasizes sin
In a charming way.
Mr Coward we know
Wrote a song or two to show
Sex was here to stay.
Richard Rodgers it's true
Takes a more romantic view
Of that sly biological urge.
But it really was Cole
Who contrived to make the whole
Thing merge.

He said that Belgians and Dutch do it,
Even Hildegarde and Hutch do it,
Let's do it, let's fall in love.
Monkeys when ever you look do it,
Aly Khan and King Farouk do it,
Let's do it, let's fall in love.
The most recherché cocottes do it
In a luxury flat,
Locks, Dunns and Scotts do it
At the drop of a hat,
Excited spinsters in spas do it,
Duchesses when opening bazaars do it,
Let's do it, let's fall in love.

Our leading writers in swarms do it,
Somerset and all the Maughams do it,
Let's do it, let's fall in love.
The Brontës felt that they must do it,
Mrs Humphry Ward could just do it,
Let's do it, let's fall in love.
Anouilh and Sartre – God knows why – do it,
As a sort of a curse
Eliot and Fry do it,
But they do it in verse.
Some mystics, as a routine do it,
Even Evelyn Waugh and Graham Greene do it,
Let's do it, let's fall in love.

In the Spring of the year
Inhibitions disappear
And our hearts beat high,
We had better face facts
Every gland that overacts
Has an alibi,
For each bird and each bee,
Each slap-happy sappy tree,

Each temptation that lures us along
Is just Nature elle-même
Merely singing us the same
Old song.

> Girls from the RADA do it,
> BBC announcers may do it,
> Let's do it, let's fall in love.
> The Ballet Jooss to a man do it,
> Alfred Lunt and Lynn Fontanne do it,
> Let's do it, let's fall in love.
> My kith and kin, more or less, do it,
> Every uncle and aunt,
> But I confess to it,
> I've one cousin who can't.
> Critics as sour as quince do it,
> Even Emile Littler and Prince do it,
> Let's do it, let's fall in love.
>
> The House of Commons en bloc do it,
> Civil Servants by the clock do it,
> Let's do it, let's fall in love.
> Deacons who've done it before do it,
> Minor canons with a roar do it,
> Let's do it, let's fall in love.
> Some rather rorty old rips do it
> When they get a bit tight,
> Government Whips do it
> If it takes them all night,
> Old mountain goats in ravines do it,
> Probably we'll live to see machines do it,
> Let's do it, let's fall in love.

Episode of Hands

The unexpected interest made him flush.
Suddenly he seemed to forget the pain, –
Consented, – and held out
One finger from the others.

The gash was bleeding, and a shaft of sun
That glittered in and out among the wheels,
Fell lightly, warmly, down into the wound.

And as the fingers of the factory owner's son,
That knew a grip for books and tennis
As well as one for iron and leather, –
As his taut, spare fingers wound the gauze
Around the thick bed of the wound,
His own hands seemed to him
Like wings of butterflies
Flickering in sunlight over summer fields.

The knots and notches, – many in the wide
Deep hand that lay in his, – seemed beautiful.
They were like the marks of wild ponies' play, –
Bunches of new green breaking a hard turf.

And factory sounds and factory thoughts
Were banished from him by that larger, quieter hand
That lay in his with the sun upon it.
And as the bandage knot was tightened
The two men smiled into each other's eyes.

'So bashful when I spied her!'

So bashful when I spied her!
So pretty – so ashamed!
So hidden in her leaflets
Lest anybody find –

So breathless till I passed her –
So helpless when I turned
And bore her struggling, blushing,
Her simple haunts beyond!

For whom I robbed the Dingle –
For whom betrayed the Dell –
Many, will doubtless ask me –
But I shall never tell!

'Her breast is fit for pearls'

Her breast is fit for pearls,
But I was not a 'Diver.'
Her brow is fit for thrones –
But I had not a crest.
Her heart is fit for home –
I – a sparrow – build there
Sweet of twigs and twine
My perennial nest.

'The Rose did caper on her cheek'

The Rose did caper on her cheek –
Her Boddice rose and fell –

Her pretty speech – like drunken men –
Did stagger pitiful –

Her fingers fumbled at her work –
Her needle would not go –
What ailed so smart a little maid –
It puzzled me to know –

Till opposite – I spied a cheek
That bore *another* Rose –
Just opposite – another speech
That like the Drunkard goes –

A Vest that like her Boddice, danced –
To the immortal tune –
Till those two troubled – little Clocks
Ticked softly into one.

'You love me – you are sure'

You love me – you are sure –
I shall not fear mistake –
I shall not *cheated* wake –
Some grinning morn –
To find the Sunrise left –
And Orchards – unbereft –
And Dollie – gone!

I need not start – you're sure –
That night will never be –
When frightened – home to Thee I run –
To find the windows dark –
And no more Dollie – mark –
Quite none?

Be sure you're sure – you know –
I'll bear it better now –

If you'll just tell me so –
Than when – a little dull Balm grown –
Over this pain of mine –
You sting – again!

'Dying! Dying in the night!'

Dying! Dying in the night!
Wont somebody bring the light
So I can see which way to go
Into the everlasting snow?

And 'Jesus'! Where is *Jesus* gone?
They said that Jesus – always came –
Perhaps he does'nt know the House –
This way, Jesus, Let him pass!

Somebody run to the great gate
And see if Dollie's coming! Wait!
I hear her feet opon the stair!
Death wont hurt – now Dollie's here!

'What shall I do – it whimpers so'

What shall I do – it whimpers so –
This little Hound within the Heart –
All day and night – with bark and start –
And yet – it will not go?

Would you untie it – were you me –
Would it stop whining, if to Thee
I sent it – even now?

It should not teaze you – by your chair –
Or on the mat – or if it dare –
To climb your dizzy knee –

Or sometimes – at your side to run –
When you were willing –
May it come –
Tell Carlo – He'll tell me!

'Wild nights – Wild nights!'

Wild nights – Wild nights!
Were I with thee
Wild nights should be
Our luxury!

Futile – the winds –
To a Heart in port –
Done with the Compass –
Done with the Chart!

Rowing in Eden –
Ah – the Sea!
Might I but moor – tonight –
In thee!

'Going to Him! Happy letter!'

Going to Him! Happy letter!
Tell Him –
Tell Him the page I did'nt write –
Tell Him – I only said the Syntax –
And left the Verb and the pronoun – out –
Tell Him just how the fingers hurried –
Then – how they waded – slow – slow –
And then you wished you had eyes in your pages –
So you could see what moved them so –

Tell Him – it was'nt a Practised Writer –
You guessed – from the way the sentence toiled –

You could hear the Boddice tug, behind you –
As if it held but the might of a child –
You almost pitied it – you – it worked so –
Tell Him – No – you may quibble there –
For it would split His Heart, to know it –
And then you and I, were silenter.

Tell Him – Night finished – before we finished –
And the Old Clock kept neighing 'Day'!
And you – got sleepy –
And begged to be ended –
What would it hinder so – to – say?
Tell Him – just how she sealed you – Cautious!
But – if He ask where you are hid
Until tomorrow – Happy letter!
Gesture Coquette – and shake your Head!

'Ourselves were wed one summer – dear'

Ourselves were wed one summer – dear –
Your Vision – was in June –
And when Your little Lifetime failed,
I wearied – too – of mine –

And overtaken in the Dark –
Where You had put me down –
By Some one carrying a Light –
I – too – received the Sign –

'Tis true – Our Futures different lay –
Your Cottage – faced the sun –
While Oceans – and the North must be –
On every side of mine

'Tis true, Your Garden led the Bloom,
For mine – in Frosts – was sown –

And yet, one Summer, we were Queens –
But You – were crowned in June –

'Precious to Me – She still shall be'

Precious to Me – She still shall be –
Though She forget the name I bear –
The fashion of the Gown I wear –
The very Color of My Hair –

So like the Meadows – now –
I dared to show a Tress of Their's
If happy – She might not despise
A Buttercup's Array –

I know the Whole – obscures the Part –
The fraction – that appeased the Heart
Till Number's Empery –
Remembered – as the Milliner's flower
When Summer's Everlasting Dower –
Confronts the dazzled Bee –

The Bait

Come live with me, and be my love,
And we will some new pleasures prove
Of golden sands, and crystal brooks,
With silken lines, and silver hooks.

There will the river whispering run
Warmed by thy eyes, more than the sun.
And there the'enamoured fish will stay,
Begging themselves they may betray.

When thou wilt swim in that live bath,
Each fish, which every channel hath,
Will amorously to thee swim,
Gladder to catch thee, than thou him.

If thou, to be so seen, be'st loth,
By sun, or moon, thou darkenest both,
And if myself have leave to see,
I need not their light, having thee.

Let others freeze with angling reeds,
And cut their legs, with shells and weeds,
Or treacherously poor fish beset,
With strangling snare, or windowy net:

Let coarse bold hands, from slimy nest
The bedded fish in banks out-wrest,
Or curious traitors, sleavesilk flies
Bewitch poor fishes' wandering eyes.

For thee, thou need'st no such deceit,
For thou thyself art thine own bait,
That fish, that is not catched thereby,
Alas, is wiser far than I.

The Broken Heart

He is stark mad, who ever says,
  That he hath been in love an hour,
Yet not that love so soon decays,
  But that it can ten in less space devour;
Who will believe me, if I swear
That I have had the plague a year?
    Who would not laugh at me, if I should say,
    I saw a flask of powder burn a day?

Ah, what a trifle is a heart,
  If once into Love's hands it come!
All other griefs allow a part
  To other griefs, and ask themselves but some,
They come to us, but us Love draws,
He swallows us, and never chaws:
    By him, as by chain-shot, whole ranks do die,
    He is the tyrant pike, our hearts the fry.

If 'twere not so, what did become
  Of my heart, when I first saw thee?
I brought a heart into the room,
  But from the room, I carried none with me;
If it had gone to thee, I know
Mine would have taught thy heart to show
    More pity unto me: but Love, alas,
    At one first blow did shiver it as glass.

Yet nothing can to nothing fall,
  Nor any place be empty quite,
Therefore I think my breast hath all
  Those pieces still, though they be not unite;
And now as broken glasses show
A hundred lesser faces, so
My rags of heart can like, wish, and adore,
But after one such love, can love no more.

The Canonization

For God's sake hold your tongue, and let me love,
  Or chide my palsy, or my gout,
My five grey hairs, or ruined fortune flout,
  With wealth your state, your mind with arts improve,
    Take you a course, get you a place,
    Observe his Honour, or his Grace,
Or the King's real, or his stamped face
  Contemplate; what you will, approve,
  So you will let me love.

Alas, alas, who's injured by my love?
  What merchant's ships have my sighs drowned?
Who says my tears have overflowed his ground?
  When did my colds a forward spring remove?
    When did the heats which my veins fill
    Add one more to the plaguy bill?
Soldiers find wars, and lawyers find out still
  Litigious men, which quarrels move,
  Though she and I do love.

Call us what you will, we are made such by love;
  Call her one, me another fly,
We are tapers too, and at our own cost die,
  And we in us find the eagle and the dove,
    The phoenix riddle hath more wit
    By us; we two being one, are it.
So to one neutral thing both sexes fit
  We die and rise the same, and prove
  Mysterious by this love.

We can die by it, if not live by love,
  And if unfit for tombs and hearse
Our legend be, it will be fit for verse;
And if no piece of chronicle we prove,
  We'll build in sonnets pretty rooms;

As well a well wrought urn becomes
The greatest ashes, as half-acre tombs,
 And by these hymns, all shall approve
 Us canonized for love:

And thus invoke us; 'You whom reverend love
 Made one another's hermitage;
You, to whom love was peace, that now is rage;
 Who did the whole world's soul contract, and drove
  Into the glasses of your eyes
  (So made such mirrors, and such spies,
That they did all to you epitomize,)
 Countries, towns, courts: beg from above
 A pattern of your love!'

The Ecstasy

Where, like a pillow on a bed,
 A pregnant bank swelled up, to rest
The violet's reclining head,
 Sat we two, one another's best;

Our hands were firmly cemented
 With a fast balm, which thence did spring,
Our eye-beams twisted, and did thread
 Our eyes, upon one double string;

So to' intergraft our hands, as yet
 Was all our means to make us one,
And pictures in our eyes to get
 Was all our propagation.

As 'twixt two equal armies, Fate
 Suspends uncertain victory,
Our souls, (which to advance their state,
 Were gone out), hung 'twixt her, and me.

And whilst our souls negotiate there,
   We like sepulchral statues lay;
All day, the same our postures were,
   And we said nothing, all the day.

If any, so by love refined,
   That he soul's language understood,
And by good love were grown all mind,
   Within convenient distance stood,

He (though he knew not which soul spake
   Because both meant, both spake the same)
Might thence a new concoction take,
   And part far purer than he came.

This ecstasy doth unperplex
   (We said) and tell us what we love,
We see by this, it was not sex,
   We see, we saw not what did move:

But as all several souls contain
   Mixture of things, they know not what,
Love, these mixed souls doth mix again,
   And makes both one, each this and that.

A single violet transplant,
   The strength, the colour, and the size,
(All which before was poor, and scant,)
   Redoubles still, and multiplies.

When love, with one another so
   Interinanimates two souls,
That abler soul, which thence doth flow,
   Defects of loneliness controls.

We then, who are this new soul, know,
   Of what we are composed, and made,
For, th' atomies of which we grow,
   Are souls, whom no change can invade.

But O alas, so long, so far
   Our bodies why do we forbear?
They are ours, though they are not we, we are
   The intelligences, they the sphere.

We owe them thanks, because they thus,
   Did us, to us, at first convey,
Yielded their forces, sense, to us,
   Nor are dross to us, but allay.

On man heaven's influence works not so,
   But that it first imprints the air,
So soul into the soul may flow,
   Though it to body first repair.

As our blood labours to beget
   Spirits, as like souls as it can,
Because such fingers need to knit
   That subtle knot, which makes us man:

So must pure lovers' souls descend
   T' affections, and to faculties,
Which sense may reach and apprehend,
   Else a great prince in prison lies.

To our bodies turn we then, that so
   Weak men on love revealed may look;
Love's mysteries in souls do grow,
   But yet the body is his book.

And if some lover, such as we,
   Have heard this dialogue of one,
Let him still mark us, he shall see
   Small change, when we're to bodies gone.

A Fever

Oh do not die, for I shall hate
   All women so, when thou art gone,

That thee I shall not celebrate,
   When I remember, thou wast one.

But yet thou canst not die, I know,
   To leave this world behind, is death,
But when thou from this world wilt go,
   The whole world vapours with thy breath.

Or if, when thou, the world's soul, go'st,
   It stay, 'tis but thy carcase then,
The fairest woman, but thy ghost,
   But corrupt worms, the worthiest men.

Oh wrangling schools, that search what fire
   Shall burn this world, had none the wit
Unto this knowledge to aspire,
   That this her fever might be it?

And yet she cannot waste by this,
   Nor long bear this torturing wrong,
For much corruption needful is
   To fuel such a fever long.

These burning fits but meteors be,
   Whose matter in thee is soon spent.
Thy beauty, and all parts, which are thee,
   Are unchangeable firmament.

Yet 'twas of my mind, seizing thee,
   Though it in thee cannot perséver.
For I had rather owner be
   Of thee one hour, than all else ever.

The Flea

Mark but this flea, and mark in this,
How little that which thou deny'st me is;
Me it sucked first, and now sucks thee,

And in this flea, our two bloods mingled be;
Confess it, this cannot be said
A sin, or shame, or loss of maidenhead,
    Yet this enjoys before it woo,
    And pampered swells with one blood made of two,
    And this, alas, is more than we would do.

Oh stay, three lives in one flea spare,
Where we almost, nay more than married are.
This flea is you and I, and this
Our marriage bed, and marriage temple is;
Though parents grudge, and you, we'are met,
And cloistered in these living walls of jet.
    Though use make you apt to kill me,
    Let not to this, self murder added be,
    And sacrilege, three sins in killing three.

Cruel and sudden, hast thou since
Purpled thy nail, in blood of innocence?
In what could this flea guilty be,
Except in that drop which it sucked from thee?
Yet thou triumph'st, and say'st that thou
Find'st not thyself, nor me the weaker now;
    'Tis true, then learn how false, fears be;
    Just so much honour, when thou yield'st to me,
    Will waste, as this flea's death took life from thee.

The Good Morrow

I wonder by my troth, what thou, and I
    Did, till we loved? were we not weaned till then,
But sucked on country pleasures, childishly?
    Or snorted we in the seven sleepers' den?
'Twas so; but this, all pleasures fancies be.
If ever any beauty I did see,
Which I desired, and got, 'twas but a dream of thee.

And now good morrow to our waking souls,
    Which watch not one another out of fear;
For love, all love of other sights controls,
    And makes one little room, an every where.
Let sea-discoverers to new worlds have gone,
Let maps to others, worlds on worlds have shown,
Let us possess one world, each hath one, and is one.

My face in thine eye, thine in mine appears,
    And true plain hearts do in the faces rest,
Where can we find two better hemispheres
    Without sharp north, without declining west?
What ever dies, was not mixed equally;
    If our two loves be one, or, thou and I
Love so alike, that none do slacken, none can die.

The Indifferent

I can love both fair and brown,
Her whom abundance melts, and her whom want betrays,
Her who loves loneness best, and her who masks and
    plays,
Her whom the country formed, and whom the town,
Her who believes, and her who tries,
Her who still weeps with spongy eyes,
And her who is dry cork, and never cries;
I can love her, and her, and you and you,
I can love any, so she be not true.

Will no other vice content you?
Will it not serve your turn to do, as did your mothers?
Have you old vices spent, and now would find out others?
Or doth a fear, that men are true, torment you?
Oh we are not, be not you so,
Let me, and do you, twenty know.
Rob me, but bind me not, and let me go.

Must I, who came to travail thorough you,
Grow your fixed subject, because you are true?

Venus heard me sigh this song,
And by love's sweetest part, variety, she swore,
She heard not this till now; and that it should be so no
    more.
She went, examined, and returned ere long,
And said, 'Alas, some two or three
Poor heretics in love there be,
Which think to establish dangerous constancy.
But I have told them, "Since you will be true,
You shall be true to them, who are false to you." '

A Nocturnal upon St Lucy's Day, being the shortest day

'Tis the year's midnight, and it is the day's,
Lucy's, who scarce seven hours herself unmasks,
   The sun is spent, and now his flasks
    Send forth light squibs, no constant rays;
      The world's whole sap is sunk:
The general balm th' hydroptic earth hath drunk,
Whither, as to the bed's-feet, life is shrunk,
Dead and interred; yet all these seem to laugh,
Compared with me, who am their epitaph.

Study me then, you who shall lovers be
At the next world, that is, at the next spring:
   For I am every dead thing,
    In whom love wrought new alchemy.
      For his art did express
A quintessence even from nothingness,
From dull privations, and lean emptiness
He ruined me, and I am re-begot
Of absence, darkness, death; things which are not.

All others, from all things, draw all that's good,
Life, soul, form, spirit, whence they being have;
   I, by love's limbeck, am the grave
   Of all, that's nothing. Oft a flood
      Have we two wept, and so
Drowned the whole world, us two; oft did we grow
To be two chaoses, when we did show
Care to aught else; and often absences
Withdrew our souls, and made us carcases.

But I am by her death (which word wrongs her)
Of the first nothing, the elixir grown;
   Were I a man, that I were one,
   I needs must know; I should prefer,
      If I were any beast,
Some ends, some means; yea plants, yea stones detest,
And love; all, all some properties invest;
If I an ordinary nothing were,
As shadow, a light, and body must be here.

But I am none; nor will my sun renew.
You lovers, for whose sake, the lesser sun
   At this time to the Goat is run
   To fetch new lust, and give it you,
      Enjoy your summer all;
Since she enjoys her long night's festival,
Let me prepare towards her, and let me call
This hour her vigil, and her eve, since this
Both the year's, and the day's deep midnight is.

Song

Go, and catch a falling star,
   Get with child a mandrake root,
Tell me, where all past years are,
   Or who cleft the Devil's foot,

Teach me to hear mermaids singing,
　　Or to keep off envy's stinging,
　　　　And find
　　　　What wind
Serves to advance an honest mind.

If thou be'est born to strange sights,
　　Things invisible to see,
Ride ten thousand days and nights,
　　Till age snow white hairs on thee,
Thou, when thou return'st, wilt tell me
All strange wonders that befell thee,
　　　　And swear
　　　　No where
Lives a woman true, and fair.

If thou find'st one, let me know,
　　Such a pilgrimage were sweet,
Yet do not, I would not go,
　　Though at next door we might meet,
Though she were true, when you met her,
And last, till you write your letter,
　　　　Yet she
　　　　Will be
False, ere I come, to two, or three.

The Sun Rising

　　Busy old fool, unruly sun,
　　Why dost thou thus,
Through windows, and through curtains call on us?
Must to thy motions lovers' seasons run?
　　Saucy pedantic wretch, go chide
　　Late school-boys, and sour prentices,
　Go tell court-huntsmen, that the King will ride,
　Call country ants to harvest offices;

Love, all alike, no season knows, nor clime,
Nor hours, days, months, which are the rags of time.

    Thy beams, so reverend, and strong
      Why shouldst thou think?
I could eclipse and cloud them with a wink,
But that I would not lose her sight so long:
    If her eyes have not blinded thine,
      Look, and tomorrow late, tell me,
    Whether both th'Indias of spice and mine
    Be where thou left'st them, or lie here with me.
Ask for those kings whom thou saw'st yesterday,
And thou shalt hear, All here in one bed lay.

    She is all states, and all princes, I,
      Nothing else is.
Princes do but play us; compared to this,
All honour's mimic; all wealth alchemy.
    Thou sun art half as happy as we,
      In that the world's contracted thus;
    Thine age asks ease, and since thy duties be
    To warm the world, that's done in warming us.
Shine here to us, and thou art everywhere;
This bed thy centre is, these walls, thy sphere.

To his Mistress Going to Bed

Come, Madam, come, all rest my powers defy,
Until I labour, I in labour lie.
The foe oft-times having the foe in sight,
Is tired with standing though they never fight.
Off with that girdle, like heaven's zone glistering,
But a far fairer world encompassing.
Unpin that spangled breastplate which you wear,
That th' eyes of busy fools may be stopped there.

Unlace yourself, for that harmonious chime
Tells me from you, that now 'tis your bed time.
Off with that happy busk, which I envy,
That still can be, and still can stand so nigh.
Your gown going off, such beauteous state reveals,
As when from flowery meads th' hill's shadow steals.
Off with that wiry coronet and show
The hairy diadem which on you doth grow;
Now off with those shoes, and then safely tread
In this love's hallowed temple, this soft bed.
In such white robes heaven's angels used to be
Received by men; thou angel bring'st with thee
A heaven like Mahomet's paradise; and though
Ill spirits walk in white, we easily know
By this these angels from an evil sprite,
Those set our hairs, but these our flesh upright.

    Licence my roving hands, and let them go
Before, behind, between, above, below.
O my America, my new found land,
My kingdom, safeliest when with one man manned,
My mine of precious stones, my empery,
How blessed am I in this discovering thee!
To enter in these bonds, is to be free;
Then where my hand is set, my seal shall be.

    Full nakedness, all joys are due to thee.
As souls unbodied, bodies unclothed must be,
To taste whole joys. Gems which you women use
Are like Atlanta's balls, cast in men's views,
That when a fool's eye lighteth on a gem,
His earthly soul may covet theirs, not them.
Like pictures, or like books' gay coverings made
For laymen, are all women thus arrayed;
Themselves are mystic books, which only we
Whom their imputed grace will dignify
Must see revealed. Then since I may know,
As liberally, as to a midwife, show

Thyself: cast all, yea, this white linen hence,
Here is no penance, much less innocence.
    To teach thee, I am naked first, why then
What needst thou have more covering than a man.

ERNEST DOWSON 1867–1900

Non Sum Qualis Eram Bonae Sub Regno Cynarae

Last night, ah, yesternight, betwixt her lips and mine
There fell thy shadow, Cynara! thy breath was shed
Upon my soul between the kisses and the wine;
And I was desolate and sick of an old passion,
     Yea, I was desolate and bowed my head:
I have been faithful to thee, Cynara! in my fashion.

All night upon mine heart I felt her warm heart beat,
Night-long within mine arms in love and sleep she lay;
Surely the kisses of her bought red mouth were sweet;
But I was desolate and sick of an old passion,
     When I awoke and found the dawn was gray:
I have been faithful to thee, Cynara! in my fashion.

I have forgot much, Cynara! gone with the wind,
Flung roses, roses riotously with the throng,
Dancing, to put thy pale, lost lilies out of mind;
But I was desolate and sick of an old passion,
     Yea, all the time, because the dance was long:
I have been faithful to thee, Cynara! in my fashion.

I cried for madder music and for stronger wine,
But when the feast is finished and the lamps expire,
Then falls thy shadow, Cynara! the night is thine;
And I am desolate and sick of an old passion,
     Yea hungry for the lips of my desire:
I have been faithful to thee, Cynara! in my fashion.

MICHAEL DRAYTON 1563–1631

'My heart was slain, and none but you and I'

My heart was slain, and none but you and I:
Who should I think the murther should commit?
Since, but yourself, there was no creature by,
But only I, guiltless of murth'ring it.
It slew it self; the verdict on the view
Do quit the dead, and me not accessary:
Well, well, I fear it will be proved by you,
The evidence so great a proof doth carry.
But O, see, see, we need inquire no further,
Upon your lips the scarlet drops are found,
And in your eye, the boy that did the murther,
Your cheeks yet pale, since first he gave the wound.
  By this I see, however things be past,
    Yet heaven will still have murther out at last.

'Nothing but no and I, and I and no'

Nothing but no and I, and I and no,
How falls it out so strangely you reply?
I tell ye, fair, I'll not be answered so,
With this affirming no, denying I.
I say, I love, you sleightly answer I:
I say, you love, you pule me out a no:
I say, I die, you echo me with I:
Save me I cry, you sigh me out a no;
Must woe and I, have nought but no and?
No I, am I, if I no more can have;
Answer no more, with silence make reply,
And let me take my self what I do crave,
  Let no and I, with I and you be so:
    Then answer no and I, and I and no.

'How many paltry, foolish, painted things'

How many paltry, foolish, painted things,
That now in coaches trouble every street,
Shall be forgotten, whom no poet sings,
Ere they be well wraped in their winding sheet?
Where I to thee eternity shall give,
When nothing else remaineth of these dayes,
And Queens hereafter shall be glad to live
Upon the alms of thy superfluous praise;
Virgins and matrons reading these my rhymes,
Shall be so much delighted with thy story,
That they shall grieve, they lived not in these times,
To have seen thee, their sexes only glory:
   So shalt thou fly above the vulgar throng,
   Still to survive in my immortal song.

'An evil spirit your beauty haunts me still'

An evil spirit your beauty haunts me still,
Wherewith (alas) I have been long possessed,
Which ceaseth not to tempt me to each ill,
Nor gives me once, but one poor minute's rest:
In me it speaks, whether I sleep or wake,
And when by means, to drive it out I try,
With greater torments, then it me doth take,
And tortures me in most extremity;
Before my face, it lays down my despairs,
And hastes me on unto a sudden death;
Now tempting me, to drown my self in tears,
And then in sighing, to give up my breath;
   Thus am I still provoked, to every evil,
   By this good wicked spirit, sweet angel devil.

'Since there's no help, come let us kiss and part'

Since there's no help, come let us kiss and part,
Nay, I have done: you get no more of me,
And I am glad, yea glad with all my heart,
That thus so cleanly, I my self can free,
Shake hands for ever, cancel all our vows,
And when we meet at any time again,
Be it not seen in either of our brows,
That we one jot of former love retain;
Now at the last gasp, of love's latest breath,
When his pulse failing, passion speechless lies,
When faith is kneeling by his bed of death,
And innocence is closing up his eyes,
   Now if thou wouldst, when all have given him over,
   From death to life, thou mightst him yet recover.

Oppenheim's Cup and Saucer

She asked me to luncheon in fur. Far from
the loud laughter of men, our secret life stirred.

I remember her eyes, the slim rope of her spine.
This is your cup, she whispered, and this mine.

We drank the sweet hot liquid and talked dirty.
As she undressed me, her breasts were a mirror

and there were mirrors in the bed. She said Place
your legs around my neck, that's right. Yes.

A Negro Love Song

Seen my lady home las' night,
   Jump back, honey, jump back.
Hel' huh han' an' sque'z it tight,
   Jump back, honey, jump back.
Hyeahd huh sigh a little sigh,
Seen a light gleam f'om huh eye,
An' a smile go flittin' by –
   Jump back, honey, jump back.

Hyeahd de win' blow thoo de pine,
   Jump back, honey, jump back.
Mockin'-bird was singin' fine,
   Jump back, honey, jump back.
An' my hea't was beatin' so,
When I reached my lady's do',
Dat I could n't ba' to go –
   Jump back, honey, jump back.

Put my ahm aroun' huh wais',
   Jump back, honey, jump back.
Raised huh lips an' took a tase,
   Jump back, honey, jump back.
Love me, honey, love me true?
Love me well ez I love you?
An' she answe'd, ' 'Cose I do' –
   Jump back, honey, jump back.

DOUGLAS DUNN 1942 —

Re-reading Katherine Mansfield's *Bliss and Other Stories*

A pressed fly, like a skeleton of gauze,
Has waited here between page 98
And 99, in the story called 'Bliss',
Since the summer of '62, its date,

Its last day in a trap of pages. Prose
Fly, what can 'Je ne parle pas français' mean
To you who died in Scotland, when I closed
These two sweet pages you were crushed between?

Here is a green bus ticket for a week
In May, my place mark in 'The Dill Pickle'.
I did not come home that Friday. I flick
Through all our years, my love, and I love you still.

These stories must have been inside my head
That day, falling in love, preparing this
Good life; and this, this fly, verbosely buried
In 'Bliss', one dry tear punctuating 'Bliss'.

Epitaph on the Monument of Sir William Dyer at Colmworth, 1641

My dearest dust, could not thy hasty day
Afford thy drowsy patience leave to stay
One hour longer: so that we might either
Sit up, or gone to bed together?
But since thy finished labour hath possessed
Thy weary limbs with early rest,
Enjoy it sweetly: and thy widow bride
Shall soon repose her by thy slumbering side.
Whose business, now, is only to prepare
My nightly dress, and call to prayer:
Mine eyes wax heavy and the day grows old,
The dew falls thick, my blood grows cold.
Draw, draw the closed curtains: and make room:
My dear, my dearest dust; I come, I come.

T. S. ELIOT 1888–1965

The Love Song of J. Alfred Prufrock

S'io credesse che mia risposta fosse
a persona che mai tornasse al mondo,
questa fiamma staria senza più scosse.
Ma per ciò che giammai di questo fondo
non tornò vivo alcun, s'i'odo il vero,
senza tema d'infamia ti rispondo.

Let us go then, you and I,
When the evening is spread out against the sky
Like a patient etherised upon a table;
Let us go, through certain half-deserted streets,
The muttering retreats
Of restless nights in one-night cheap hotels
And sawdust restaurants with oyster-shells:
Streets that follow like a tedious argument
Of insidious intent
To lead you to an overwhelming question . . .
Oh, do not ask, 'What is it?'
Let us go and make our visit.

In the room the women come and go
Talking of Michelangelo.

The yellow fog that rubs its back upon the window-panes,
The yellow smoke that rubs its muzzle on the window-panes
Licked its tongue into the corners of the evening,
Lingered upon the pools that stand in drains,
Let fall upon its back the soot that falls from chimneys,
Slipped by the terrace, made a sudden leap,
And seeing that it was a soft October night,
Curled once about the house, and fell asleep.

And indeed there will be time
For the yellow smoke that slides along the street,

Rubbing its back upon the window-panes;
There will be time, there will be time
To prepare a face to meet the faces that you meet;
There will be time to murder and create.
And time for all the works and days of hands
That lift and drop a question on your plate;
Time for you and time for me,
And time yet for a hundred indecisions,
And for a hundred visions and revisions,
Before the taking of a toast and tea.

In the room the women come and go
Talking of Michelangelo.

And indeed there will be time
To wonder, 'Do I dare?' and, 'Do I dare?'
Time to turn back and descend the stair,
With a bald spot in the middle of my hair –
(They will say: 'How his hair is growing thin!')
My morning coat, my collar mounting firmly to the chin,
My necktie rich and modest, but asserted by a simple pin –
(They will say: 'But how his arms and legs are thin!')
Do I dare
Disturb the universe?
In a minute there is time
For decisions and revisions which a minute will reverse.

For I have known them all already, known them all –
Have known the evenings, mornings, afternoons,
I have measured out my life with coffee spoons;
I know the voices dying with a dying fall
Beneath the music from a farther room.
  So how should I presume?

And I have known the eyes already, known them all –
The eyes that fix you in a formulated phrase,
And when I am formulated, sprawling on a pin,
When I am pinned and wriggling on the wall,

Then how should I begin
To spit out all the butt-ends of my days and ways?
   And how should I presume?

And I have known the arms already, known them all –
Arms that are braceleted and white and bare
(But in the lamplight, downed with light brown hair!)
Is it perfume from a dress
That makes me so digress?
Arms that lie along a table, or wrap about a shawl.
   And should I then presume?
   And how should I begin?

                 .   .   .   .   .

Shall I say, I have gone at dusk through narrow streets
And watched the smoke that rises from the pipes
Of lonely men in shirt-sleeves, leaning out of windows? . . .

I should have been a pair of ragged claws
Scuttling across the floors of silent seas.

                 .   .   .   .   .

And the afternoon, the evening, sleeps so peacefully!
Smoothed by long fingers.
Asleep . . . tired . . . or it malingers.
Stretched on the floor, here beside you and me.
Should I, after tea and cakes and ices,
Have the strength to force the moment to its crisis?
But though I have wept and fasted, wept and prayed,
Though I have seen my head (grown slightly bald) brought
   in upon a platter,
I am no prophet – and here's no great matter;
I have seen the moment of my greatness flicker,
And I have seen the eternal Footman hold my coat, and
   snicker,
And in short, I was afraid.

And would it have been worth it, after all,
After the cups, the marmalade, the tea,
Among the porcelain, among some talk of you and me,
Would it have been worth while,
To have bitten off the matter with a smile,
To have squeezed the universe into a ball
To roll it toward some overwhelming question,
To say: 'I am Lazarus, come from the dead,
Come back to tell you all, I shall tell you all' –
If one, settling a pillow by her head,
    Should say: 'That is not what I meant at all.
    That is not it, at all.'

And would it have been worth it, after all,
Would it have been worth while,
After the sunsets and the dooryards and the sprinkled streets,
After the novels, after the teacups, after the skirts that trail
    along the floor –
And this, and so much more? –
It is impossible to say just what I mean!
But as if a magic lantern threw the nerves in patterns on a
    screen:
Would it have been worth while
If one, settling a pillow or throwing off a shawl,
And turning toward the window, should say:
    'That is not it at all,
    That is not what I meant, at all.'

.   .   .   .   .

No! I am not Prince Hamlet, nor was meant to be;
Am an attendant lord, one that will do
To swell a progress, start a scene or two,
Advise the prince; no doubt, an easy tool,
Deferential, glad to be of use,
Politic, cautious, and meticulous;
Full of high sentence, but a bit obtuse;

At times, indeed, almost ridiculous –
Almost, at times, the Fool.

I grow old . . . I grow old . . .
I shall wear the bottoms of my trousers rolled.

Shall I part my hair behind? Do I dare to eat a peach?
I shall wear white flannel trousers, and walk upon the beach.
I have heard the mermaids singing, each to each.

I do not think that they will sing to me.

I have seen them riding seaward on the waves
Combing the white hair of the waves blown back
When the wind blows the water white and black.

We have lingered in the chambers of the sea
By sea-girls wreathed with seaweed red and brown
Till human voices wake us, and we drown.

Portrait of a Lady

Thou hast committed –
Fornication: but that was in another country,
And besides, the wench is dead.

THE JEW OF MALTA

I

Among the smoke and fog of a December afternoon
You have the scene arrange itself – as it will seem to do –
With 'I have saved this afternoon for you';
And four wax candles in the darkened room,
Four rings of light upon the ceiling overhead,
An atmosphere of Juliet's tomb
Prepared for all the things to be said, or left unsaid.
We have been, let us say, to hear the latest Pole
Transmit the Preludes, through his hair and fingertips.
'So intimate, this Chopin, that I think his soul

Should be resurrected only among friends
Some two or three, who will not touch the bloom
That is rubbed and questioned in the concert room.'
– And so the conversation slips
Among velleities and carefully caught regrets
Through attenuated tones of violins
Mingled with remote cornets
And begins.
'You do not know how much they mean to me, my friends,
And how, how rare and strange it is, to find
In a life composed so much, so much of odds and ends,
(For indeed I do not love it . . . you knew? you are not
    blind!
How keen you are!)
To find a friend who has these qualities,
Who has, and gives
Those qualities upon which friendship lives.
How much it means that I say this to you –
Without these friendships – life, what *cauchemar!*'

    Among the windings of the violins
And the ariettes
Of cracked cornets
Inside my brain a dull tom-tom begins
Absurdly hammering a prelude of its own,
Capricious monotone
That is at least one definite 'false note.'
– Let us take the air, in a tobacco trance,
Admire the monuments,
Discuss the late events,
Correct our watches by the public clocks.
Then sit for half an hour and drink our bocks.

II

Now that lilacs are in bloom
She has a bowl of lilacs in her room

And twists one in her fingers while she talks.
'Ah, my friend, you do not know, you do not know
What life is, you who hold it in your hands';
(Slowly twisting the lilac stalks)
'You let it flow from you, you let it flow,
And youth is cruel, and has no remorse
And smiles at situations which it cannot see.'
I smile, of course,
And go on drinking tea.
'Yet with these April sunsets, that somehow recall
My buried life, and Paris in the Spring,
I feel immeasurably at peace, and find the world
To be wonderful and youthful, after all.'

The voice returns like the insistent out-of-tune
Of a broken violin on an August afternoon:
'I am always sure that you understand
My feelings, always sure that you feel,
Sure that across the gulf you reach your hand.

    You are invulnerable, you have no Achilles' heel.
You will go on, and when you have prevailed
You can say: at this point many a one has failed.
But what have I, but what have I, my friend,
To give you, what can you receive from me?
Only the friendship and the sympathy
Of one about to reach her journey's end.

I shall sit here, serving tea to friends. . . .'

I take my hat: how can I make a cowardly amends
For what she has said to me?
You will see me any morning in the park
Reading the comics and the sporting page.
Particularly I remark
An English countess goes upon the stage.
A Greek was murdered at a Polish dance,
Another bank defaulter has confessed.

I keep my countenance,
I remain self-possessed
Except when a street piano, mechanical and tired
Reiterates some worn-out common song
With the smell of hyacinths across the garden
Recalling things that other people have desired.
Are these ideas right or wrong?

III

The October night comes down; returning as before
Except for a slight sensation of being ill at ease
I mount the stairs and turn the handle of the door
And feel as if I had mounted on my hands and knees.
'And so you are going abroad; and when do you return?
But that's a useless question.
You hardly know when you are coming back,
You will find so much to learn.'
My smile falls heavily among the bric-à-brac.

'Perhaps you can write to me.'
My self-possession flares up for a second;
This is as I had reckoned.
'I have been wondering frequently of late
(But our beginnings never know our ends!)
Why we have not developed into friends.'
I feel like one who smiles, and turning shall remark
Suddenly, his expression in a glass.
My self-possession gutters; we are really in the dark.

'For everybody said so, all our friends,
They all were sure our feelings would relate
So closely! I myself can hardly understand.
We must leave it now to fate.
You will write, at any rate.
Perhaps it is not too late.
I shall sit here, serving tea to friends.'

And I must borrow every changing shape
To find expression . . . dance, dance
Like a dancing bear,
Cry like a parrot, chatter like an ape.
Let us take the air, in a tobacco trance –

Well! and what if she should die some afternoon,
Afternoon grey and smoky, evening yellow and rose;
Should die and leave me sitting pen in hand
With the smoke coming down above the housetops;
Doubtful, for a while
Not knowing what to feel or if I understand
Or whether wise or foolish, tardy or too soon . . .
Would she not have the advantage, after all?
This music is successful with a 'dying fall'
Now that we talk of dying –
And should I have the right to smile?

La Figlia Che Piange

  O quam te memorem virgo . . .

Stand on the highest pavement of the stair –
Lean on a garden urn –
Weave, weave the sunlight in your hair –
Clasp your flowers to you with a pained surprise –
Fling them to the ground and turn
With a fugitive resentment in your eyes:
But weave, weave the sunlight in your hair.

So I would have had him leave,
So I would have had her stand and grieve,
So he would have left
As the soul leaves the body torn and bruised,
As the mind deserts the body it has used.
I should find
Some way incomparably light and deft,

Some way we both should understand,
Simple and faithless as a smile and shake of the hand.

She turned away, but with the autumn weather
Compelled my imagination many days,
Many days and many hours:
Her hair over her arms and her arms full of flowers.
And I wonder how they should have been together!
I should have lost a gesture and a pose.
Sometimes these cogitations still amaze
The troubled midnight and the noon's repose.

Out of Danger

Heart be kind and sign the release
As the trees their loss approve.
Learn as leaves must learn to fall
Out of danger, out of love.

What belongs to frost and thaw
Sullen winter will not harm.
What belongs to wind and rain
Is out of danger from the storm.

Jealous passion, cruel need
Betray the heart they feed upon.
But what belongs to earth and death
Is out of danger from the sun.

I was cruel, I was wrong –
Hard to say and hard to know.
You do not belong to me.
You are out of danger now –

Out of danger from the wind,
Out of danger from the wave,
Out of danger from the heart
Falling, falling out of love.

Hinterhof

Stay near to me and I'll stay near to you –
As near as you are dear to me will do,
    Near as the rainbow to the rain,
    The west wind to the windowpane,
As fire to the hearth, as dawn to dew.

Stay true to me and I'll stay true to you –
As true as you are new to me will do,
    New as the rainbow in the spray,
    Utterly new in every way,
New in the way that what you say is true.

Stay near to me, stay true to me. I'll stay
As near, as true to you as heart could pray.
    Heart never hoped that one might be
    Half of the things you are to me –
The dawn, the fire, the rainbow and the day.

I'll Explain

It's something you say at your peril.
It's something you shouldn't contain.
It's a truth for the dark and a pillow.
Turn out the light and I'll explain.

It's the obvious truth of the morning
Bitten back as the sun turns to rain,
To the rain, to the dark, to the pillow.
Turn out the light and I'll explain.

   It's what I was hoping to tell you.
   It's what I was hoping you'd guess.
   It's what I was hoping you *wouldn't* guess
   Or you wouldn't mind.
   It's a kind
   Of hopelessness.

It's the hope that you hope at your peril.
It's the hope that you fear to attain.
It's the obvious truth of the evening.
Turn out the light and I'll explain.

In Paris With You

Don't talk to me of love. I've had an earful
And I get tearful when I've downed a drink or two.
I'm one of your talking wounded.
I'm a hostage. I'm maroonded.
But I'm in Paris with you.

Yes I'm angry at the way I've been bamboozled
And resentful at the mess that I've been through.
I admit I'm on the rebound
And I don't care where are *we* bound.
I'm in Paris with you.

Do you mind if we do *not* go to the Louvre,
If we say sod off to sodding Notre Dame,
If we skip the Champs Elysées
And remain here in this sleazy
Old hotel room
Doing this and that
To what and whom
Learning who you are,
Learning what I am.

Don't talk to me of love. Let's talk of Paris,
The little bit of Paris in our view.
There's that crack across the ceiling
And the hotel walls are peeling
And I'm in Paris with you.

Don't talk to me of love. Let's talk of Paris.
I'm in Paris with the slightest thing you do.
I'm in Paris with your eyes, your mouth,
I'm in Paris with . . . all points south.
Am I embarrassing you?
I'm in Paris with you.

Yellow Tulips

Looking into the vase, into the calyx, into the water drop,
Looking into the throat of the flower, at the pollen stain,
I can see the ambush love sprung once in the summery wood.
I can see the casualties where they lay, till they set forth again.

I can see the lips, parted first in surprise, parted in desire,
Smile now as a silence falls on the yellow-dappled ride
For each thinks the other can hear each receding thought
On each receding tide.

They have come out of the wood now. They are skirting the
fields
Between the tall wheat and the hedge, on the unploughed strips,
And they believe anyone who saw them would know
Every secret of their limbs and of their lips,
As if, like creatures of legend, they had come down out of the
mist
Back to their native city, and stood in the square,
And they were seen to be marked at the throat with a certain
sign
Whose meaning all could share.

      .   .   .   .   .

These flowers came from a shop. Really they looked nothing
much
Till they opened as if in surprise at the heat of this hotel.
Then the surprise turned to a shout, and the girl said, 'Shall I
chuck them now
Or give them one more day? They've not lasted so well.'

'Oh give them one more day. They've lasted well enough.
They've lasted as love lasts, which is longer than most
maintain.
Look at the sign it has left here at the throat of the flower
And on your tablecloth – look at the pollen stain.'

The Alibi

My mind was racing.
It was some years from now.
We were together again in our old flat.
You were admiring yourself adjusting your hat.
'Oh of course I was mad then,' you said with a
    forgiving smile,
'Something snapped in me and I was mad for a
    while.'

But this madness of yours disgusted me,
This alibi,
This gorgeous madness like a tinkling sleigh,
It carried you away
Snug in your fur, snug in your muff and cape.
You made your escape
Through the night, over the dry powdery snow.
I watched you go.

Truly the mad deserve our sympathy.
And you were driven mad you said by me
And then you drove away
The cushions and the furs piled high,
Snug with your madness alibi,
Injured and forgiven on your loaded sleigh.

ROBERT FROST 1874-1963

Love and a Question

A Stranger came to the door at eve,
   And he spoke the bridegroom fair.
He bore a green-white stick in his hand,
   And, for all burden, care.
He asked with the eyes more than the lips
   For a shelter for the night,
And he turned and looked at the road afar
   Without a window light.

The bridegroom came forth into the porch
   With 'Let us look at the sky,
And question what of the night to be,
   Stranger, you and I.'
The woodbine leaves littered the yard,
   The woodbine berries were blue,
Autumn, yes, winter was in the wind;
   'Stranger, I wish I knew.'

Within, the bride in the dusk alone
   Bent over the open fire,
Her face rose-red with the glowing coal
   And the thought of the heart's desire.
The bridegroom looked at the weary road,
   Yet saw but her within,
And wished her heart in a case of gold
   And pinned with a silver pin.

The bridegroom thought it little to give
   A dole of bread, a purse,
A heartfelt prayer for the poor of God,
   Or for the rich a curse;
But whether or not a man was asked

To mar the love of two
By harboring woe in the bridal house,
   The bridegroom wished he knew.

The Telephone

'When I was just as far as I could walk
From here today,
There was an hour
All still
When leaning with my head against a flower
I heard you talk.
Don't say I didn't, for I heard you say –
You spoke from that flower on the window sill –
Do you remember what it was you said?'

'First tell me what it was you thought you heard.'

'Having found the flower and driven a bee away,
I leaned my head,
And holding by the stalk,
I listened and I thought I caught the word –
What was it? Did you call me by my name?
Or did you say –
Someone said "Come" – I heard it as I bowed.'

'I may have thought as much, but not aloud.'

'Well, so I came.'

JOHN FULLER

The Kiss

Who are you,
You who may
Die one day,

Who saw the
Fat bee and
The owl fly

And the sad
Ivy put out
One sly arm?

Not the eye,
Not the ear
Can say Yes:

One eye has
Its lid and
Can get shy;

One ear can
Run out and
Off the map;

One eye can
Aim too low
And not hit;

One ear can
Hug the air,
Get too hot.

But lip and
Red lip are
Two and two,

His lip and
Her lip mix
And are wed,

Lip and lip
Can now say:
'You may die

But not yet.
Yes, you die
But not yet.'

The old lie.

Two Voices

'Love is a large hope in what,
Unfound, imaginary, leaves us
With a beautifying presence.
Love always grieves us.'

So sang youth to the consenting air
While age in deathly silence, thus:

'Love is a regret for what,
Lost or never was, assails us
With a beautifying presence.
Love never fails us.'

Valentine

The things about you I appreciate
    May seem indelicate:
I'd like to find you in the shower
And chase the soap for half an hour.
I'd like to have you in my power

And see your eyes dilate.
I'd like to have your back to scour
And other parts to lubricate.
Sometimes I feel it is my fate
To chase you screaming up a tower
   Or make you cower
By asking you to differentiate
   Nietzsche from Schopenhauer.
I'd like successfully to guess your weight
   And win you at a fête.
I'd like to offer you a flower.

I like the hair upon your shoulders,
Falling like water over boulders.
I like the shoulders, too: they are essential.
Your collar-bones have great potential
(I'd like all your particulars in folders
   Marked *Confidential*).

I like your cheeks, I like your nose,
I like the way your lips disclose
The neat arrangement of your teeth
(Half above and half beneath)
   In rows.

I like your eyes, I like their fringes.
The way they focus on me gives me twinges.
Your upper arms drive me berserk.
I like the way your elbows work,
   On hinges.

I like your wrists, I like your glands,
I like the fingers on your hands.
I'd like to teach them how to count,
And certain things we might exchange,
Something familiar for something strange.
I'd like to give you just the right amount
   And get some change.

I like it when you tilt your cheek up.
I like the way you nod and hold a teacup.
I like your legs when you unwind them.
Even in trousers I don't mind them.
I like each softly-moulded kneecap.
I like the little crease behind them.
I'd always know, without a recap,
    Where to find them.

I like the sculpture of your ears.
I like the way your profile disappears
Whenever you decide to turn and face me.
I'd like to cross two hemispheres
    And have you chase me.
I'd like to smuggle you across frontiers
Or sail with you at night into Tangiers.
    I'd like you to embrace me.

I'd like to see you ironing your skirt
    And cancelling other dates.
I'd like to button up your shirt.
I like the way your chest inflates.
I'd like to soothe you when you're hurt
Or frightened senseless by invertebrates.

I'd like you even if you were malign
And had a yen for sudden homicide.
I'd let you put insecticide
    Into my wine.
I'd even like you if you were the Bride
    Of Frankenstein
Or something ghoulish out of Mamoulian's
    Jekyll and Hyde.
I'd even like you as my Julian
Of Norwich or Cathleen ni Houlihan.
    How melodramatic
If you were something muttering in attics

Like Mrs Rochester or a student of Boolean
  Mathematics.

You are the end of self-abuse.
You are the eternal feminine.
I'd like to find a good excuse
To call on you and find you in.
I'd like to put my hand beneath your chin,
  And see you grin.
I'd like to taste your Charlotte Russe,
I'd like to feel my lips upon your skin,
I'd like to make you reproduce.

I'd like you in my confidence.
I'd like to be your second look.
I'd like to let you try the French Defence
  And mate you with my rook.
I'd like to be your preference
  And hence
I'd like to be around when you unhook.
I'd like to be your only audience,
The final name in your appointment book,
  Your future tense.

GEORGE GASCOIGNE 1542–77

The Lullaby of a Lover

Sing lullaby, as women do,
  Wherewith they bring their babes to rest;
And lullaby can I sing too,
  As womanly as can the best.
With lullaby they still the child;
And, if I be not much beguiled,
Full many wanton babes have I,
Which must be stilled with lullaby.

First, lullaby my youthful years,
  It is now time to go to bed;
For crooked age and hoary hairs
  Have won the haven within my head.
With lullaby, then, youth, be still!
With lullaby content thy will!
Since courage quails and comes behind,
Go sleep, and so beguile thy mind!

Next, lullaby my gazing eyes,
  Which wonted were to glance apace;
For every glass may now suffice
  To show the furrows in my face.
With lullaby, then, wink awhile!
With lullaby your looks beguile!
Let no fair face, nor beauty bright,
Entice you eft with vain delight.

And lullaby my wanton will;
  Let reason's rule now reign thy thought,
Since all too late I find by skill
  How dear I have thy fancies bought.
With lullaby now take thine ease!

With lullaby thy doubts appease!
For trust to this, if thou be still,
My body shall obey thy will.

Eke lullaby my loving boy;
  My little Robin, take thy rest!
Since age is cold and nothing coy,
  Keep close thy coin, for so is best.
With lullaby be thou content!
With lullaby thy lusts relent!
Let others pay which have mo pence,
Thou art too poor for such expense.

Thus, lullaby my youth, mine eyes,
  My will, my ware, and all that was:
I can no mo delays devise;
  But welcome pain, let pleasure pass.
With lullaby now take your leave!
With lullaby your dreams deceive!
And when you rise with waking eye,
Remember then this lullaby!

'And if I did, what then?'

'And if I did, what then?
Are you aggrieved therefore?
The sea hath fish for every man,
And what would you have more?'

Thus did my mistress once
Amaze my mind with doubt;
And popped a question for the nonce,
To beat my brains about.

Whereto I thus replied:
'Each fisherman can wish

That all the seas at every tide
Were his alone to fish;

And so did I, in vain;
But since it may not be,
Let such fish there as find the gain,
And leave the loss for me.

And with such luck and loss
I will content myself,
Till tides of turning time may toss
Such fishers on the shelf.

And when they stick on sands,
That every man may see,
Then will I laugh and clap my hands,
As they do now at me.'

To My Wife at Midnight

1

Are you to say goodnight
And turn away under
The blanket of your delight?

Are you to let me go
Alone to sleep beside you
Into the drifting snow?

Where we each reach,
Sleeping alone together,
Nobody can touch.

Is the cat's window open?
Shall I turn into your back?
And what is to happen?

What is to happen to us
And what is to happen to each
Of us asleep in our places?

2

I mean us both going
Into sleep at our ages
To sleep and get our fairing.

They have all gone home.
Night beasts are coming out.
The black wood of Madron

Is just waking up.
I hear the rain outside
To help me to go to sleep.

Nessie, dont let my soul
Skip and miss a beat
And cause me to fall.

3

Are you asleep I say
Into the back of your neck
For you not to hear me.

Are you asleep? I hear
Your heart under the pillow
Saying my dear my dear

My dear for all it's worth.
Where is the dun's moor
Which began your breath?

4

Ness, to tell you the truth
I am drifting away
Down to fish for the saithe.

Is the cat's window open?
The weather is on my shoulder
And I am drifting down

Into O can you hear me
Among your Dunsmuir Clan?
Are you coming out to play?

5

Did I behave badly
On the field at Culloden?
I lie sore-wounded now

By all activities, and
The terrible acts of my time
Are only a distant sound.

With responsibility
I am drifting off
Breathing regularly

Into my younger days
To play the games of Greenock
Beside the sugar-house quays.

6

Nessie Dunsmuir, I say
Wheesht wheesht to myself
To help me now to go

Under into somewhere
In the redcoat rain.
Buckle me for the war.

Are you to say goodnight
And kiss me and fasten
My drowsy armour tight?

My dear camp-follower,
Hap the blanket round me
And tuck in a flower.

Maybe from my sleep
In the stoure at Culloden
I'll see you here asleep

In your lonely place.

Love Without Hope

Love without hope, as when the young bird-catcher
Swept off his tall hat to the Squire's own daughter,
So let the imprisoned larks escape and fly
Singing about her head, as she rode by.

At First Sight

'Love at first sight,' some say, misnaming
Discovery of twinned helplessness
Against the huge tug of procreation.

But friendship at first sight? This also
Catches fiercely at the surprised heart
So that the cheek blanches and then blushes.

Down, Wanton, Down!

Down, wanton, down! Have you no shame
That at the whisper of Love's name,
Or Beauty's, presto! up you raise
Your angry head and stand at gaze?

Poor Bombard-captain, sworn to reach
The ravelin and effect a breach –
Indifferent what you storm or why,
So be that in the breach you die!

Love may be blind, but Love at least
Knows what is man and what mere beast;
Or Beauty wayward, but requires
More delicacy from her squires.

Tell me, my witless, whose one boast
Could be your staunchness at the post,
When were you made a man of parts
To think fine and profess the arts?

Will many-gifted Beauty come
Bowing to your bald rule of thumb,
Or Love swear loyalty to your crown?
Be gone, have done! Down, wanton, down!

A Former Attachment

And glad to find, on again looking at it,
It meant even less to me than I had thought –
You know the ship is moving when you see
The boxes on the quayside sliding away
And become smaller – and feel a calm delight
When the port's cleared and the coast out of sight,
And ships are few, each on its proper course,
With no occasion for approach or discourse.

A Jealous Man

To be homeless is a pride
To the jealous man prowling
Hungry down the night lanes,

Who has no steel at his side,
No drink hot in his mouth,
But a mind dream-enlarged,

Who witnesses warfare,
Man with woman, hugely
Raging from hedge to hedge:

The raw knotted oak-club
Clenched in the raw fist,
The ivy-noose well flung,

The thronged din of battle,
Gaspings of the throat-snared,
Snores of the battered dying,

Tall corpses, braced together,
Fallen in clammy furrows,
Male and female,

Or, among haulms of nettle
Humped, in noisome heaps,
Male and female.

He glowers in the choked roadway
Between twin churchyards,
Like a turnip ghost.

(Here, the rain-worn headstone,
There, the Celtic cross
In rank white marble.)

This jealous man is smitten,
His fear-jerked forehead
Sweats a fine musk;

A score of bats bewitched
By the ruttish odour
Swoop singing at his head;

Nuns bricked up alive
Within the neighbouring wall
Wail in cat-like longing.

Crow, cocks, crow loud,
Reprieve the doomed devil –
Has he not died enough?

Now, out of careless sleep,
She wakes and greets him coldly,
The woman at home,

She, with a private wonder
At shoes bemired and bloody –
His war was not hers.

With Her Lips Only

This honest wife, challenged at dusk
At the garden gate, under a moon perhaps,
In scent of honeysuckle, dared to deny
Love to an urgent lover: with her lips only,
Not with her heart. It was no assignation;
Taken aback, what could she say else?
For the children's sake, the lie was venial;
'For the children's sake', she argued with her conscience.

Yet a mortal lie must follow before dawn:
Challenged as usual in her own bed,
She protests love to an urgent husband,
Not with her heart but with her lips only;
'For the children's sake', she argues with her conscience,
'For the children' – turning suddenly cold towards them.

She is No Liar

She is no liar, yet she will wash away
Honey from her lips, blood from her shadowy hand,
And, dressed at dawn in clean white robes will say,
Trusting the ignorant world to understand:
'Such things no longer are; this is today.'

THOMAS GRAY 1716–71

Sonnet: On the Death of Richard West

In vain to me the smileing Mornings shine,
   And redning Phoebus lifts his golden Fire:
The Birds in vain their amorous Descant joyn;
   Or chearful Fields resume their green Attire:
These Ears, alas! for other Notes repine,
   A different Object do these Eyes require.
My lonely Anguish melts no Heart, but mine;
   And in my Breast the imperfect Joys expire.
Yet Morning smiles the busy Race to chear,
   And new-born Pleasure brings to happier Men:
The Fields to all their wonted Tribute bear:
   To warm their little Loves the Birds complain:
I fruitless mourn to him, that cannot hear,
   And weep the more because I weep in vain.

'I with whose colours Myra dressed her head'

I with whose colours Myra dressed her head,
I, that ware posies of her own hand making,
I, that mine own name in the chimneys read
By Myra finely wrought ere I was waking:
Must I look on, in hope time coming may
With change bring back my turn again to play?

I, that on Sunday at the church-stile found
A garland sweet, with true-love knots in flowers,
Which I to wear about mine arm was bound
That each of us might know that all was ours:
Must I now lead an idle life in wishes?
And follow Cupid for his loaves and fishes?

I, that did wear the ring her mother left,
I, for whose love she gloried to be blamed,
I, with whose eyes her eyes committed theft,
I, who did make her blush when I was named;
Must I lose ring, flowers, blush, theft and go naked,
Watching with sighs, till dead love be awaked?

I, that when drowsy Argus fell asleep,
Like Jealousy o'erwatched with desire,
Was even warned modesty to keep,
While her breath, speaking, kindled nature's fire:
Must I look on a-cold, while others warm them?
Do Vulcan's brothers in such fine nets arm them?

Was it for this that I might Myra see
Washing the water with her beauties, white?
Yet would she never write her love to me;
Thinks wit of change while thoughts are in delight?
Mad girls must safely love, as they may leave,
No man can print a kiss, lines may deceive.

THOM GUNN 1929–2004

Touch

You are already
asleep. I lower
myself in next to
you, my skin slightly
numb with the restraint
of habits, the patina of
self, the black frost
of outsideness, so that even
unclothed it is
a resilient chilly
hardness, a superficially
malleable, dead
rubbery texture.

You are a mound
of bedclothes, where the cat
in sleep braces
its paws against your
calf through the blankets,
and kneads each paw in turn.

Meanwhile and slowly
I feel a is it
my own warmth surfacing or
the ferment of your whole
body that in darkness beneath
the cover is stealing
bit by bit to break
down that chill.
           You turn and
hold me tightly, do
you know who

I am or am I
your mother or
the nearest human being to
hold on to in a
dreamed pogrom.

What I, now loosened,
sink into is an old
big place, it is
there already, for
you are already
there, and the cat
got there before you, yet
it is hard to locate.
What is more, the place is
not found but seeps
from our touch in
continuous creation, dark
enclosing cocoon round
ourselves alone, dark
wide realm where we
walk with everyone.

The Bed

    The pulsing stops where time has been,
        The garden is snow-bound,
The branches weighed down and the paths filled in,
        Drifts quilt the ground.

    We lie soft-caught, still now it's done,
        Loose-twined across the bed
Like wrestling statues; but it still goes on
        Inside my head.

The Hug

It was your birthday, we had drunk and dined
  Half of the night with our old friend
    Who'd showed us in the end
  To a bed I reached in one drunk stride.
    Already I lay snug,
And drowsy with the wine dozed on one side.

I dozed, I slept. My sleep broke on a hug,
    Suddenly, from behind,
In which the full lengths of our bodies pressed:
    Your instep to my heel,
  My shoulder-blades against your chest.
  It was not sex, but I could feel
  The whole strength of your body set,
      Or braced, to mine,
    And locking me to you
  As if we were still twenty-two
  When our grand passion had not yet
    Become familial.
  My quick sleep had deleted all
  Of intervening time and place.
    I only knew
The stay of your secure firm dry embrace.

A Blank

The year of griefs being through, they had to merge
In one last grief, with one last property:
To view itself like loosened cloud lose edge,
And pull apart, and leave a voided sky.

Watching Victorian porches through the glass,
From the 6 bus, I caught sight of a friend
Stopped on a corner-kerb to let us pass,

A four-year-old blond child tugging his hand,
Which tug he held against with a slight smile.
I knew the smile from certain passages
Two years ago, thus did not know him well,
Since they took place in my bedroom and his.

A sturdy-looking admirable young man.
He said 'I chose to do this with my life.'
Casually met he said it of the plan
He undertook without a friend or wife.

Now visibly tugged upon by his decision,
Wayward and eager. So this was his son!
What I admired about his self-permission
Was that he turned from nothing he had done,
Or was, or had been, even while he transposed
The expectations he took out at dark
– Of Eros playing, features undisclosed –
Into another pitch, where he might work
With the same melody, and opted so
To educate, permit, guide, feed, keep warm,
And love a child to be adopted, though
The child was still a blank then on a form.

The blank was flesh now, running on its nerve,
This fair-topped organism dense with charm,
Its braided muscle grabbing what would serve,
His countering pull, his own devoted arm.

Rapallo

Before the heavy hotel sink
I lost myself a minute.
I paused as people do who think,
And gazed at what was in it.

Rinsed from my swimming trunks, the sand
Wavered down grain by grain
To settle at the bottom stunned,
Distinct on thick porcelain.

As if my happiness was tired
And sought that strange mild pause,
It still observantly endured
And yet forgot its cause.

But then from habit I looked round
For what I thought it lacked.
Of course: for without you as ground,
How could it stay intact?

Turned to miss you, amnesiac,
I was restored when you
Across the floor were given back,
– Changing for dinner too,

For those discoveries still ahead
To match those of our play
Upon the beach where we had led
All of a spacious day.

That summer I was twenty-three,
You about twenty-one,
We hoped to live together, as we
(Not to be smug) have done.

If in four decades matter-of-factly
Coming to be resigned
To separate beds was not exactly
What we then had in mind,

Something of our first impetus,
Something of what we planned
Remains of what was given us
On the Rapallo sand.

Against our house of floors and beams
A mannerless wind strains
Down from the North, and cold rain streams
Across the window panes.

The structure creaks we hold together.
Water blurs all detail.
This wood will speak beneath worse weather
Yet than the Yukon's hail.

In Trust

    You go from me
  In June for months on end
 To study equanimity
    Among high trees alone;
 I go out with a new boyfriend
And stay all summer in the city where
    Home mostly on my own
    I watch the sunflowers flare.

    You travel East
  To help your relatives.
The rainy season's start, at least,
    Brings you from banishment:
And from the hall a doorway gives
A glimpse of you, writing I don't know what,
    Through winter, with head bent
    In the lamp's yellow spot.

    To some fresh task
  Some improvising skill
Your face is turned, of which I ask
    Nothing except the presence:
Beneath white hair your clear eyes still

Are candid as the cat's fixed narrowing gaze
   – Its pale-blue incandescence
   In your room nowadays.

    Sociable cat:
  Without much noise or fuss
 We left the kitchen where he sat,
   And suddenly we find
 He happens still to be with us,
In this room now, though firmly faced away,
   Not to be left behind,
   Though all the night he'll stray.

    As you began
  You'll end the year with me.
 We'll hug each other while we can,
   Work or stray while we must.
 Nothing is, or will ever be,
Mine, I suppose. No one can hold a heart,
   But what we hold in trust
   We do hold, even apart.

IVOR GURNEY 1890–1937

To His Love

He's gone, and all our plans
   Are useless indeed.
We'll walk no more on Cotswold
   Where the sheep feed
   Quietly and take no heed.

His body that was so quick
   Is not as you
Knew it, on Severn river
   Under the blue
   Driving our small boat through.

You would not know him now . . .
   But still he died
Nobly, so cover him over
   With violets of pride
   Purple from Severn side.

Cover him, cover him soon!
   And with thick-set
Masses of memoried flowers –
   Hide that red wet
   Thing I must somehow forget.

The Love Song

Out of the blackthorn edges
I caught a tune
And before it could vanish, seized
It, wrote it down.

Gave to a girl, so praising
Her eyes, lips and hair
She had little knowing, it was only thorn
Had dreamed of a girl there.

Prettily she thanked me, and never
Guessed any of my deceit . . .
But O Earth is this the only way
Man may conquer, a girl surrender her sweet?

St. Louis Blues

I hate to see de ev'nin' sun go down,
Hate to see de ev'nin' sun go down,
'Cause ma baby, he done lef dis town.

Feelin' tomorrow lak ah feel today,
Feel tomorrow lak ah feel today,
I'll pack my trunk, make ma gitaway.

St. Louis woman, wid her diamon' rings,
Pulls dat man roun' by her apron strings.
'Twant for powder an' for store-bought hair,
De man ah love would not gone nowhere, nowhere.

Got de St. Louis Blues jes as blue as ah can be,
Dat man got a heart lak a rock cast in the sea,
Or else he wouldn't have gone so far from me.

Been to de Gypsy to get ma fortune tole,
To de Gypsy done got ma fortune tole,
'Cause I'm most wile 'bout ma Jelly Roll.

Gypsy done tole me, 'Don't you wear no black.'
Yes she done tole me, 'Don't you wear no black,
Go to St. Louis. You can win him back.'

Help me to Cairo, make St. Louis by maself,
Git to Cairo, find ma ole friend Jeff.
Gwine to pin maself close to his side,
If ah flag his train, I sho' can ride.

I loves dat man lak a schoolboy loves his pie,
Lak a Kentucky Col'nel loves his mint an' rye,
I'll love ma baby till the day ah die.

You ought to see dat stovepipe brown of mine,
Lak he owns de Dimon Joseph line,
He'd make a cross-eyed 'oman go stone blin'.

Blacker than midnight, teeth lak flags of truce,
Blackest man in de whole St. Louis,
Blacker de berry, sweeter am de juice.

About a crap game, he knows a pow'ful lot,
But when work-time comes, he's on de dot.
Gwine to ask him for a cold ten-spot,
What it takes to git it, he's cert'nly got.

A black-headed gal makes a freight train jump the track,
Said a black-headed gal makes a freight train jump the
    track,
But a long tall gal makes a preacher ball the Jack.

Lawd, a blonde-headed woman makes a good man leave
    the town,
I said blonde-headed woman makes a good man leave the
    town,
But a red-headed woman makes a boy slap his papa down.

Oh ashes to ashes and dust to dust,
I said ashes to ashes and dust to dust,
If my blues don't get you my jazzing must.

Beale Street Blues

I've seen the lights of gay Broadway,
Old Market Street down by the Frisco Bay,
I've strolled the Prado, I've gambled on the Bourse
The seven wonders of the world I've seen
And many are the places I have been.

Take my advice folks and see Beale Street first.

You'll see pretty Browns in beautiful gowns,
You'll see tailor-mades and hand-me-downs
You'll meet honest men and pickpockets skilled,
You'll find that bus'ness never closes till somebody gets killed.

I'd rather be here than any place I know,
I'd rather be here than any place I know
It's goin' to take the Sargent
For to make me go,

Goin' to the river,
Maybe, bye and bye,
Goin' to the river, and there's a reason why,
Because the river's wet,
And Beale Street's done gone dry.

You'll see Hog-Nose rest'rants and Chitlin' Cafés,
You'll see Jugs that tell of by-gone days,
And places, once places, now just a sham,
You'll see Golden Balls enough to pave the New Jerusalem.

I'd rather be here than any place I know,
I'd rather be here than any place I know
It's goin' to take the Sargent
For to make me go,

Goin' to the river,
Maybe, bye and bye,
Goin' to the river, and there's a reason why,
Because the river's wet,
And Beale Street's done gone dry.

If Beale Street could talk,
If Beale Street could talk,
Married men would have to take their beds and walk,
Except one or two, who never drink booze,
And the blind man on the corner who sings the Beale Street
    Blues.

I'd rather be here than any place I know,
I'd rather be here than any place I know
It's goin' to take the Sargent
For to make me go,

Goin' to the river,
Maybe, bye and bye,
Goin' to the river, and there's a reason why,
Because the river's wet,
And Beale Street's done gone dry.

Loveless Love

Love is like a gold brick in a bunco game
Like a banknote with a bogus name
Both have caused many downfalls
Love has done the same
Love has for its emblem Cupid with his bow
Loveless love has lots and lots of dough
So carry lots of Jack and pick 'em as you go.

For Love, oh love, oh loveness love
Has set our hearts on goalless goals
From milk-less milk, and silk-less silk
We are growing used to soul-less souls
Such grafting times we never saw
That's why we have a pure food law
In ev'rything we find a flaw
Even love, oh love, oh loveless love.

Love is like a hydrant, it turns off and on
Like some friendships when your money's gone
Love stands in with the loan sharks when your heart's in
     pawn
If I had some strong wings like an aeroplane
Had some broad wings like an aeroplane
I would fly away forever ne'er to come again.

For Love, oh love, oh loveless love
You set our hearts on goalless goals
With dreamless dreams and scheme-less schemes
We wreck our love boats on the shoals
We S.O.S. by wireless wire
And in the wreckage of desire
We sigh for wings like Noah's dove
Just to fly away from loveless love.

THOMAS HARDY 1840–1928

Neutral Tones

We stood by a pond that winter day,
And the sun was white, as though chidden of God,
And a few leaves lay on the starving sod;
    – They had fallen from an ash, and were gray.

Your eyes on me were as eyes that rove
Over tedious riddles of years ago;
And some words played between us to and fro
    On which lost the more by our love.

The smile on your mouth was the deadest thing
Alive enough to have strength to die;
And a grin of bitterness swept thereby
    Like an ominous bird a-wing. . . .

Since then, keen lessons that love deceives,
And wrings with wrong, have shaped to me
Your face, and the God-curst sun, and a tree,
    And a pond edged with grayish leaves.

A Church Romance
  (Mellstock, circa 1835)

She turned in the high pew, until her sight
Swept the west gallery, and caught its row
Of music-men with viol, book, and bow
Against the sinking sad tower-window light.

She turned again; and in her pride's despite
One strenuous viol's inspirer seemed to throw
A message from his string to her below,
Which said: 'I claim thee as my own forthright!'

Thus their hearts' bond began, in due time signed.
And long years thence, when Age had scared Romance,
At some old attitude of his or glance
That gallery-scene would break upon her mind,
With him as minstrel, ardent, young, and trim,
Bowing 'New Sabbath' or 'Mount Ephraim'.

A Thunderstorm in Town
(A Reminiscence: 1893)

She wore a new 'terra-cotta' dress,
And we stayed, because of the pelting storm,
Within the hansom's dry recess,
Though the horse had stopped; yea, motionless
    We sat on, snug and warm.

Then the downpour ceased, to my sharp sad pain,
And the glass that had screened our forms before
Flew up, and out she sprang to her door:
I should have kissed her if the rain
    Had lasted a minute more.

The Going

Why did you give no hint that night
That quickly after the morrow's dawn,
And calmly, as if indifferent quite,
You would close your term here, up and be gone
    Where I could not follow
    With wing of swallow
To gain one glimpse of you ever anon!

    Never to bid good-bye,
    Or lip me the softest call,
Or utter a wish for a word, while I

Saw morning harden upon the wall,
    Unmoved, unknowing
    That your great going
Had place that moment, and altered all.

Why do you make me leave the house
And think for a breath it is you I see
At the end of the alley of bending boughs
Where so often at dusk you used to be;
    Till in darkening dankness
    The yawning blankness
Of the perspective sickens me!

  You were she who abode
  By those red-veined rocks far West,
You were the swan-necked one who rode
Along the beetling Beeny Crest,
    And, reining nigh me,
    Would muse and eye me,
While Life unrolled us its very best.

Why, then, latterly did we not speak,
Did we not think of those days long dead,
And ere your vanishing strive to seek
That time's renewal? We might have said,
    'In this bright spring weather
    We'll visit together
Those places that once we visited.'

    Well, well! All's past amend,
    Unchangeable. It must go.
I seem but a dead man held on end
To sink down soon. . . . O you could not know
    That such swift fleeing
    No soul foreseeing –
Not even I – would undo me so!

Your Last Drive

Here by the moorway you returned,
And saw the borough lights ahead
That lit your face – all undiscerned
To be in a week the face of the dead,
And you told of the charm of that haloed view
That never again would beam on you.

And on your left you passed the spot
Where eight days later you were to lie,
And be spoken of as one who was not;
Beholding it with a heedless eye
As alien from you, though under its tree
You soon would halt everlastingly.

I drove not with you. . . . Yet had I sat
At your side that eve I should not have seen
That the countenance I was glancing at
Had a last-time look in the flickering sheen,
Nor have read the writing upon your face,
'I go hence soon to my resting-place;

'You may miss me then. But I shall not know
How many times you visit me there,
Or what your thoughts are, or if you go
There never at all. And I shall not care.
Should you censure me I shall take no heed
And even your praises no more shall need.'

True: never you'll know. And you will not mind.
But shall I then slight you because of such?
Dear ghost, in the past did you ever find
The thought 'What profit,' move me much?
Yet abides the fact, indeed, the same, –
You are past love, praise, indifference, blame.

The Walk

   You did not walk with me
   Of late to the hill-top tree
      By the gated ways,
      As in earlier days;
      You were weak and lame,
      So you never came,
And I went alone, and I did not mind,
Not thinking of you as left behind.

   I walked up there to-day
   Just in the former way:
      Surveyed around
      The familiar ground
      By myself again:
      What difference, then?
Only that underlying sense
Of the look of a room on returning thence.

Without Ceremony

It was your way, my dear,
To vanish without a word
When callers, friends, or kin
Had left, and I hastened in
To rejoin you, as I inferred.

And when you'd a mind to career
Off anywhere – say to town –
You were all on a sudden gone
Before I had thought thereon,
Or noticed your trunks were down.

So, now that you disappear
For ever in that swift style,

Your meaning seems to me
Just as it used to be:
'Good-bye is not worth while!'

After a Journey

Hereto I come to view a voiceless ghost;
   Whither, O whither will its whim now draw me?
Up the cliff, down, till I'm lonely, lost,
   And the unseen waters' ejaculations awe me.
Where you will next be there's no knowing,
    Facing round about me everywhere,
       With your nut-coloured hair,
And gray eyes, and rose-flush coming and going.

Yes: I have re-entered your olden haunts at last;
   Through the years, through the dead scenes I have tracked
     you;
What have you now found to say of our past –
   Scanned across the dark space wherein I have lacked you?
Summer gave us sweets, but autumn wrought division?
    Things were not lastly as firstly well
       With us twain, you tell?
But all's closed now, despite Time's derision.

I see what you are doing: you are leading me on
   To the spots we knew when we haunted here together,
The waterfall, above which the mist-bow shone
   At the then fair hour in the then fair weather,
And the cave just under, with a voice still so hollow
    That it seems to call out to me from forty years ago,
      When you were all aglow,
And not the thin ghost that I now fraily follow!

Ignorant of what there is flitting here to see,
   The waked birds preen and the seals flop lazily,

Soon you will have, Dear, to vanish from me,
For the stars close their shutters and the dawn whitens
hazily.
Trust me, I mind not, though Life lours,
The bringing me here; nay, bring me here again!
I am just the same as when
Our days were a joy, and our paths through flowers.

Pentargan Bay

At Castle Boterel

As I drive to the junction of lane and highway,
And the drizzle bedrenches the waggonette,
I look behind at the fading byway,
And see on its slope, now glistening wet,
Distinctly yet

Myself and a girlish form benighted
In dry March weather. We climb the road
Beside a chaise. We had just alighted
To ease the sturdy pony's load
When he sighed and slowed.

What we did as we climbed, and what we talked of
Matters not much, nor to what it led, –
Something that life will not be balked of
Without rude reason till hope is dead,
And feeling fled.

It filled but a minute. But was there ever
A time of such quality, since or before,
In that hill's story? To one mind never,
Though it has been climbed, foot-swift, foot-sore,
By thousands more.

Primaeval rocks form the road's steep border,

And much have they faced there, first and last,
Of the transitory in Earth's long order;
    But what they record in colour and cast
        Is – that we two passed.

And to me, though Time's unflinching rigour,
    In mindless rote, has ruled from sight
The substance now, one phantom figure
    Remains on the slope, as when that night
        Saw us alight.

I look and see it there, shrinking, shrinking,
    I look back at it amid the rain
For the very last time; for my sand is sinking,
    And I shall traverse old love's domain
        Never again.

Where the Picnic Was

Where we made the fire
In the summer time
Of branch and briar
On the hill to the sea,
I slowly climb
Through winter mire,
And scan and trace
The forsaken place
Quite readily.

Now a cold wind blows,
And the grass is gray,
But the spot still shows
As a burnt circle – aye,
And stick-ends, charred,
Still strew the sward
Whereon I stand,

Last relic of the band
Who came that day!

Yes, I am here
Just as last year,
And the sea breathes brine
From its strange straight line
Up hither, the same
As when we four came.
– But two have wandered far
From this grassy rise
Into urban roar
Where no picnics are,
And one – has shut her eyes
For evermore.

Wedding Day

I am afraid.
Sound has stopped in the day
And the images reel over
And over. Why all those tears,

The wild grief on his face
Outside the taxi? The sap
Of mourning rises
In our waving guests.

You sing behind the tall cake
Like a deserted bride
Who persists, demented,
And goes through the ritual.

When I went to the Gents
There was a skewered heart
And a legend of love. Let me
Sleep on your breast to the airport.

Act of Union

I

Tonight, a first movement, a pulse,
As if the rain in bogland gathered head
To slip and flood: a bog-burst,
A gash breaking open the ferny bed.
Your back is a firm line of eastern coast
And arms and legs are thrown
Beyond your gradual hills. I caress
The heaving province where our past has grown.

I am the tall kingdom over your shoulder
That you would neither cajole nor ignore.
Conquest is a lie. I grow older
Conceding your half-independent shore
Within whose borders now my legacy
Culminates inexorably.

II

And I am still imperially
Male, leaving you with the pain,
The rending process in the colony,
The battering ram, the boom burst from within.
The act sprouted an obstinate fifth column
Whose stance is growing unilateral.
His heart beneath your heart is a wardrum
Mustering force. His parasitical
And ignorant little fists already
Beat at your borders and I know they're cocked
At me across the water. No treaty
I foresee will salve completely your tracked
And stretchmarked body, the big pain
That leaves you raw, like opened ground, again.

The Otter

When you plunged
The light of Tuscany wavered
And swung through the pool
From top to bottom.

I loved your wet head and smashing crawl,
Your fine swimmer's back and shoulders
Surfacing and surfacing again
This year and every year since.

I sat dry-throated on the warm stones.
You were beyond me.
The mellowed clarities, the grape-deep air
Thinned and disappointed.

Thank God for the slow loadening:
When I hold you now
We are close and deep
As the atmosphere on water.

My two hands are plumbed water.
You are my palpable, lithe
Otter of memory
In the pool of the moment,

Turning to swim on your back,
Each silent, thigh-shaking kick
Retilting the light,
Heaving the cool at your neck.

And suddenly you're out,
Back again, intent as ever,
Heavy and frisky in your freshened pelt,
Printing the stones.

The Skunk

Up, black, striped and damasked like the chasuble
At a funeral Mass, the skunk's tail
Paraded the skunk. Night after night
I expected her like a visitor.

The refrigerator whinnied into silence.
My desk light softened beyond the verandah.
Small oranges loomed in the orange tree.
I began to be tense as a voyeur.

After eleven years I was composing
Love-letters again, broaching the word 'wife'

Like a stored cask, as if its slender vowel
Had mutated into the night earth and air

Of California. The beautiful, useless
Tang of eucalyptus spelt your absence.
The aftermath of a mouthful of wine
Was like inhaling you off a cold pillow.

And there she was, the intent and glamorous,
Ordinary, mysterious skunk,
Mythologized, demythologized,
Snuffing the boards five feet beyond me.

It all came back to me last night, stirred
By the sootfall of your things at bedtime,
Your head-down, tail-up hunt in a bottom drawer
For the black plunge-line nightdress.

The Underground

There we were in the vaulted tunnel running,
You in your going-away coat speeding ahead
And me, me then like a fleet god gaining
Upon you before you turned to a reed

Or some new white flower japped with crimson
As the coat flapped wild and button after button
Sprang off and fell in a trail
Between the Underground and the Albert Hall.

Honeymooning, mooning around, late for the Proms,
Our echoes die in that corridor and now
I come as Hansel came on the moonlit stones
Retracing the path back, lifting the buttons

To end up in a draughty lamplit station
After the trains have gone, the wet track
Bared and tensed as I am, all attention
For your step following and damned if I look back.

The Frozen Heart

I Freeze, I freeze, and nothing dwels
In me but Snow, and *icicles*.
For pitties sake give your advice,
To melt this snow, and thaw this ice;
I'll drink down Flames, but if so be
Nothing but love can supple me;
I'll rather keep this frost, and snow,
Then to be thaw'd, or heated so.

No Loathsomnesse in love

What I fancy, I approve,
No Dislike there is in love:
Be my Mistress short or tall,
And distorted there-withall:
Be she likewise one of those,
That an *Acre* hath of Nose:
Be her forehead, and her eyes
Full of incongruities:
Be her cheeks so shallow too,
As to shew her *Tongue* wag through:
Be her lips ill hung, or set,
And her grinders black as jet;
Hath she thin hair, hath she none,
She's to me a *Paragon*.

The shoe tying

Anthea bade me tie her shoe;
I did; and kissed the Instep too:
And would have kissed unto her knee,
Had not her Blush rebuked me.

The Vine

I Dream'd this mortal part of mine
Was Metamorphoz'd to a Vine;
Which crawling one and every way,
Enthrall'd my dainty *Lucia*.
Me thought, her long small legs and thighs
I with my *Tendrils* did surprize;
Her Belly, Buttocks, and her Waste
By my soft *Nerv'lits* were embrac'd:
About her head I writhing hung,
And with rich clusters (hid among
The leaves) her temples I behung:
So that my *Lucia* seem'd to me
Young *Bacchus* ravished by his tree.
My curls about her neck did crawl,
And arms and hands they did enthral:
So that she could not freely stir,
(All parts there made one prisoner.)
But when I crept with leaves to hide
Those parts, which maids keep unespy'd,
Such fleeting pleasures there I took,
That with the fancy I awook;
And found (Ah me!) this flesh of mine
More like a *Stock*, then like a *Vine*.

Love perfumes all Parts

If I kiss *Anthea's* brest,
There I smell the Phoenix nest:
If her lip, the most sincere
Altar of Incense, I smell there.
Hands, and thighs, and legs, are all
Richly Aromatical.
Goddess *Isis* can't transfer
Musks and Ambers more from her:
Nor can *Juno* sweeter be,
When she lies with *Jove*, then she.

Her Legs

Fain would I kiss my *Julia's* dainty Leg,
Which is as white and hair-less as an egg.

Fresh Cheese and Cream

Wo'd yee have fresh Cheese and Cream?
Julia's Breast can give you them:
And if more; Each *Nipple* cries,
To your *Cream*, here's *Strawberries*.

Upon Julia's Clothes

When as in silks my *Julia* goes,
Then, then (me thinks) how sweetly flows
That liquefaction of her clothes.

Next, when I cast mine eyes and see
That brave Vibration each way free;
O how that glittering taketh me!

Upon Love

Love brought me to a silent Grove,
    And show'd me there a Tree,
Where some had hang'd themselves for love,
    And gave a Twist to me.

The Halter was of silk, and gold,
    That he reach'd forth unto me:
No otherwise, then if he would
    By dainty things undo me.

He bade me then that Necklace use;
    And told me too, he maketh
A glorious end by such a Noose,
    His Death for Love that taketh.

'Twas but a dream; but had I been
    There really alone;
My desp'rate fears, in love, had seen
    Mine Execution.

Kisses Loathsome

I Abhor the slimy kiss,
(Which to me most loathsome is.)
Those lips please me which are placed
Close, but not too strictly laced:
Yielding I would have them; yet
Not a wimbling Tongue admit:
What should poking-sticks make there,
When the ruff is set elsewhere?

The Turtle Dove

Love that drained her drained him she'd loved, though each
For the other's sake forged passion upon speech,
Bore their close days through sufferance towards night
Where she at length grasped sleep and he lay quiet

As though needing no questions, now, to guess
What her secreting heart could not well hide.
Her caught face flinched in half-sleep at his side.
Yet she, by day, modelled her real distress,

Poised, turned her cheek to the attending world
Of children and intriguers and the old,
Conversed freely, exercised, was admired,
Being strong to dazzle. All this she endured

To affront him. He watched her rough grief work
Under the formed surface of habit. She spoke
Like one long undeceived but she was hurt.
She denied more love, yet her starved eyes caught

His, devouring, at times. Then, as one self-dared,
She went to him, plied there; like a furious dove
Bore down with visitations of such love
As his lithe, fathoming heart absorbed and buried.

A. E. HOUSMAN 1859–1936

'Is my team ploughing'

'Is my team ploughing,
    That I was used to drive
And hear the harness jingle
    When I was man alive?'

Ay, the horses trample,
    The harness jingles now;
No change though you lie under
    The land you used to plough.

'Is football playing
    Along the river shore,
With lads to chase the leather,
    Now I stand up no more?'

Ay, the ball is flying,
    The lads play heart and soul;
The goal stands up, the keeper
    Stands up to keep the goal.

'Is my girl happy,
    That I thought hard to leave,
And has she tired of weeping
    As she lies down at eve?'

Ay, she lies down lightly,
    She lies not down to weep:
Your girl is well contented.
    Be still, my lad, and sleep.

'Is my friend hearty,
    Now I am thin and pine,
And has he found to sleep in
    A better bed than mine?'

Yes, lad, I lie easy,
    I lie as lads would choose;
I cheer a dead man's sweetheart,
    Never ask me whose.

'If truth in hearts that perish'

If truth in hearts that perish
    Could move the powers on high,
I think the love I bear you
    Should make you not to die.

Sure, sure, if stedfast meaning,
    If single thought could save,
The world might end to-morrow,
    You should not see the grave.

This long and sure-set liking,
    This boundless will to please,
– Oh, you should live for ever
    If there were help in these.

But now, since all is idle,
    To this lost heart be kind,
Ere to a town you journey
    Where friends are ill to find.

'Shot? so quick, so clean an ending?'

Shot? so quick, so clean an ending?
    Oh that was right, lad, that was brave:
Yours was not an ill for mending,
    'Twas best to take it to the grave.

Oh you had forethought, you could reason,
    And saw your road and where it led,

And early wise and brave in season
    Put the pistol to your head.

Oh soon, and better so than later
    After long disgrace and scorn,
You shot dead the household traitor,
    The soul that should not have been born.

Right you guessed the rising morrow
    And scorned to tread the mire you must:
Dust's your wages, son of sorrow,
    But men may come to worse than dust.

Souls undone, undoing others, –
    Long time since the tale began.
You would not live to wrong your brothers:
    Oh lad, you died as fits a man.

Now to your grave shall friend and stranger
    With ruth and some with envy come:
Undishonoured, clear of danger,
    Clean of guilt, pass hence and home.

Turn safe to rest, no dreams, no waking;
    And here, man, here's the wreath I've made:
'Tis not a gift that's worth the taking,
    But wear it and it will not fade.

'Her strong enchantments failing'

Her strong enchantments failing,
    Her towers of fear in wreck,
Her limbecks dried of poisons
    And the knife at her neck,

The Queen of air and darkness
    Begins to shrill and cry,

'O young man, O my slayer,
  To-morrow you shall die.'

O Queen of air and darkness,
  I think 'tis truth you say,
And I shall die to-morrow;
  But you will die to-day.

Sinner's Rue

I walked alone and thinking,
  And faint the nightwind blew
And stirred on mounds at crossways
  The flower of sinner's rue.

Where the roads part they bury
  Him that his own hand slays,
And so the weed of sorrow
  Springs at the four cross ways.

By night I plucked it hueless,
  When morning broke 'twas blue:
Blue at my breast I fastened
  The flower of sinner's rue.

It seemed a herb of healing,
  A balsam and a sign,
Flower of a heart whose trouble
  Must have been worse than mine.

Dead clay that did me kindness,
  I can do none to you,
But only wear for breastknot
  The flower of sinner's rue.

'Ho, everyone that thirsteth'

Ho, everyone that thirsteth
  And hath the price to give,
Come to the stolen waters,
  Drink and your soul shall live.

Come to the stolen waters,
  And leap the guarded pale,
And pull the flower in season
  Before desire shall fail.

It shall not last for ever,
  No more than earth and skies;
But he that drinks in season
  Shall live before he dies.

June suns, you cannot store them
  To warm the winter's cold,
The lad that hopes for heaven
  Shall fill his mouth with mould.

'Shake hands, we shall never be friends, all's over'

Shake hands, we shall never be friends, all's over,
    I only vex you the more I try.
All's wrong that ever I've done or said,
And nought to help it in this dull head:
    Shake hands, here's luck, good-bye.

But if you come to a road where danger
    Or guilt or anguish or shame's to share,
Be good to the lad that loves you true
And the soul that was born to die for you.
    And whistle and I'll be there.

'Because I liked you better'

Because I liked you better
   Than suits a man to say,
It irked you, and I promised
   To throw the thought away.

To put the world between us
   We parted, stiff and dry;
'Good-bye,' said you, 'forget me.'
   'I will, no fear,' said I.

If here, where clover whitens
   The dead man's knoll, you pass,
And no tall flower to meet you
   Starts in the trefoiled grass,

Halt by the headstone naming
   The heart no longer stirred,
And say the lad that loved you
   Was one that kept his word.

'He looked at me with eyes I thought'

He looked at me with eyes I thought
   I was not like to find,
The voice he begged for pence with brought
   Another man to mind.

Oh no, lad, never touch your cap;
   It is not my half-crown:
You have it from a better chap
   That long ago lay down.

Turn east and over Thames to Kent
   And come to the sea's brim,
And find his everlasting tent
   And touch your cap to him.

'He would not stay for me; and who can wonder?'

He would not stay for me; and who can wonder?
  He would not stay for me to stand and gaze.
I shook his hand and tore my heart in sunder
  And went with half my life about my ways.

Evil Woman

I ain't gonna mistreat ma
Good gal any more.
I'm just gonna kill her
Next time she makes me sore.

I treats her kind but
She don't do me right.
She fights an' quarrels most
Ever night.

I can't have no woman's
Got such low-down ways,
Cause a blue-gummed woman
Ain't de style now days.

I brought her from de South
An' she's goin' on back
Else I'll use her head
For a carpet tack.

Lament over Love

I hope ma chile'll
Never love a man.
I say I hope ma chile'll
Never love a man.
Cause love can hurt you
Mo'n anything else can.

I'm goin' down to de river
An' I ain't goin' there to swim.

Goin' down to de river,
Ain't goin' there to swim.
Ma true love's left me, an'
I'm goin' there to think about him.

Love is like whiskey,
Love is like red, red wine.
Love is like whiskey,
O, like sweet red wine.
If you wants to be happy
You got to love all de time.

I'm goin' up in a tower
Tall as a tree is tall.
Say up in a tower
Tall as a tree is tall.
Gonna think about ma man an'
Let ma fool self fall.

Brief Encounter

I was lookin' for a sandwich, Judge,
Any old thing to eat.
I was walkin' down de street, Judge,
Lookin' for any old thing to eat –
When I come across that woman
That I didn't want to meet.

Judge, she is de woman
That put de miz on me.
She is de woman, Judge,
That put de miz on me.
If there's anybody on this earth, Judge,
I didn't want to see!

Fact that I hurt her, Judge,
De fact that she is dead,

Fact that I hurt her,
Fact that she is dead –
She was de wrongest thing, Judge,
That I ever had!

KATHLEEN JAMIE 1963–

Perfect Day

I am just a woman of the shore
wearing your coat against the snow
that falls on the oyster-catcher's tracks
and on our own; falls
on the still grey waters
of Loch Morar, and on our shoulders
gentle as restraint: a perfect weight
of snow as tree-boughs
and fences bear against a loaded sky:
one flake more, they'd break.

Fado

How all things cohere, some days, how all things conspire –
if I had not been walking past the window of a sushi bar
in Soho just as the sunset caught it in a flash of fire
I would not have noticed its backdrop flag of Japan,
would not have thought of her, of that song (*Wherever
   you are,*
it's 3 a.m.) or of the time she died, she was so embarrassed,
thirteen, walking the aisle of the airbus in her best white
harem-pants, realising that a patch of red
had begun to seep, to seep and darken and spread
and she had to walk the length of that aisle to find her seat
and reach to stow a bag before she could sit and hide her
   shame;
or of the photograph I took of her lying bare-assed
on my bed, waving me away with one hand that holds
a cigarette in fingers that are daubed and dabbled red;
would not have noticed how the sunset drained and bled
into itself, how it drained itself of purples, golds
and crimsons to become a dull rust-red-brown (the same
rust-red-brown as radiator-water, as blood washed out of a
   sheet);
would not have thought of her driving all day in the heat
to a hill-town in Portugal, a cellar bar, those two Japanese
who laughed all through the fado-singer's guttural sobs . . .
Of how I lay unmoving in the dark beneath the fan
in our hotel room while she came and went, all night,
came and went, would not have thought of those gobbets
   and gobs
of red that drained down the bowl from which, bent
almost double, she looked at me, finally, on my knees;
of that song, *How did it ever come so far . . .*

BEN JONSON 1572–1637

Why I Write Not of Love

Some act of Love's bound to rehearse,
I thought to bind him in my verse;
Which when he felt, Away! quoth he,
Can poets hope to fetter me?
It is enough they once did get
Mars and my mother in their net:
I wear not these my wings in vain.
With which he fled me; and again
Into my rhymes could ne'er be got
By any art. Then wonder not
That since, my numbers are so cold,
When Love is fled, and I grow old.

Song

To Celia

Drink to me only with thine eyes,
    And I will pledge with mine;
Or leave a kiss but in the cup,
    And I'll not look for wine.
The thirst that from the soul doth rise
    Doth ask a drink divine;
But might I of Jove's nectar sup,
    I would not change for thine.
I sent thee late a rosy wreath,
    Not so much honouring thee
As giving it a hope that there
    It could not withered be.
But thou thereon didst only breathe,
    And sent'st it back to me;
Since when it grows, and smells, I swear,
    Not of itself, but thee.

The Hour-Glass

Do but consider this small dust
   Here running in the glass,
      By atoms moved:
Could you believe that this
   The body ever was
      Of one that loved?
And in his mistress' flame, playing like a fly,
   Turned to cinders by her eye?
     Yes; and in death, as life, unblessed,
      To have 't expressed,
Even ashes of lovers find no rest.

My Picture Left in Scotland

I now think Love is rather deaf than blind,
   For else it could not be
      That she
Whom I adore so much should so slight me,
   And cast my love behind;
I'm sure my language to her was as sweet,
     And every close did meet
     In sentence of as subtle feet,
      As hath the youngest he
   That sits in shadow of Apollo's tree.

   Oh, but my conscious fears
     That fly my thoughts between,
     Tell me that she hath seen
     My hundred of grey hairs,
     Told seven-and-forty years,
   Read so much waste, as she cannot embrace
     My mountain belly, and my rocky face;
And all these through her eyes have stopped her ears.

Against Jealousy

Wretched and foolish jealousy
How cam'st thou thus to enter me?
    I ne'er was of thy kind,
  Nor have I yet the narrow mind
    To vent that poor desire
That others should not warm them at my fire;
    I wish the sun should shine
On all men's fruit and flowers, as well as mine.

The Dream

Or scorn, or pity on me take,
I must the true relation make:
    I am undone tonight;
  Love in a subtle dream disguised
  Hath both my heart and me surprised,
Whom never yet he durst attempt awake;
Nor will he tell me for whose sake
    He did me the delight,
      Or spite,
  But leaves me to inquire,
  In all my wild desire
    Of sleep again, who was his aid;
    And sleep so guilty and afraid
As, since, he dares not come within my sight.

PATRICK KAVANAGH 1905-67

On Raglan Road
(Air: The Dawning of The Day)

On Raglan Road on an autumn day I met her first and knew
That her dark hair would weave a snare that I might one day
rue;
I saw the danger, yet I walked along the enchanted way,
And I said, let grief be a fallen leaf at the dawning of the day.

On Grafton Street in November we tripped lightly along the
ledge
Of the deep ravine where can be seen the worth of passion's
pledge,
The Queen of Hearts still making tarts and I not making hay
O I loved too much and by such by such is happiness thrown
away.

I gave her gifts of the mind I gave her the secret sign that's
known
To the artists who have known the true gods of sound and
stone
And word and tint. I did not stint for I gave her poems to
say.
With her own name there and her own dark hair like clouds
over fields of May

On a quiet street where old ghosts meet I see her walking
now
Away from me so hurriedly my reason must allow
That I had wooed not as I should a creature made of clay –
When the angel woos the clay he'd lose his wings at the
dawn of day.

La Belle Dame sans Merci. A Ballad

I

O what can ail thee, knight-at-arms,
  Alone and palely loitering?
The sedge has withered from the lake,
  And no birds sing.

II

O what can ail thee, knight-at-arms,
  So haggard and so woe-begone?
The squirrel's granary is full,
  And the harvest's done.

III

I see a lily on thy brow,
  With anguish moist and fever-dew,
And on thy cheeks a fading rose
  Fast withereth too.

IV

I met a lady in the meads,
  Full beautiful – a faery's child,
Her hair was long, her foot was light,
  And her eyes were wild.

V

I made a garland for her head,
  And bracelets too, and fragrant zone;
She looked at me as she did love,
  And made sweet moan.

VI

I set her on my pacing steed,
  And nothing else saw all day long,
For sidelong would she bend, and sing
  A faery's song.

VII

She found me roots of relish sweet,
  And honey wild, and manna-dew,
And sure in language strange she said –
  'I love thee true'.

VIII

She took me to her elfin grot,
  And there she wept and sighed full sore,
And there I shut her wild wild eyes
  With kisses four.

IX

And there she lullèd me asleep
  And there I dreamed – Ah! woe betide! –
The latest dream I ever dreamt
  On the cold hill side.

X

I saw pale kings and princes too,
  Pale warriors, death-pale were they all;
They cried – 'La Belle Dame sans Merci
  Thee hath in thrall!'

XI

I saw their starved lips in the gloam,
  With horrid warning gapèd wide,

And I awoke and found me here,
　　On the cold hill's side.

XII

And this is why I sojourn here
　　Alone and palely loitering,
Though the sedge is withered from the lake,
　　And no birds sing.

'Bright Star! would I were steadfast as thou art'

Bright star! would I were steadfast as thou art –
　　Not in lone splendour hung aloft the night
And watching, with eternal lids apart,
　　Like nature's patient, sleepless Eremite,
The moving waters at their priestlike task
　　Of pure ablution round earth's human shores,
Or gazing on the new soft-fallen mask
　　Of snow upon the mountains and the moors –
No – yet still steadfast, still unchangeable,
　　Pillowed upon my fair love's ripening breast,
To feel for ever its soft swell and fall,
　　Awake for ever in a sweet unrest,
Still, still to hear her tender-taken breath,
And so live ever – or else swoon to death.

The Exequy. To his Matchless never to be forgotten Friend

Accept thou Shrine of my dead Saint,
Insteed of Dirges this complaint;
And for sweet flowers to crown thy hearse,
Receive a strew of weeping verse
From thy grieved friend, whom thou mightst see
Quite melted into tears for thee.

   Dear loss! since thy untimely fate
My task hath been to meditate
On thee, on thee: thou art the book,
The library whereon I look
Though almost blind. For thee (loved clay)
I languish out, not live the day,
Using no other exercise
But what I practise with mine eyes:
By which wet glasses I find out
How lazily time creeps about
To one that mourns: this, only this
My exercise and business is:
So I compute the weary hours
With sighs dissolved into showers.

   Nor wonder if my time go thus
Backward and most preposterous;
Thou hast benighted me, thy set
This Eve of blackness did beget,
Who wast my day, (though overcast
Before thou had'st thy Noon-tide past)
And I remember must in tears,
Thou scarce had'st seen so many years
As Day tells hours. By thy clear Sun

My life and fortune first did run;
But thou wilt never more appear
Folded within my Hemisphere,
Since both thy light and motion
Like a fled Star is fallen and gone,
And twixt me and my soul's dear wish
The earth now interposed is,
Which such a strange eclipse doth make
As ne're was read in Almanac.

I could allow thee for a time
To darken me and my sad Clime,
Were it a month, a year, or ten,
I would thy exile live till then;
And all that space my mirth adjourn,
So thou wouldst promise to return;
And putting off thy ashy shroud
At length disperse this sorrows cloud.

But woe is me! the longest date
Too narrow is to calculate
These empty hopes: never shall I
Be so much blessed as to descry
A glimpse of thee, till that day come
Which shall the earth to cinders doom,
And a fierce Feaver must calcine
The body of this world like thine,
(My little World!). That fit of fire
Once off, our bodies shall aspire
To our souls' bliss: then we shall rise
And view our selves with clearer eyes
In that calm Region, where no night
Can hide us from each others sight.

Mean time, thou hast her, earth: much good
May my harm do thee. Since it stood
With Heavens will I might not call

Her longer mine, I give thee all
My short-lived right and interest
In her, whom living I loved best:
With a most free and bounteous grief,
I give thee what I could not keep.
Be kind to her, and prithee look
Thou write into thy Doomsday book
Each parcel of this Rarity
Which in thy Casket shrined doth lie:
See that thou make thy reckoning straight,
And yield her back again by weight;
For thou must audit on thy trust
Each grain and atom of this dust,
As thou wilt answer *Him* that lent,
Not gave thee, my dear Monument.

So close the ground, and 'bout her shade
Black curtains draw, my *Bride* is laid.

Sleep on my *Love* in thy cold bed
Never to be disquieted!
My last good night! Thou wilt not wake
Till I thy fate shall overtake:
Till age, or grief, or sickness must
Marry my body to that dust
It so much loves; and fill the room
My heart keeps empty in thy Tomb.
Stay for me there; I will not fail
To meet thee in that hollow Vale.
And think not much of my delay;
I am already on the way,
And follow thee with all the speed
Desire can make, or sorrows breed.
Each minute is a short degree,
And every hour a step towards thee.
At night when I betake to rest,
Next morn I rise nearer my West

Of life, almost by eight hours sail,
Than when sleep breathed his drowsy gale.

Thus from the Sun my Bottom steers,
And my dayes Compass downward bears:
Nor labour I to stem the tide
Through which to *Thee* I swiftly glide.

Tis true, with shame and grief I yield,
Thou like the *Vann* first took'st the field,
And gotten hast the victory
In thus adventuring to die
Before me, whose more years might crave
A just precedence in the grave.
But hark! My pulse like a soft Drum
Beats my approch, tells *Thee* I come;
And slow howe're my marches be,
I shall at last sit down by *Thee*.

The thought of this bids me go on,
And wait my dissolution
With hope and comfort. *Dear* (forgive
The crime) I am content to live
Divided, with but half a heart,
Till we shall meet and never part.

The Oldest Song

'For before Eve was Lilith.' – OLD TALE

'These were never your true love's eyes.
    Why do you feign that you love them?
You that broke from their constancies,
    And the wide calm brows above them!

This was never your true love's speech.
    Why do you thrill when you hear it?
You that have ridden out of its reach
    The width of the world or near it!

This was never your true love's hair, –
    You that chafed when it bound you
Screened from knowledge or shame or care,
    In the night that it made around you!'

'All these things I know, I know.
    And that's why my heart is breaking!'
'Then what do you gain by pretending so?'
    'The joy of an old wound waking.'

Mandalay

By the old Moulmein Pagoda, lookin' lazy at the sea,
There's a Burma girl a-settin', and I know she thinks o' me;
For the wind is in the palm-trees, and the temple-bells they say:
'Come you back, you British soldier; come you back to
    Mandalay!'
      Come you back to Mandalay,
      Where the old Flotilla lay:
      Can't you 'ear their paddles chunkin' from Rangoon to
        Mandalay?

> On the road to Mandalay,
> Where the flyin'-fishes play,
> An' the dawn comes up like thunder outer China 'crost
> the Bay!

'Er petticoat was yaller an' 'er little cap was green,
An' 'er name was Supi-yaw-lat – jes' the same as Theebaw's
Queen,
An' I seed her first a-smokin' of a whackin' white cheroot,
An' a-wastin' Christian kisses on an 'eathen idol's foot:
> Bloomin' idol made o' mud –
> Wot they called the Great Gawd Budd –
> Plucky lot she cared for idols when I kissed 'er where
> she stud!
> On the road to Mandalay . . .

When the mist was on the rice-fields an' the sun was droppin'
slow,
She'd git 'er little banjo an' she'd sing '*Kulla-lo-lo!*'
With 'er arm upon my shoulder an' 'er cheek agin my cheek
We useter watch the steamers an' the *hathis* pilin' teak.
> Elephints a-pilin' teak
> In the sludgy, squdgy creek,
> Where the silence 'ung that 'eavy you was 'arf afraid to
> speak!
> On the road to Mandalay . . .

But that's all shove be'ind me – long ago an' fur away,
An' there ain't no 'buses runnin' from the Bank to Mandalay;
An' I'm learnin' 'ere in London what the ten-year soldier
tells:
'If you've 'eard the East a-callin', you won't never 'eed
naught else.'
> No! you won't 'eed nothin' else
> But them spicy garlic smells,
> An' the sunshine an' the palm-trees an' the tinkly
> temple-bells;
> On the road to Mandalay . . .

I am sick o' wastin' leather on these gritty pavin'-stones,
An' the blasted English drizzle wakes the fever in my bones;
Tho' I walks with fifty 'ousemaids outer Chelsea to the
    Strand,
An' they talks a lot o' lovin', but wot do they understand?
      Beefy face an' grubby 'and –
      Law! wot do they understand?
      I've a neater, sweeter maiden in a cleaner, greener land!
      On the road to Mandalay . . .

Ship me somewheres east of Suez, where the best is like the
    worst,
Where there aren't no Ten Commandments an' a man can
    raise a thirst;
For the temple-bells are callin', an' it's there that I would be
    –
By the old Moulmein Pagoda, looking lazy at the sea;
      On the road to Mandalay,
      Where the old Flotilla lay,
      With our sick beneath the awnings when we went to
        Mandalay!
      O the road to Mandalay,
      Where the flyin'-fishes play,
      An' the dawn comes up like thunder outer China 'crost
        the Bay!

'Mary, Pity Women!'

You call yourself a man,
   For all you used to swear,
An' leave me, as you can,
   My certain shame to bear?
   I 'ear! You do not care –
You done the worst you know.
   I 'ate you, grinnin' there. . . .
Ah, Gawd, I love you so!

Nice while it lasted, an' now it is over –
Tear out your 'eart an' good-bye to your lover!
What's the use o' grievin', when the mother that bore you
(Mary, pity women!) knew it all before you?

It aren't no false alarm,
　The finish to your fun;
You – you 'ave brung the 'arm,
　An' I'm the ruined one!
　An' now you'll off an' run
With some new fool in tow.
　Your 'eart? You 'aven't none. . . .
Ah, Gawd, I love you so!

When a man is tired there is naught will bind 'im;
All 'e solemn promised 'e will shove be'ind 'im.
What's the good o' prayin' for The Wrath to strike 'im
(Mary, pity women!), when the rest are like 'im?

What 'ope for me or – it?
　What's left for us to do?
I've walked with men a bit,
　But this – but this is you.
　So 'elp me, Christ, it's true!
Where can I 'ide or go?
　You coward through and through! . . .
Ah, Gawd, I love you so!

All the more you give 'em the less are they for givin' –
Love lies dead, an' you cannot kiss 'im livin'.
Down the road 'e led you there is no returnin'
(Mary, pity women!), but you're late in learnin'!

You'd like to treat me fair?
　You can't, because we're pore?
We'd starve? What do I care!
　We might, but *this* is shore!
　I want the name – no more –

The name, an' lines to show,
 An' not to be an 'ore. . . .
Ah, Gawd, I love you so!

What's the good o' pleadin', when the mother that bore you
(Mary, pity women!) knew it all before you?
Sleep on 'is promises an' wake to your sorrow
(Mary, pity women!), for we sail to-morrow!

The Widower

For a season there must be pain –
For a little, little space
I shall lose the sight of her face,
Take back the old life again
While She is at rest in her place.

For a season this pain must endure,
For a little, little while
I shall sigh more often than smile
Till Time shall work me a cure,
And the pitiful days beguile.

For that season we must be apart,
For a little length of years,
Till my life's last hour nears,
And, above the beat of my heart,
I hear Her voice in my ears.

But I shall not understand –
Being set on some later love,
Shall not know her for whom I strove,
Till she reach me forth her hand,
Saying, 'Who but I have the right?'
And out of a troubled night
Shall draw me safe to the land.

Rahere

('The Wish House')

Rahere, King Henry's Jester, feared by all the Norman Lords
For his eye that pierced their bosoms, for his tongue that
    shamed their swords;
Feed and flattered by the Churchmen – well they knew how
    deep he stood
In dark Henry's crooked counsels – fell upon an evil mood.

Suddenly, his days before him and behind him seemed to
    stand
Stripped and barren, fixed and fruitless, as those leagues of
    naked sand
When St. Michael's ebb slinks outward to the bleak horizon-
    bound,
And the trampling wide-mouthed waters are withdrawn from
    sight and sound.

Then a Horror of Great Darkness sunk his spirit and, anon,
(Who had seen him wince and whiten as he turned to walk
    alone)
Followed Gilbert the Physician, and muttered in his ear,
'Thou hast it, O my brother?' 'Yea, I have it,' said Rahere.

'So it comes,' said Gilbert smoothly, 'man's most immanent
    distress.
'Tis a humour of the Spirit which abhorreth all excess;
And, whatever breed the surfeit – Wealth, or Wit, or Power,
    or Fame
(And thou hast each) the Spirit laboureth to expel the same.

'Hence the dulled eye's deep self-loathing – hence the loaded
    leaden brow;
Hence the burden of Wanhope that aches thy soul and body
    now.
Ay, the merriest fool must face it, and the wisest Doctor
    learn;

For it comes – it comes,' said Gilbert, 'as it passes – to
  return.'

But Rahere was in his torment, and he wandered, dumb and far,
Till he came to reeking Smithfield where the crowded
  gallows are,
(Followed Gilbert the Physician) and beneath the wry-necked
  dead,
Sat a leper and his woman, very merry, breaking bread.

He was cloaked from chin to ankle – faceless, fingerless,
  obscene –
Mere corruption swaddled man-wise, but the woman whole
  and clean;
And she waited on him crooning, and Rahere beheld the
  twain,
Each delighting in the other, and he checked and groaned again.

'So it comes, – it comes,' said Gilbert, 'as it came when Life
  began.
'Tis a motion of the Spirit that revealeth God to man.
In the shape of Love exceeding, which regards not taint or fall,
Since in perfect Love, saith Scripture, can be no excess at all.

'Hence the eye that sees no blemish – hence the hour that
  holds no shame.
Hence the Soul assured the Essence and the Substance are the
  same.
Nay, the meanest need not miss it, though the mightier pass
  it by;
For it comes – it comes,' said Gilbert, 'and, thou seest, it does
  not die!'

PHILIP LARKIN 1922–85

Lines on a Young Lady's Photograph Album

At last you yielded up the album, which,
Once open, sent me distracted. All your ages
Matt and glossy on the thick black pages!
Too much confectionery, too rich:
I choke on such nutritious images.

My swivel eye hungers from pose to pose –
In pigtails, clutching a reluctant cat;
Or furred yourself, a sweet girl-graduate;
Or lifting a heavy-headed rose
Beneath a trellis, or in a trilby hat

(Faintly disturbing, that, in several ways) –
From every side you strike at my control,
Not least through these disquieting chaps who loll
At ease about your earlier days:
Not quite your class, I'd say, dear, on the whole.

But o, photography! as no art is,
Faithful and disappointing! that records
Dull days as dull, and hold-it smiles as frauds,
And will not censor blemishes
Like washing-lines, and Hall's-Distemper boards,

But shows the cat as disinclined, and shades
A chin as doubled when it is, what grace
Your candour thus confers upon her face!
How overwhelmingly persuades
That this is a real girl in a real place,

In every sense empirically true!
Or is it just *the past*? Those flowers, that gate,
These misty parks and motors, lacerate

Simply by being over; you
Contract my heart by looking out of date.

Yes, true; but in the end, surely, we cry
Not only at exclusion, but because
It leaves us free to cry. We know *what was*
Won't call on us to justify
Our grief, however hard we yowl across

The gap from eye to page. So I am left
To mourn (without a chance of consequence)
You, balanced on a bike against a fence;
To wonder if you'd spot the theft
Of this one of you bathing; to condense,

In short, a past that no one now can share,
No matter whose your future; calm and dry,
It holds you like a heaven, and you lie
Unvariably lovely there,
Smaller and clearer as the years go by.

An Arundel Tomb

Side by side, their faces blurred,
The earl and countess lie in stone,
Their proper habits vaguely shown
As jointed armour, stiffened pleat,
And that faint hint of the absurd –
The little dogs under their feet.

Such plainness of the pre-baroque
Hardly involves the eye, until
It meets his left-hand gauntlet, still
Clasped empty in the other; and
One sees, with a sharp tender shock,
His hand withdrawn, holding her hand.

They would not think to lie so long.
Such faithfulness in effigy
Was just a detail friends would see:
A sculptor's sweet commissioned grace
Thrown off in helping to prolong
The Latin names around the base.

They would not guess how early in
Their supine stationary voyage
The air would change to soundless damage,
Turn the old tenantry away;
How soon succeeding eyes begin
To look, not read. Rigidly they

Persisted, linked, through lengths and breadths
Of time. Snow fell, undated. Light
Each summer thronged the glass. A bright
Litter of birdcalls strewed the same
Bone-riddled ground. And up the paths
The endless altered people came,

Washing at their identity.
Now, helpless in the hollow of
An unarmorial age, a trough
Of smoke in slow suspended skeins
Above their scrap of history,
Only an attitude remains:

Time has transfigured them into
Untruth. The stone fidelity
They hardly meant has come to be
Their final blazon, and to prove
Our almost-instinct almost true:
What will survive of us is love.

Talking in Bed

Talking in bed ought to be easiest,
Lying together there goes back so far,
An emblem of two people being honest.

Yet more and more time passes silently.
Outside, the wind's incomplete unrest
Builds and disperses clouds about the sky,

And dark towns heap up on the horizon.
None of this cares for us. Nothing shows why
At this unique distance from isolation

It becomes still more difficult to find
Words at once true and kind,
Or not untrue and not unkind.

Broadcast

Giant whispering and coughing from
Vast Sunday-full and organ-frowned-on spaces
Precede a sudden scuttle on the drum,
'The Queen', and huge resettling. Then begins
A snivel on the violins:
I think of your face among all those faces,

Beautiful and devout before
Cascades of monumental slithering,
One of your gloves unnoticed on the floor
Beside those new, slightly-outmoded shoes.
Here it goes quickly dark. I lose
All but the outline of the still and withering

Leaves on half-emptied trees. Behind
The glowing wavebands, rabid storms of chording
By being distant overpower my mind

All the more shamelessly, their cut-off shout
Leaving me desperate to pick out
Your hands, tiny in all that air, applauding.

Cherry Robbers

Under the long dark boughs, like jewels red
  In the hair of an Eastern girl
Hang strings of crimson cherries, as if had bled
  Blood-drops beneath each curl.

Under the glistening cherries, with folded wings
  Three dead birds lie:
Pale-breasted throstles and a blackbird, robberlings
  Stained with red dye.

Against the haystack a girl stands laughing at me,
  Cherries hung round her ears.
Offers me her scarlet fruit: I will see
  If she has any tears.

Violets

Sister, tha knows while we was on th' planks
  Aside o' t' grave, an' th' coffin set
On th' yaller clay, wi' th' white flowers top of it
  Waitin' ter be buried out o' th' wet?

An' t' parson makin' haste, an' a' t' black
  Huddlin' up i' t' rain,
Did t' 'appen ter notice a bit of a lass way back
  Hoverin', lookin' poor an' plain?

    – How should I be lookin' round!
      An' me standin' there on th' plank,
    An' our Ted's coffin set on th' ground,
      Waitin' to be sank!

I'd as much as I could do, to think
    Of 'im bein' gone
That young, an' a' the fault of drink
    An' carryin's on! –

Let that be; 'appen it worna th' drink, neither,
Nor th' carryin' on as killed 'im.
                       – No, 'appen not,
My sirs! But I say 'twas! For a blither
Lad never stepped, till 'e got in with your lot. –

All right, all right, it's my fault! But let
Me tell about that lass. When you'd all gone
Ah stopped behind on t' pad, i' t' pourin' wet
An' watched what 'er 'ad on.

Tha should ha' seed 'er slive up when yer'd gone!
Tha should ha' seed 'er kneel an' look in
At th' sloppy grave! an' 'er little neck shone
That white, an' 'er cried that much, I'd like to begin

Scraightin' mysen as well. 'Er undid 'er black
Jacket at th' bosom, an' took out
Over a double 'andful o' violets, a' in a pack
An' white an' blue in a ravel, like a clout.

An' warm, for th' smell come waftin' to me. 'Er put 'er face
Right in 'em, an' scraighted a bit again,
Then after a bit 'er dropped 'em down that place,
An' I come away, acause o' th' teemin' rain.

But I thowt ter mysen, as that wor th' only bit
O' warmth as 'e got down theer; th' rest wor stone cold.
From that bit of a wench's bosom; 'e'd be glad of it,
Gladder nor of thy lilies, if tha maun be told.

Piano

Softly, in the dusk, a woman is singing to me;
Taking me back down the vista of years, till I see
A child sitting under the piano, in the boom of the tingling
    strings
And pressing the small, poised feet of a mother who smiles as
    she sings.

In spite of myself, the insidious mastery of song
Betrays me back, till the heart of me weeps to belong
To the old Sunday evenings at home, with winter outside
And hymns in the cosy parlour, the tinkling piano our guide.

So now it is vain for the singer to burst into clamour
With the great black piano appassionato. The glamour
Of childish days is upon me, my manhood is cast
Down in the flood of remembrance, I weep like a child for
    the past.

Gloire de Dijon

When she rises in the morning
I linger to watch her;
She spreads the bath-cloth underneath the window
And the sunbeams catch her
Glistening white on the shoulders,
While down her sides the mellow
Golden shadow glows as
She stoops to the sponge, and her swung breasts
Sway like full-blown yellow
Gloire de Dijon roses.

She drips herself with water, and her shoulders
Glisten as silver, they crumple up
Like wet and falling roses, and I listen

For the sluicing of their rain-dishevelled petals.
In the window full of sunlight
Concentrates her golden shadow
Fold on fold, until it glows as
Mellow as the glory roses.

A Youth Mowing

There are four men mowing down by the Isar;
I can hear the swish of the scythe-strokes, four
Sharp breaths taken: yea, and I
Am sorry for what's in store.

The first man out of the four that's mowing
Is mine, I claim him once and for all;
Though it's sorry I am, on his young feet, knowing
None of the trouble he's led to stall.

As he sees me bringing the dinner, he lifts
His head as proud as a deer that looks
Shoulder-deep out of the corn; and wipes
His scythe-blade bright, unhooks

The scythe-stone and over the stubble to me.
Lad, thou hast gotten a child in me,
Laddie, a man thou'lt ha'e to be,
Yea, though I'm sorry for thee.

The Mess of Love

We've made a great mess of love
since we made an ideal of it.

The moment I swear to love a woman, a certain woman,
   all my life
that moment I begin to hate her.

The moment I even say to a woman: I love you! –
my love dies down considerably.

The moment love is an understood thing between us, we are
    sure of it,
it's a cold egg, it isn't love any more.

Love is like a flower, it must flower and fade;
if it doesn't fade, it is not a flower,
it's either an artificial rag blossom, or an immortelle, for the
    cemetery.

The moment the mind interferes with love, or the will fixes
    on it,
or the personality assumes it as an attribute, or the ego takes
    possession of it,
it is not love any more, it's just a mess.
And we've made a great mess of love, mind-perverted, will-
    perverted, ego-perverted love.

Intimates

Don't you care for my love? she said bitterly.

I handed her the mirror, and said:
Please address these questions to the proper person!
Please make all requests to head-quarters!
In all matters of emotional importance
please approach the supreme authority direct! –
So I handed her the mirror.

And she would have broken it over my head,
but she caught sight of her own reflection
and that held her spellbound for two seconds
while I fled.

Prove It On Me Blues

Went out last night,
Had a great big fight,
Everything seemed to go a-wrong.
I looked up,
To my surprise,
The gal I was with was gone.

Why she went
I don't know,
I mean to follow everywhere she goes.
Folks say I'm crooked,
I don't know where she took it,
I want the whole world to know.

CHORUS
They say I do it,
Ain't nobody caught me,
You all got to prove it on me.

Went out last night,
With a crowd of my friends,
They must bin womens
Cause I don't like no mens.
It's true I wear a collar and a tie,
Make the women-folk
Go all wild.
You all say I do it,
Ain't nobody caught me,
You sure got to prove it on me.

They say I do it,
Ain't nobody caught me,
You all got to prove it on me.

I went out last night,
With a crowd of my friends,
They must bin womens
As I don't like no mens.
Wear my clothes
Just like a man,
Talk to the gals,
Just like any old man.
Cause they say I do it,
Ain't nobody caught me,
You sure got to prove it on me.

B.D. Women Blues

Comin' a time,
B.D. women they ain't goin' need no men,
Comin' a time,
B.D. women they ain't goin' need no men,
Oh the way they treat us
Is a lowdown and dirty thing.

B.D. women
You sure can't understand,
B.D. women
You sure can't understand,
They got a head like [a machine gun?]
And they walk just like a natural man.

B.D. women,
They all done laid their claim,
B.D. women,

They all done laid their claim,
They can lay their jive
Just like a natural man.

B.D. women,
B.D. women you know they sure is rough,
B.D. women,
B.D. women you know they sure is rough,
They all drink up many a whiskey
And they sure do strut their stuff.

B.D. women,
You know they work and make their dough,
B.D. women,
You know they work and make their dough,
And when they get ready to spend it,
They know just where to go.

Has Anybody Seen My Corinne?

Has anybody seen my Corinne?
Aw, she's a dream,
Just like a vampire
She set my heart on fire.

I regret the day,
The day that she was born,
Since my lovin' Corinna's been gone.

If anybody sees my Corinne,
No matter where Corinna may be,
Tell my Corinna
To hurry back to me.

My gal went away last night,
I did my best to treat her right,
For no reason I could see,

I was wild about my gal,
Thought she was wild about me.

Has anybody seen my Corinne?
Aw, she's a dream,
Just like a vampire
She set my heart on fire.

I regret the day,
The day that she was born,
Since my lovin' Corinna's been gone.

If anybody sees my Corinne,
No matter where Corinna may be,
Tell my Corinna
To hurry back to me.

Has anybody seen my Corinne?
Aw, she's a dream,
Just like a vampire
She set my heart on fire.

I regret the day,
The day that she's been gone,
Ever since Corinna's been gone.

If anybody sees my Corinne,
No matter where Corinna may be,
Tell my Corinna
To hurry home to me.

To Lallie
(Outside the British Museum)

Up those Museum steps you came,
And straightway all my blood was flame,
  O Lallie, Lallie!

The world (I had been feeling low)
In one short moment's space did grow
  A happy valley.

There was a friend, my friend, with you;
A meagre dame, in peacock blue
  Apparelled quaintly;

This poet-heart went pit-a-pat;
I bowed and smiled and raised my hat;
  You nodded – faintly.

My heart was full as full could be;
You had not got a word for me,
  Not one short greeting;

That nonchalant small nod you gave
(The tyrant's motion to the slave)
  Sole mark'd our meeting.

Is it so long? Do you forget
That first and last time that we met?
  The time was summer;

The trees were green; the sky was blue;
Our host presented me to you –
  A tardy comer.

You look'd demure, but when you spoke
You made a little, funny joke,
  Yet half pathetic.

Your gown was grey, I recollect,
I think you patronized the sect
    They call 'esthetic.'

I brought you strawberries and cream,
I plied you long about a stream
    With duckweed laden;

We solemnly discussed the – heat.
I found you shy and very sweet,
    A rosebud maiden.

Ah me, to-day! You passed inside
To where the marble gods abide:
    Hermes, Apollo,

Sweet Aphrodite, Pan; and where,
For aye reclined, a headless fair
    Beats all fairs hollow.

And I, I went upon my way,
Well – rather sadder, let us say;
    The world looked flatter.

I had been sad enough before,
A little less, a little more,
    What does it matter?

At a Dinner Party

With fruit and flowers the board is deckt,
The wine and laughter flow;
I'll not complain – could one expect
So dull a world to know?

You look across the fruit and flowers,
My glance your glances find. –
It is our secret, only ours,
Since all the world is blind.

MICHAEL LONGLEY 1939–

The Rope-Makers

Sometimes you and I are like rope-makers
Twisting straw into a golden cable,
So gradual my walking backwards
You fail to notice when I reach the door,
Each step infinitesimal, a delay,
Neither a coming nor a going when
Across the lane-way I face you still
Or, at large at last in the sunny fields,
Struggle to pick you out of the darkness
Where, close to the dresser, the scrubbed table,
Fingers securing the other end, you
Watch me diminish in a square of light.

The Bat

We returned to the empty ballroom
And found a bat demented there, quite
Out of its mind, flashing round and round
Where earlier the dancers had moved.

We opened a window and shouted
To jam the signals and, so we thought,
Inspire a tangent in the tired skull,
A swerve, a saving miscalculation.

We had come to make love secretly
Without disturbance or obstacle,
And fell like shadows across the bat's
Singlemindedness, sheer insanity.

I told you of the blind snake that thrives
In total darkness by eating bats,

Of centuries measured in bat droppings,
The light bones that fall out of the air.

You called it a sky-mouse and described
Long fingers, anaesthetising teeth,
How it clung to the night by its thumbs,
And suggested that we leave it there.

Suspended between floor and ceiling
It would continue in our absence
And drop exhausted, a full stop
At the centre of the ballroom floor.

The Linen Industry

Pulling up flax after the blue flowers have fallen
And laying our handfuls in the peaty water
To rot those grasses to the bone, or building stooks
That recall the skirts of an invisible dancer,

We become a part of the linen industry
And follow its processes to the grubby town
Where fields are compacted into window-boxes
And there is little room among the big machines.

But even in our attic under the skylight
We make love on a bleach green, the whole meadow
Draped with material turning white in the sun
As though snow reluctant to melt were our attire.

What's passion but a battering of stubborn stalks,
Then a gentle combing out of fibres like hair
And a weaving of these into christening robes,
Into garments for a marriage or funeral?

Since it's like a bereavement once the labour's done
To find ourselves last workers in a dying trade,

Let flax be our matchmaker, our undertaker,
The provider of sheets for whatever the bed –

And be shy of your breasts in the presence of death,
Say that you look more beautiful in linen
Wearing white petticoats, the bow on your bodice
A butterfly attending the embroidered flowers.

The Pattern

Thirty-six years, to the day, after our wedding
When a cold figure-revealing wind blew against you
And lifted your veil, I find in its fat envelope
The six-shilling *Vogue* pattern for your bride's dress,
Complicated instructions for stitching bodice
And skirt, box pleats and hems, tissue-paper outlines,
Semblances of skin which I nervously unfold
And hold up in snow light, for snow has been falling
On this windless day, and I glimpse your wedding dress
And white shoes outside in the transformed garden
Where the clothesline and every twig have been covered.

To Lucasta. Going to the Wars

Tell me not, sweet, I am unkind,
  That from the nunnery
Of thy chaste breast, and quiet mind,
  To war and arms I fly.

True, a new mistress now I chase,
  The first foe in the field;
And with a stronger faith embrace
  A sword, a horse, a shield.

Yet this inconstancy is such,
  As you too shall adore;
I could not love thee, dear, so much,
  Loved I not honor more.

To Althea. From Prison

When Love with unconfinéd wings
  Hovers within my gates,
And my divine Althea brings
  To whisper at the grates;
When I lie tangled in her hair
  And fettered to her eye,
The gods that wanton in the air
  Know no such liberty.

When flowing cups run swiftly round,
  With no allaying Thames,
Our careless heads with roses bound,
  Our hearts with loyal flames;
When thirsty grief in wine we steep,

When healths and draughts go free,
Fishes that tipple in the deep
   Know no such liberty.

When, like committed linnets, I
   With shriller throat shall sing
The sweetness, mercy, majesty,
   And glories of my King;
When I shall voice aloud how good
   He is, how great should be,
Enlargéd winds that curl the flood
   Know no such liberty.

Stone walls do not a prison make,
   Nor iron bars a cage:
Minds innocent and quiet take
   That for an hermitage.
If I have freedom in my love,
   And in my soul am free,
Angels alone, that soar above,
   Enjoy such liberty.

La Bella Bona Roba

I cannot tell who loves the skeleton
Of a poor marmoset, nought but bone, bone.
Give me a nakedness with her clothes on.

Such whose white satin upper coat of skin,
Cut upon velvet rich incarnadine,
Has yet a body (and of flesh) within.

Sure it is meant good husbandry in men
Who do incorporate with airy lean,
T' repair their sides, and get their rib again.

Hard hap unto that huntsman that decrees
Fat joys for all his sweat, whenas he sees,
After his assay, nought but his keeper's fees.

Then Love, I beg, when next thou tak'st thy bow,
Thy angry shafts, and dost heart-chasing go,
Pass rascal deer, strike me the largest doe.

Friendship

When we were charming *Backfisch*
  With curls and velvet bows
We shared a charming kitten
  With tiny velvet toes.

It was so gay and playful;
  It flew like a woolly ball
From my lap to your shoulder –
  And, oh, it was so small,

So warm – and so obedient
  If we cried: 'That's enough!'
It lay and slept between us,
  A purring ball of fluff.

But now that I am thirty
  And she is thirty-one,
I shudder to discover
  How wild our cat has run.

It's bigger than a Tiger,
  Its eyes are jets of flame,
Its claws are gleaming daggers,
  Could it have once been tame?

Take it away; I'm frightened!
  But she, with placid brow,
Cries: 'This is our Kitty-witty!
  Why don't you love her now?'

CHRISTOPHER MARLOWE 1564–93

The Passionate Shepherd to His Love

Come live with me, and be my love,
And we will all the pleasures prove
That valleys, groves, hills and fields,
Woods, or steepy mountain yields.

And we will sit upon the rocks,
Seeing the shepherds feed their flocks
By shallow rivers, to whose falls
Melodious birds sing madrigals.

And I will make thee beds of roses,
And a thousand fragrant posies,
A cap of flowers, and a kirtle,
Embroidered all with leaves of myrtle.

A gown made of the finest wool
Which from our pretty lambs we pull,
Fair linèd slippers for the cold,
With buckles of the purest gold.

A belt of straw and ivy-buds,
With coral clasps and amber studs,
And if these pleasures may thee move,
Come live with me, and be my love.

The shepherd swains shall dance and sing
For thy delight each May morning.
If these delights thy mind may move,
Then live with me, and be my love.

ANDREW MARVELL 1621–78

The Unfortunate Lover

1

Alas, how pleasant are their days
With whom the infant Love yet plays!
Sorted by pairs, they still are seen
By fountains cool, and shadows green.
But soon these flames do lose their light,
Like meteors of a summer's night:
Nor can they to that region climb,
To make impression upon time.

2

'Twas in a shipwreck, when the seas
Ruled, and the winds did what they please,
That my poor lover floating lay,
And, ere brought forth, was cast away:
Till at the last the master-wave
Upon the rock his mother drave;
And there she split against the stone,
In a Caesarean séction.

3

The sea him lent those bitter tears
Which at his eyes he always wears;
And from the winds the sighs he bore,
Which through his surging breast do roar.
No day he saw but that which breaks
Through frighted clouds in forkèd streaks,
While round the rattling thunder hurled,
As at the funeral of the world.

4

While Nature to his birth presents
This masque of quarrelling elements,
A numerous fleet of cormorants black,
That sailed insulting o'er the wrack,
Received into their cruel care
Th' unfortunate and abject heir:
Guardians most fit to entertain
The orphan of the hurricane.

5

They fed him up with hopes and air,
Which soon digested to despair,
And as one cormorant fed him, still
Another on his heart did bill,
Thus while they famish him, and feast,
He both consumèd, and increased:
And languishèd with doubtful breath,
The amphibíum of life and death.

6

And now, when angry heaven would
Behold a spectacle of blood,
Fortune and he are called to play
At sharp before it all the day:
And tyrant Love his breast does ply
With all his winged artillery,
Whilst he, betwixt the flames and waves,
Like Ajax, the mad tempest braves.

7

See how he nak'd and fierce does stand,
Cuffing the thunder with one hand,
While with the other he does lock,

And grapple, with the stubborn rock:
From which he with each wave rebounds,
Torn into flames, and ragg'd with wounds,
And all he says, a lover dressed
In his own blood does relish best.

8

This is the only banneret
That ever Love created yet:
Who though, by the malignant stars,
Forcèd to live in storms and wars,
Yet dying leaves a perfume here,
And music within every ear:
And he in story only rules,
In a field sable a lover gules.

The Definition of Love

1

My love is of a birth as rare
As 'tis for object strange and high:
It was begotten by Despair
Upon Impossibility.

2

Magnanimous Despair alone
Could show me so divine a thing,
Where feeble Hope could ne'er have flown
But vainly flapped its tinsel wing.

3

And yet I quickly might arrive
Where my extended soul is fixed,

But Fate does iron wedges drive,
And always crowds itself betwixt.

4

For Fate with jealous eye does see
Two perfect loves, nor lets them close:
Their union would her ruin be,
And her tyrannic power depose.

5

And therefore her decrees of steel
Us as the distant Poles have placed,
(Though Love's whole world on us doth wheel)
Not by themselves to be embraced,

6

Unless the giddy heaven fall,
And earth some new convulsion tear;
And, us to join, the world should all
Be cramped into a planisphere.

7

As lines (so loves) oblique may well
Themselves in every angle greet:
But ours so truly parallel,
Though infinite, can never meet.

8

Therefore the love which us doth bind,
But Fate so enviously debars,
Is the conjunction of the mind,
And opposition of the stars.

To His Coy Mistress

Had we but world enough, and time,
This coyness, Lady, were no crime.
We would sit down, and think which way
To walk, and pass our long love's day.
Thou by the Indian Ganges' side
Shouldst rubies find: I by the tide
Of Humber would complain. I would
Love you ten years before the flood:
And you should, if you please, refuse
Till the conversion of the Jews.
My vegetable love should grow
Vaster than empires, and more slow.
An hundred years should go to praise
Thine eyes, and on thy forehead gaze.
Two hundred to adore each breast:
But thirty thousand to the rest.
An age at least to every part,
And the last age should show your heart:
For, Lady, you deserve this state;
Nor would I love at lower rate.

But at my back I always hear
Time's wingèd chariot hurrying near:
And yonder all before us lie
Deserts of vast eternity.
Thy beauty shall no more be found;
Nor, in thy marble vault, shall sound
My echoing song: then worms shall try
That long-preserved virginity:
And your quaint honour turn to dust;
And into ashes all my lust.
The grave's a fine and private place,
But none, I think, do there embrace.

Now, therefore, while the youthful glue
Sits on thy skin like morning dew,

And while thy willing soul transpires
At every pore with instant fires,
Now let us sport us while we may;
And now, like amorous birds of prey,
Rather at once our time devour,
Than languish in his slow-chapped power.
Let us roll all our strength, and all
Our sweetness, up into one ball:
And tear our pleasures with rough strife,
Thorough the iron grates of life.
Thus, though we cannot make our sun
Stand still, yet we will make him run.

Damon the Mower

1

Hark how the Mower Damon sung,
With love of Juliana stung!
While everything did seem to paint
The scene more fit for his complaint.
Like her fair eyes the day was fair,
But scorching like his am'rous care.
Sharp like his scythe his sorrow was,
And withered like his hopes the grass.

2

'Oh what unusual heats are here,
Which thus our sunburned meadows sear!
The grasshopper its pipe gives o'er;
And hamstringed frogs can dance no more.
But in the brook the green frog wades;
And grasshoppers seek out the shades.
Only the snake, that kept within,
Now glitters in its second skin.

3

'This heat the sun could never raise,
Nor Dog Star so inflame the days.
It from an higher beauty grow'th,
Which burns the fields and mower both:
Which mads the dog, and makes the sun
Hotter than his own Phaëton.
Not July causeth these extremes,
But Juliana's scorching beams.

4

'Tell me where I may pass the fires
Of the hot day, or hot desires.
To what cool cave shall I descend,
Or to what gelid fountain bend?
Alas! I look for ease in vain,
When remedies themselves complain.
No moisture but my tears do rest,
Nor cold but in her icy breast.

5

'How long wilt thou, fair shepherdess,
Esteem me, and my presents less?
To thee the harmless snake I bring,
Disarmèd of its teeth and sting;
To thee chameleons, changing hue,
And oak leaves tipped with honey dew.
Yet thou, ungrateful, hast not sought
Nor what they are, nor who them brought.

6

'I am the Mower Damon, known
Through all the meadows I have mown.
On me the morn her dew distills

Before her darling daffodils.
And, if at noon my toil me heat,
The sun himself licks off my sweat.
While, going home, the evening sweet
In cowslip-water bathes my feet.

7

'What, though the piping shepherd stock
The plains with an unnumbered flock,
This scythe of mine discovers wide
More ground than all his sheep do hide.
With this the golden fleece I shear
Of all these closes every year.
And though in wool more poor than they,
Yet am I richer far in hay.

8

'Nor am I so deformed to sight,
If in my scythe I lookèd right;
In which I see my picture done,
As in a crescent moon the sun.
The deathless fairies take me oft
To lead them in their dances soft:
And, when I tune myself to sing,
About me they contract their ring.

9

'How happy might I still have mowed,
Had not Love here his thistles sowed!
But now I all the day complain,
Joining my labour to my pain;
And with my scythe cut down the grass,
Yet still my grief is where it was:
But, when the iron blunter grows,
Sighing, I whet my scythe and woes.'

While thus he threw his elbow round,
Depopulating all the ground,
And, with his whistling scythe, does cut
Each stroke between the earth and root,
The edgèd steel by careless chance
Did into his own ankle glance;
And there among the grass fell down,
By his own scythe, the Mower mown.

11

'Alas!' said he, 'these hurts are slight
To those that die by love's despite.
With shepherd's-purse, and clown's-all-heal,
The blood I staunch, and wound I seal.
Only for him no cure is found,
Whom Juliana's eyes do wound.
'Tis death alone that this must do:
For Death thou art a Mower too.'

The Mower to the Glowworms

1

Ye living lamps, by whose dear light
The nightingale does sit so late,
And studying all the summer night,
Her matchless songs does meditate;

2

Ye country comets, that portend
No war, nor prince's funeral,
Shining unto no higher end
Than to presage the grass's fall;

3

Ye glowworms, whose officious flame
To wandering mowers shows the way,
That in the night have lost their aim,
And after foolish fires do stray;

4

Your courteous lights in vain you waste,
Since Juliana here is come,
For she my mind hath so displaced
That I shall never find my home.

GEORGE MEREDITH 1828–1909

from Modern Love

I

By this he knew she wept with waking eyes:
That, at his hand's light quiver by her head,
The strange low sobs that shook their common bed
Were called into her with a sharp surprise,
And strangled mute, like little gaping snakes,
Dreadfully venomous to him. She lay
Stone-still, and the long darkness flowed away
With muffled pulses. Then, as midnight makes
Her giant heart of Memory and Tears
Drink the pale drug of silence, and so beat
Sleep's heavy measure, they from head to feet
Were moveless, looking through their dead black years
By vain regret scrawled over the blank wall.
Like sculptured effigies they might be seen
Upon their marriage-tomb, the sword between;
Each wishing for the sword that severs all.

II

It ended, and the morrow brought the task.
Her eyes were guilty gates, that let him in
By shutting all too zealous for their sin:
Each sucked a secret, and each wore a mask.
But, oh, the bitter taste her beauty had!
He sickened as at breath of poison-flowers:
A languid humour stole among the hours,
And if their smiles encountered, he went mad,
And raged deep inward, till the light was brown
Before his vision, and the world, forgot,
Looked wicked as some old dull murder-spot.

A star with lurid beams, she seemed to crown
The pit of infamy: and then again
He fainted on his vengefulness, and strove
To ape the magnanimity of love,
And smote himself, a shuddering heap of pain.

V

A message from her set his brain aflame.
A world of household matters filled her mind,
Wherein he saw hypocrisy designed:
She treated him as something that is tame,
And but at other provocation bites.
Familiar was her shoulder in the glass,
Through that dark rain: yet it may come to pass
That a changed eye finds such familiar sights
More keenly tempting than new loveliness.
The 'What has been' a moment seemed his own:
The splendours, mysteries, dearer because known,
Nor less divine: Love's inmost sacredness
Called to him, 'Come!' – In his restraining start.
Eyes nurtured to be looked at scarce could see
A wave of the great waves of Destiny
Convulsed at a checked impulse of the heart.

VII

She issues radiant from her dressing-room,
Like one prepared to scale an upper sphere:
– By stirring up a lower, much I fear!
How deftly that oiled barber lays his bloom!
That long-shanked dapper Cupid with frisked curls
Can make known women torturingly fair;
The gold-eyed serpent dwelling in rich hair
Awakes beneath his magic whisks and twirls.
His art can take the eyes from out my head,
Until I see with eyes of other men;

While deeper knowledge crouches in its den,
And sends a spark up: – is it true we are wed?
Yea! filthiness of body is most vile,
But faithlessness of heart I do hold worse.
The former, it were not so great a curse
To read on the steel-mirror of her smile,

IX

He felt the wild beast in him betweenwhiles
So masterfully rude, that he would grieve
To see the helpless delicate thing receive
His guardianship through certain dark defiles.
Had he not teeth to rend, and hunger too?
But still he spared her. Once: 'Have you no fear?'
He said: 'twas dusk; she in his grasp; none near.
She laughed: 'No, surely; am I not with you?'
And uttering that soft starry 'you,' she leaned
Her gentle body near him, looking up;
And from her eyes, as from a poison-cup,
He drank until the flittering eyelids screened.
Devilish malignant witch; and oh, young beam
Of heaven's circle-glory! Here thy shape
To squeeze like an intoxicating grape –
I might, and yet thou goest safe, supreme.

XV

I think she sleeps: it must be sleep, when low
Hangs that abandoned arm toward the floor;
The face turned with it. Now make fast the door.
Sleep on: it is your husband, not your foe.
The Poet's black stage-lion of wronged love
Frights not our modern dames: – well if he did!
Now will I pour new light upon that lid,
Full-sloping like the breasts beneath. 'Sweet dove,
Your sleep is pure. Nay, pardon: I disturb.

I do not? good!' Her waking infant-stare
Grows woman to the burden my hands bear:
Her own handwriting to me when no curb
Was left on Passion's tongue. She trembles through;
A woman's tremble – the whole instrument: –
I show another letter lately sent.
The words are very like: the name is new.

CHARLOTTE MEW 1869–1928

The Farmer's Bride

Three Summers since I chose a maid,
Too young maybe – but more's to do
At harvest-time than bide and woo.
        When us was wed she turned afraid
Of love and me and all things human;
Like the shut of a winter's day.
Her smile went out, and 'twasn't a woman –
        More like a little frightened fay.
            One night, in the Fall, she runned away.

'Out 'mong the sheep, her be,' they said,
'Should properly have been abed;
But sure enough she wasn't there
Lying awake with her wide brown stare.
So over seven-acre field and up-along across the down
        We chased her, flying like a hare
        Before our lanterns. To Church-Town
            All in a shiver and a scare
        We caught her, fetched her home at last
            And turned the key upon her, fast.

She does the work about the house
As well as most, but like a mouse:
        Happy enough to chat and play
        With birds and rabbits and such as they,
        So long as men-folk keep away.
'Not near, not near!' her eyes beseech
When one of us comes within reach.
        The women say that beasts in stall
        Look round like children at her call.
        I've hardly heard her speak at all.

Shy as a leveret, swift as he,
Straight and slight as a young larch tree,
Sweet as the first wild violets, she,
To her wild self. But what to me?

The short days shorten and the oaks are brown,
    The blue smoke rises to the low grey sky,
One leaf in the still air falls slowly down,
    A magpie's spotted feathers lie
On the black earth spread white with rime,
The berries redden up to Christmas-time.
    What's Christmas-time without there be
    Some other in the house than we!

    She sleeps up in the attic there
    Alone, poor maid. 'Tis but a stair
Betwixt us. Oh! my God! the down,
The soft young down of her, the brown,
The brown of her – her eyes, her hair, her hair!

In Nunhead Cemetery

It is the clay that makes the earth stick to his spade;
    He fills in holes like this year after year;
The others have gone; they were tired, and half afraid
    But I would rather be standing here;

There is nowhere else to go. I have seen this place
    From the windows of the train that's going past
Against the sky. This is rain on my face –
    It was raining here when I saw it last.

There is something horrible about a flower;
    This, broken in my hand, is one of those
He threw in just now: it will not live another hour;
    There are thousands more: you do not miss a rose.

One of the children hanging about
　　Pointed at the whole dreadful heap and smiled
This morning, after THAT was carried out;
　　There is something terrible about a child.

We were like children, last week, in the Strand;
　　That was the day you laughed at me
Because I tried to make you understand
　　The cheap, stale chap I used to be
　　Before I saw the things you made me see.

This is not a real place; perhaps by-and-by
　　I shall wake – I am getting drenched with all this rain:
Tomorrow I will tell you about the eyes of the Crystal Palace
　　　　train
　　Looking down on us, and you will laugh and I shall see
　　　　what you see again.

　　Not here, not now. We said 'Not yet
　　Across our low stone parapet
Will the quick shadows of the sparrows fall.'

　　But still it was a lovely thing
　　Through the grey months to wait for Spring
　　With the birds that go a-gypsying
In the parks till the blue seas call.
　　And next to these, you used to care
　　For the lions in Trafalgar Square,
Who'll stand and speak for London when her bell of
　　　　Judgment tolls –
　　And the gulls at Westminster that were
　　The old sea-captains' souls.
Today again the brown tide splashes, step by step, the river
　　　　stair,
　　And the gulls are there!

By a month we have missed our Day:
　　The children would have hung about

Round the carriage and over the way
    As you and I came out.

We should have stood on the gulls' black cliffs and heard
      the sea
    And seen the moon's white track,
I would have called, you would have come to me
    And kissed me back.

You have never done that: I do not know
    Why I stood staring at your bed
And heard you, though you spoke so low,
    But could not reach your hands, your little head.
There was nothing we could not do, you said,
    And you went, and I let you go!

Now I will burn you back, I will burn you through,
    Though I am damned for it we two will lie
    And burn, here where the starlings fly
    To these white stones from the wet sky – ;
    Dear, you will say this is not I –
It would not be you, it would not be you!

If for only a little while
    You will think of it you will understand,
      If you will touch my sleeve and smile
    As you did that morning in the Strand
      I can wait quietly with you
      Or go away if you want me to –
God! What is God? but your face has gone and your hand!
      Let me stay here too.

      When I was quite a little lad
    At Christmas time we went half mad
      For joy of all the toys we had,
And then we used to sing about the sheep
      The shepherds watched by night;
We used to pray to Christ to keep

Our small souls safe till morning light – ;
I am scared, I am staying with you to-night –
                    Put me to sleep.

I shall stay here: here you can see the sky;
The houses in the streets are much too high;
    There is no one left to speak to there;
    Here they are everywhere,
And just above them fields and fields of roses lie –
If he would dig it all up again they would not die.

À Quoi Bon Dire

    Seventeen years ago you said
Something that sounded like Good-bye;
    And everybody thinks that you are dead,
                    But I.

    So I, as I grow stiff and cold
To this and that say Good-bye too;
    And everybody sees that I am old
                    But you.

    And one fine morning in a sunny lane
Some boy and girl will meet and kiss and swear
    That nobody can love their way again
                    While over there
You will have smiled, I shall have tossed your hair.

The Road to Kérity

Do you remember the two old people we passed on the road
    to Kérity,
Resting their sack on the stones, by the drenched
    wayside,

Looking at us with their lightless eyes through the driving
   rain, and then out
                         again
To the rocks, and the long white line of the tide:
Frozen ghosts that were children once, husband and wife,
   father, and mother,
Looking at us with those frozen eyes; have you ever seen
   anything quite so
                         chilled or so old?
              But we – with our arms about each other,
              We did not feel the cold!

From a Window

    Up here, with June, the sycamore throws
    Across the window a whispering screen;
  I shall miss the sycamore more, I suppose,
Than anything else on this earth that is out in green.
    But I mean to go through the door without fear,
    Not caring much what happens here
         When I'm away: –
How green the screen is across the panes
    Or who goes laughing along the lanes
With my old lover all the summer day.

My Heart is Lame

My heart is lame with running after yours so fast
         Such a long way,
Shall we walk slowly home, looking at all the things we
   passed
         Perhaps to-day?

Home down the quiet evening roads under the quiet skies,
         Not saying much,

You for a moment giving me your eyes
      When you could bear my touch.

But not to-morrow. This has taken all my breath;
      Then, though you look the same,
There may be something lovelier in Love's face in
    death
As your heart sees it, running back the way we came;
      My heart is lame.

JOHN MILTON 1608–74

Sonnet I

O nightingale, that on yon bloomy spray
   Warblest at eve, when all the woods are still,
   Thou with fresh hope the lover's heart dost fill,
   While the jolly hours lead on propitious May,
Thy liquid notes that close the eye of day,
   First heard before the shallow cuckoo's bill
   Portend success in love; O if Jove's will
   Have linked that amorous power to thy soft lay,
Now timely sing, ere the rude bird of hate
   Foretell my hopeless doom in some grove nigh:
   As thou from year to year hast sung too late
For my relief; yet hadst no reason why,
   Whether the Muse, or Love call thee his mate,
   Both them I serve, and of their train am I.

Sonnet XIX

Methought I saw my late espoused saint
   Brought to me like Alcestis from the grave,
   Whom Jove's great son to her glad husband gave,
   Rescued from death by force though pale and faint.
Mine as whom washed from spot of childbed taint,
   Purification in the old Law did save,
   And such, as yet once more I trust to have
   Full sight of her in heaven without restraint,
Came vested all in white, pure as her mind:
   Her face was veiled, yet to my fancied sight,
   Love, sweetness, goodness in her person shined
So clear, as in no face with more delight.
   But O as to embrace me she inclined
   I waked, she fled, and day brought back my night.

LADY MARY WORTLEY MONTAGU 1689–1762

The Lover: A Ballad

At length, by so much importunity pressed,
Take, Molly, at once, the inside of my breast;
This stupid indifference so often you blame
Is not owing to nature, to fear, or to shame:
I am not as cold as a virgin in lead,
Nor is Sunday's sermon so strong in my head:
I know but too well how time flies along,
That we live but few years, and yet fewer are young.

But I hate to be cheated, and never will buy
Long years of repentance for moments of joy.
Oh! was there a man (but where shall I find
Good sense and good nature so equally joined?)
Would value his pleasure, contribute to mine;
Not meanly would boast, nor lewdly design;
Not over severe, yet not stupidly vain,
For I would have the power, though not give the pain.

No pedant, yet learnèd; not rake-helly gay,
Or laughing, because he has nothing to say;
To all my whole sex obliging and free,
Yet never be fond of any but me;
In public, preserve the decorums are just,
And show in his eyes he is true to his trust;
Then rarely approach, and respectfully bow,
Yet not fulsomely pert, nor yet foppishly low.

But when the long hours of public are past,
And we meet with champagne and a chicken at last,
May every fond pleasure that hour endear;
Be banished afar both discretion and fear.
Forgetting or scorning the airs of the crowd,

He may cease to be formal, and I to be proud,
Till lost in the joy, we confess that we live,
And he may be rude, and yet I may forgive.

And that my delight may be solidly fixed,
Let the friend and the lover be handsomely mixed;
In whose tender bosom my soul might confide,
Whose kindness can soothe me, whose counsel could guide.
From such a dear lover, as here I describe,
No danger should fright me, no millions should bribe;
But till this astonishing creature I know,
As I long have lived chaste, I will keep myself so.

I never will share with the wanton coquette,
Or be caught by a vain affectation of wit.
The toasters and songsters may try all their art,
But never shall enter the pass of my heart.
I loathe the lewd rake, the dressed fopling despise:
Before such pursuers the nice virgin flies:
And as Ovid has sweetly in parables told,
We harden like trees, and like rivers are cold.

PAUL MULDOON 1951–

Paris

A table for two will scarcely seat
The pair of us! All the people we have been
Are here as guests, strategically deployed
As to who will go best with whom.
A convent girl, a crashing bore, the couple

Who aren't quite all they seem.
A last shrimp curls and winces on your plate
Like an embryo. 'Is that a little overdone?'
And these country faces at the window
That were once our own. They study the menu,

Smile faintly, and are gone.
Chicken Marengo! It's a far cry from the Moy.
'There's no such person as Saint Christopher,
Father Talbot gave it out at Mass.
Same as there's no such place as Limbo.'

The world's less simple for being travelled,
Though. In each fresh, neutral place
Where our differences might have been settled
There were men sitting down to talk of peace
Who began with the shape of the table.

Bran

While he looks into the eyes of women
Who have let themselves go,
While they sigh and they moan
For pure joy,

He weeps for the boy on that small farm
Who takes an oatmeal Labrador
In his arms,
Who knows all there is of rapture.

History

Where and when exactly did we first have sex?
Do you remember? Was it Fitzroy Avenue,
Or Cromwell Road, or Notting Hill?
Your place or mine? Marseilles or Aix?
Or as long ago as that Thursday evening
When you and I climbed through the bay window
On the ground floor of Aquinas Hall
And into the room where MacNeice wrote 'Snow',
Or the room where they say he wrote 'Snow'.

The Avenue

Now that we've come to the end
I've been trying to piece it together,
Not that distance makes anything clearer.
It began in the half-light
While we walked through the dawn chorus
After a party that lasted all night,
With the blackbird, the wood-pigeon,
The song-thrush taking a bludgeon
To a snail, our taking each other's hand
As if the whole world lay before us.

ALICE OSWALD 1966–

Wedding

From time to time our love is like a sail
and when the sail begins to alternate
from tack to tack, it's like a swallowtail
and when the swallow flies it's like a coat;
and if the coat is yours, it has a tear
like a wide mouth and when the mouth begins
to draw the wind, it's like a trumpeter
and when the trumpet blows, it blows like millions . . .
and this, my love, when millions come and go
beyond the need of us, is like a trick;
and when the trick begins, it's like a toe
tip-toeing on a rope, which is like luck;
and when the luck begins, it's like a wedding,
which is like love, which is like everything.

'I saw his round mouth's crimson deepen as it fell'

I saw his round mouth's crimson deepen as it fell,
 Like a sun, in his last deep hour;
Watched the magnificent recession of farewell,
 Clouding, half gleam, half glower,
And a last splendour burn the heavens of his cheek.
 And in his eyes
The cold stars lighting, very old and bleak,
 In different skies.

'I am the Ghost of Shadwell Stair'

I am the ghost of Shadwell Stair.
 Along the wharves by the water-house,
 And through the cavernous slaughter-house,
I am the shadow that walks there.

Yet I have flesh both firm and cool,
 And eyes tumultuous as the gems
 Of moons and lamps in the full Thames
When dusk sails wavering down the Pool.

Shuddering, a purple street-arc burns
 Where I watch always. From the banks
 Dolorously the shipping clanks.
And after me a strange tide turns.

I walk till the stars of London wane,
 And dawn creeps up the Shadwell Stair.
 But when the crowing sirens blare,
I with another ghost am lain.

DOROTHY PARKER 1893–1967

One Perfect Rose

A single flow'r he sent me, since we met.
   All tenderly his messenger he chose;
Deep-hearted, pure, with scented dew still wet
   One perfect rose.

I knew the language of the floweret;
   'My fragile leaves,' it said, 'his heart enclose.'
Love long has taken for his amulet
   One perfect rose.

Why is it no one ever sent me yet
   One perfect limousine, do you suppose?
Ah no, it's always just my luck to get
   One perfect rose.

A Gift

That night she called his name, not mine
    and could not call it back
I shamed myself, and thought of that blind
    girl in Kodiak

who sat out on the stoop each night
    to watch the daylight fade
and lift her child down to the gate cut
    in the palisade

and what old caution love resigned
    when through that misty stare
she passed the boy to not her bearskinned
    husband but the bear

GEORGE PEELE 1556-96

What Thing is Love?

What thing is love? for, well I wot, love is a thing.
It is a prick, it is a sting,
It is a pretty pretty thing;
It is a fire, it is a coal,
Whose flame creeps in at every hole;
And as my wit doth best devise,
Love's dwelling is in ladies' eyes:
From whence do glance love's piercing darts
That make such holes into our hearts;
And all the world herein accord
Love is a great and mighty lord,
And when he list to mount so high,
With Venus he in heaven doth lie,
And evermore hath been a god
Since Mars and she played even and odd.

Song

Whenas the rye reach to the chin,
And chopcherry, chopcherry ripe within,
Strawberries swimming in the cream,
And schoolboys playing in the stream;
Then oh, then oh, then oh, my true Love said,
Till that time come again
She could not live a maid.

COLE PORTER 1891–1964

Let's Do It, Let's Fall in Love

When the little bluebird,
Who has never said a word,
Starts to sing 'Spring, spring,'
When the little bluebell,
In the bottom of the dell,
Starts to ring 'Ding, ding,'
When the little blue clerk,
In the middle of his work,
Starts a tune to the moon up above,
It is nature, that's all,
Simply telling us to fall
In love.

Birds do it, Bees do it,
Even educated fleas do it,
Let's do it, let's fall in love.
In Spain, the best upper sets do it,
Lithuanians and Letts do it,
Let's do it, let's fall in love.
The Dutch in old Amsterdam do it,
Not to mention the Finns,
Folks in Siam do it,
Think of Siamese twins.
Some Argentines, without means, do it,
People say, in Boston, even beans do it,
Let's do it, let's fall in love.

The nightingales, in the dark, do it,
Larks, k-razy for a lark, do it,
Let's do it, let's fall in love.
Canaries, caged in the house, do it,
When they're out of season, grouse do it,

Let's do it, let's fall in love.
The most sedate barnyard fowls do it,
When a chanticleer cries,
High-browed old owls do it,
They're supposed to be wise,
Penguins in flocks, on the rocks, do it,
Even little cuckoos, in their clocks, do it,
Let's do it, let's fall in love.

Romantic sponges, they say, do it,
Oysters, down in Oyster Bay, do it,
Let's do it, let's fall in love.
Cold Cape Cod clams, 'gainst their wish, do it,
Even lazy jellyfish do it,
Let's do it, let's fall in love.
Electric eels, I might add, do it,
Though it shocks 'em, I know.
Why ask if shad do it?
Waiter, bring me shad roe.
In shallow shoals, English soles do it.
Goldfish, in the privacy of bowls, do it.
Let's do it, let's fall in love.

Young whelks and winkles, in pubs, do it.
Little sponges, in their tubs, do it,
Let's do it, let's fall in love.
Cold salmon, quite 'gainst their wish, do it,
Even lazy jellyfish do it,
Let's do it, let's fall in love.
The most select schools of cod do it,
Though it shocks 'em, I fear,
Sturgeon, thank God, do it,
Have some caviar, dear.
In shady shoals, English soles do it,
Goldfish, in the privacy of bowls, do it,
Let's do it, let's fall in love.

The dragonflies, in the reeds, do it,
Sentimental centipedes do it,
Let's do it, let's fall in love.
Mosquitoes, heaven forbid, do it,
So does ev'ry katydid, do it,
Let's do it, let's fall in love.
The most refined lady bugs do it,
When a gentleman calls,
Moths in your rugs, do it,
What's the use of moth balls?
Locusts in trees do it, bees do it,
Even overeducated fleas do it,
Let's do it, let's fall in love.

The chimpanzees, in the zoos, do it,
Some courageous kangaroos do it,
Let's do it, let's fall in love.
I'm sure giraffes, on the sly, do it,
Heavy hippopotami do it,
Let's do it, let's fall in love.
Old sloths who hang down from twigs do it,
Though the effort is great,
Sweet guinea pigs do it,
Buy a couple and wait.
The world admits bears in pits do it,
Even pekineses in the Ritz, do it,
Let's do it, let's fall in love.

Night and Day

Like the beat beat beat of the tom-tom
When the jungle shadows fall,
Like the tick tick tock of the stately clock
As it stands against the wall,
Like the drip drip drip of the raindrops

When the sum'r show'r is through,
So a voice within me keeps repeating
You – You – You.

Night and day you are the one,
Only you beneath the moon and under the sun.
Whether near to me or far
It's no matter, darling, where you are,
I think of you, night and day.
Day and night, why is it so
That this longing for you follows wherever I go?
In the roaring traffic's boom,
In the silence of my lonely room,
I think of you, night and day.
Night and day under the hide of me
There's an, oh, such a hungry yearning burning inside of me,
And its torment won't be through
Till you let me spend my life making love to you
Day and night, night and day.

CRAIG RAINE 1944-

The Onion, Memory

Divorced, but friends again at last,
we walk old ground together
in bright blue uncomplicated weather.
We laugh and pause
to hack to bits these tiny dinosaurs,
prehistoric, crenellated, cast
between the tractor ruts in mud.

On the green, a junior Douglas Fairbanks,
swinging on the chestnut's unlit chandelier,
defies the corporation spears –
a single rank around the bole,
rusty with blood.
Green, tacky phalluses curve up, romance.
A gust – the old flag blazes on its pole.

In the village bakery
the pasty babies pass
from milky slump to crusty cadaver,
from crib to coffin – without palaver.
All's over in a flash,
too silently . . .

Tonight the arum lilies fold
back napkins monogrammed in gold,
crisp and laundered fresh.
Those crustaceous gladioli, on the sly,
reveal the crimson flower-flesh
inside their emerald armour plate.
The uncooked herrings blink a tearful eye.
The candles palpitate.
The Oistrakhs bow and scrape

in evening dress, on Emi-tape.

Outside the trees are bending over backwards
to please the wind: the shining sword
grass flattens on its belly.
The white-thorn's frillies offer no resistance.
In the fridge, a heart-shaped jelly
strives to keep a sense of balance.

I slice up the onions. You sew up a dress.
This is the quiet echo – flesh –
white muscle on white muscle,
intimately folded skin,
finished with a satin rustle.
One button only to undo, sewn up with shabby thread.
It is the onion, memory,
that makes me cry.

Because there's everything and nothing to be said,
the clock with hands held up before its face,
stammers softly on, trying to complete a phrase –
while we, together and apart,
repeat unfinished gestures got by heart.

And afterwards, I blunder with the washing on the line –
headless torsos, faceless lovers, friends of mine.

Southern Blues

House catch on fire
                and ain't no water 'round
If your house catch on fire
                  ain't no water 'round
Throw your trunk out the window
                    building burn on down

I went to the Gypsy
              to have my fortune told
I went to the Gypsy
              to have my fortune told
He said, Doggone you, girlie
                doggone your bad luck soul

I turned around
            went to the Gypsy next door
I turned around
            went to the Gypsy next door
He said, You'll get a man
              any where you go

Let me be your rag-doll
                until your chiny come
Let me be your rag-doll till
              your chiny come
If he beats me ragged
            he's got to rag it some

CHRISTOPHER REID 1949–

At the Wrong Door

A bank-manager's rapid signature
of hair on the bath enamel, twist
and tail, to confirm that I have missed
you by a minute; mat on the floor,

stamped vigorously with wet; your
absence palpable in the misty,
trickling, inexorcizable ghost
that occupies the whole mirror –

I cannot rub it away – the room
clings to me with such a perfume
of soap and sweat, that I can only

stop to think how somewhere else
you may be standing, naked, lonely,
amid a downfall of dampish towels.

ELIZABETH MADOX ROBERTS 1881–1941

An Old Love in Song

'Oh, my truelove,' is part of it,
Or was it 'My truelove and I?' . . .
It trembles on old memories
And walks on by.

I asked an old man and he said,
'That song? Why everybody knows . . .'
He said, but when he tried to sing,
'I can't remember how it goes.'

He said, 'My father used to sing
A verse of it,' and then he said,
'It really came before my day
And those that used it all are dead.'

It walks tiptoe on other thoughts.
It's hardly there for you to touch,
But once, – my hand was on the door,
It leaned against the latch.

'Oh, my truelove' is dead and lost,
And no one sings it now at all,
But once I saw it on a shelf;
It curved against an ancient bowl.

They used to sing it by the doors
On summer nights, and yet, and yet,
It wasn't anything to keep;
It was something to forget.

I saw it lying in the ground
In a deep hole that I had made. . . .
I dug beside an old rose bush –
I touched it with my spade.

Winter: My Secret

I tell my secret? No indeed, not I:
Perhaps some day, who knows?
But not today; it froze, and blows, and snows,
And you're too curious: fie!
You want to hear it? well:
Only, my secret's mine, and I won't tell.

Or, after all, perhaps there's none:
Suppose there is no secret after all,
But only just my fun.
Today's a nipping day, a biting day;
In which one wants a shawl,
A veil, a cloak, and other wraps:
I cannot ope to every one who taps,
And let the draughts come whistling thro' my hall;
Come bounding and surrounding me,
Come buffeting, astounding me,
Nipping and clipping thro' my wraps and all.
I wear my mask for warmth: who ever shows
His nose to Russian snows
To be pecked at by every wind that blows?
You would not peck? I thank you for good will,
Believe, but leave that truth untested still.

Spring's an expansive time: yet I don't trust
March with its peck of dust,
Nor April with its rainbow-crowned brief showers,
Nor even May, whose flowers
One frost may wither thro' the sunless hours.

Perhaps some languid summer day,
When drowsy birds sing less and less,

And golden fruit is ripening to excess,
If there's not too much sun nor too much cloud,
And the warm wind is neither still nor loud,
Perhaps my secret I may say,
Or you may guess.

'No, Thank You, John'

I never said I loved you, John:
  Why will you teaze me day by day,
And wax a weariness to think upon
    With always 'do' and 'pray'?

You know I never loved you, John;
  No fault of mine made me your toast:
Why will you haunt me with a face as wan
    As shows an hour-old ghost?

I dare say Meg or Moll would take
  Pity upon you, if you'd ask:
And pray don't remain single for my sake
    Who can't perform that task.

I have no heart? – Perhaps I have not;
  But then you're mad to take offence
That I don't give you what I have not got:
    Use your own common sense.

Let bygones be bygones:
  Don't call me false, who owed not to be true:
I'd rather answer 'No' to fifty Johns
    Than answer 'Yes' to you.

Let's mar our pleasant days no more,
  Song-birds of passage, days of youth:
Catch at today, forget the days before:
    I'll wink at your untruth.

Let us strike hands as hearty friends;
   No more no less; and friendship's good:
Only don't keep in view ulterior ends,
    And points not understood

In open treaty. Rise above
   Quibbles and shuffling off and on:
Here's friendship for you if you like; but love, –
   No, thank you, John.

Without Her

What of her glass without her? The blank grey
　　There where the pool is blind of the moon's face.
　　Her dress without her? The tossed empty space
Of cloud-rack whence the moon has passed away
Her paths without her? Day's appointed sway
　　Usurped by desolate night. Her pillowed place
　　Without her? Tears, ah me! for love's good grace,
And cold forgetfulness of night or day.

What of the heart without her? Nay, poor heart,
　　Of thee what word remains ere speech be still?
　　A wayfarer by barren ways and chill,
Steep ways and weary, without her thou art,
Where the long cloud, the long wood's counterpart,
　　Sheds doubled darkness up the labouring hill.

Sudden Light

　　I have been here before,
　　　　But when or how I cannot tell:
　　I know the grass beyond the door,
　　　　The sweet keen smell,
The sighing sound, the lights around the shore.

　　You have been mine before, –
　　　　How long ago I may not know:
　　But just when at that swallow's soar
　　　　Your neck turned so,
Some veil did fall, – I knew it all of yore.

　　Then, now, – perchance again! . . .
　　　　O round mine eyes your tresses shake!

Shall we not lie as we have lain
    Thus for Love's sake,
And sleep, and wake, yet never break the chain?

The Orchard-Pit

Piled deep below the screening apple-branch
    They lie with bitter apples in their hands:
And some are only ancient bones that blanch,
And some had ships that last year's wind did launch,
    And some were yesterday the lords of lands.

In the soft dell, among the apple-trees,
    High up above the hidden pit she stands,
And there for ever sings, who gave to these,
That lie below, her magic hour of ease,
    And those her apples holden in their hands.

This in my dreams is shown me; and her hair
    Crosses my lips and draws my burning breath;
Her song spreads golden wings upon the air,
Life's eyes are gleaming from her forehead fair,
    And from her breasts the ravishing eyes of Death.

Men say to me that sleep hath many dreams,
    Yet I knew never but this dream alone:
There, from a dried-up channel, once the stream's,
The glen slopes up; even such in sleep it seems
    As to my waking sight the place well known.

    *

My love I call her, and she loves me well:
    But I love her as in the maelstrom's cup
The whirled stone loves the leaf inseparable
That clings to it round all the circling swell,
    And that the same last eddy swallows up.

Together

Splashing along the boggy woods all day,
And over brambled hedge and holding clay,
I shall not think of him:
But when the watery fields grow brown and dim,
And hounds have lost their fox, and horses tire,
I know that he'll be with me on my way
Home through the darkness to the evening fire.
He's jumped each stile along the glistening lanes;
His hand will be upon the mud-soaked reins;
Hearing the saddle creak,
He'll wonder if the frost will come next week.
I shall forget him in the morning light;
And while we gallop on he will not speak:
But at the stable-door he'll say good-night.

The Dug-Out

Why do you lie with your legs ungainly huddled,
And one arm bent across your sullen, cold,
Exhausted face? It hurts my heart to watch you,
Deep-shadow'd from the candle's guttering gold;
And you wonder why I shake you by the shoulder;
Drowsy, you mumble and sigh and turn your head . . .
You are too young to fall asleep for ever;
And when you sleep you remind me of the dead.

WILLIAM SHAKESPEARE 1564–1616

Sonnets

18

Shall I compare thee to a summer's day?
Thou art more lovely and more temperate.
Rough winds do shake the darling buds of May,
And summer's lease hath all too short a date.
Sometime too hot the eye of heaven shines,
And often is his gold complexion dimmed,
And every fair from fair some time declines,
By chance or nature's changing course untrimmed;
But thy eternal summer shall not fade
Nor lose possession of that fair thou ow'st,
Nor shall death brag thou wander'st in his shade
When in eternal lines to time thou grow'st.
 So long as men can breathe or eyes can see,
 So long lives this, and this gives life to thee.

20

A woman's face with nature's own hand painted
Hast thou, the master-mistress of my passion;
A woman's gentle heart, but not acquainted
With shifting change as is false women's fashion;
An eye more bright than theirs, less false in rolling,
Gilding the object whereupon it gazeth;
A man in hue, all hues in his controlling,
Which steals men's eyes and women's souls amazeth.
And for a woman wert thou first created,
Till nature as she wrought thee fell a-doting,
And by addition me of thee defeated
By adding one thing to my purpose nothing.

But since she pricked thee out for women's pleasure,
Mine be thy love and thy love's use their treasure.

27

Weary with toil I haste me to my bed,
The dear repose for limbs with travel tired;
But then begins a journey in my head
To work my mind when body's work's expired;
For then my thoughts, from far where I abide,
Intend a zealous pilgrimage to thee,
And keep my drooping eyelids open wide,
Looking on darkness which the blind do see:
Save that my soul's imaginary sight
Presents thy shadow to my sightless view,
Which like a jewel hung in ghastly night
Makes black night beauteous and her old face new.
  Lo, thus by day my limbs, by night my mind,
  For thee, and for myself, no quiet find.

29

When, in disgrace with fortune and men's eyes,
I all alone beweep my outcast state,
And trouble deaf heaven with my bootless cries,
And look upon myself and curse my fate,
Wishing me like to one more rich in hope,
Featured like him, like him with friends possessed,
Desiring this man's art and that man's scope,
With what I most enjoy contented least:
Yet in these thoughts myself almost despising,
Haply I think on thee, and then my state,
Like to the lark at break of day arising
From sullen earth, sings hymns at heaven's gate;
  For thy sweet love remembered such wealth brings
  That then I scorn to change my state with kings'.

34

Why didst thou promise such a beauteous day
And make me travel forth without my cloak,
To let base clouds o'ertake me in my way,
Hiding thy brav'ry in their rotten smoke?
'Tis not enough that through the cloud thou break
To dry the rain on my storm-beaten face,
For no man well of such a salve can speak
That heals the wound and cures not the disgrace.
Nor can thy shame give physic to my grief;
Though thou repent, yet I have still the loss.
Th'offender's sorrow lends but weak relief
To him that bears the strong offence's cross.
   Ah, but those tears are pearl which thy love sheds,
   And they are rich, and ransom all ill deeds.

35

No more be grieved at that which thou hast done:
Roses have thorns, and silver fountains mud.
Clouds and eclipses stain both moon and sun,
And loathsome canker lives in sweetest bud.
All men make faults, and even I in this,
Authorizing thy trespass with compare,
Myself corrupting salving thy amiss,
Excusing thy sins more than thy sins are;
For to thy sensual fault I bring in sense –
Thy adverse party is thy advocate –
And 'gainst myself a lawful plea commence.
Such civil war is in my love and hate
   That I an accessory needs must be
   To that sweet thief which sourly robs from me.

40

Take all my loves, my love, yea, take them all:
What hast thou then more than thou hadst before?

No love, my love, that thou mayst true love call –
All mine was thine before thou hadst this more.
Then if for my love thou my love receivest,
I cannot blame thee for my love thou usest;
But yet be blamed if thou this self deceivest
By wilful taste of what thyself refusest.
I do forgive thy robb'ry, gentle thief,
Although thou steal thee all my poverty;
And yet love knows it is a greater grief
To bear love's wrong than hate's known injury.
  Lascivious grace, in whom all ill well shows,
  Kill me with spites, yet we must not be foes.

42

That thou hast her, it is not all my grief,
And yet it may be said I loved her dearly;
That she hath thee is of my wailing chief,
A loss in love that touches me more nearly.
Loving offenders, thus I will excuse ye:
Thou dost love her because thou know'st I love her,
And for my sake even so doth she abuse me,
Suff'ring my friend for my sake to approve her.
If I lose thee, my loss is my love's gain,
And losing her, my friend hath found that loss:
Both find each other, and I lose both twain,
And both for my sake lay on me this cross.
  But here's the joy: my friend and I are one.
  Sweet flattery! Then she loves but me alone.

53

What is your substance, whereof are you made,
That millions of strange shadows on you tend?
Since every one hath, every one, one shade,
And you, but one, can every shadow lend.
Describe Adonis, and the counterfeit

Is poorly imitated after you.
On Helen's cheek all art of beauty set,
And you in Grecian tires are painted new.
Speak of the spring and foison of the year:
The one doth shadow of your beauty show,
The other as your bounty doth appear;
And you in every blessèd shape we know.
   In all external grace you have some part,
    But you like none, none you, for constant heart.

55

Not marble nor the gilded monuments
Of princes shall outlive this powerful rhyme,
But you shall shine more bright in these contents
Than unswept stone besmeared with sluttish time.
When wasteful war shall statues overturn,
And broils root out the work of masonry,
Nor Mars his sword nor war's quick fire shall burn
The living record of your memory.
'Gainst death and all oblivious enmity
Shall you pace forth; your praise shall still find room
Even in the eyes of all posterity
That wear this world out to the ending doom.
   So, till the judgement that yourself arise,
    You live in this, and dwell in lovers' eyes.

61

Is it thy will thy image should keep open
My heavy eyelids to the weary night?
Dost thou desire my slumbers should be broken
While shadows like to thee do mock my sight?
Is it thy spirit that thou send'st from thee
So far from home into my deeds to pry,
To find out shames and idle hours in me,
The scope and tenor of thy jealousy?

O no; thy love, though much, is not so great.
It is my love that keeps mine eye awake,
Mine own true love that doth my rest defeat,
To play the watchman ever for thy sake.
　　For thee watch I whilst thou dost wake elsewhere,
　　From me far off, with others all too near.

66

Tired with all these, for restful death I cry:
As, to behold desert a beggar born,
And needy nothing trimmed in jollity,
And purest faith unhappily forsworn,
And gilded honour shamefully misplaced,
And maiden virtue rudely strumpeted,
And right perfection wrongfully disgraced,
And strength by limping sway disablèd,
And art made tongue-tied by authority,
And folly, doctor-like, controlling skill,
And simple truth miscalled simplicity,
And captive good attending captain ill.
　　Tired with all these, from these would I be gone,
　　Save that to die I leave my love alone.

71

No longer mourn for me when I am dead
Than you shall hear the surly sullen bell
Give warning to the world that I am fled
From this vile world with vilest worms to dwell.
Nay, if you read this line, remember not
The hand that writ it; for I love you so
That I in your sweet thoughts would be forgot
If thinking on me then should make you woe.
O, if, I say, you look upon this verse
When I perhaps compounded am with clay,
Do not so much as my poor name rehearse,

But let your love even with my life decay,
 Lest the wise world should look into your moan
 And mock you with me after I am gone.

73

That time of year thou mayst in me behold
When yellow leaves, or none, or few, do hang
Upon those boughs which shake against the cold,
Bare ruined choirs where late the sweet birds sang.
In me thou seest the twilight of such day
As after sunset fadeth in the west,
Which by and by black night doth take away,
Death's second self, that seals up all in rest.
In me thou seest the glowing of such fire
That on the ashes of his youth doth lie
As the death-bed whereon it must expire,
Consumed with that which it was nourished by.
 This thou perceiv'st, which makes thy love more strong,
 To love that well which thou must leave ere long.

87

Farewell – thou art too dear for my possessing,
And like enough thou know'st thy estimate.
The charter of thy worth gives thee releasing;
My bonds in thee are all determinate.
For how do I hold thee but by thy granting,
And for that riches where is my deserving?
The cause of this fair gift in me is wanting,
And so my patent back again is swerving.
Thyself thou gav'st, thy own worth then not knowing,
Or me to whom thou gav'st it else mistaking;
So thy great gift, upon misprision growing,
Comes home again, on better judgement making.
 Thus have I had thee as a dream doth flatter:
 In sleep a king, but waking no such matter.

97

How like a winter hath my absence been
From thee, the pleasure of the fleeting year!
What freezings have I felt, what dark days seen,
What old December's bareness everywhere!
And yet this time removed was summer's time,
The teeming autumn big with rich increase,
Bearing the wanton burden of the prime
Like widowed wombs after their lords' decease.
Yet this abundant issue seemed to me
But hope of orphans and unfathered fruit,
For summer and his pleasures wait on thee,
And thou away, the very birds are mute;
   Or if they sing, 'tis with so dull a cheer
   That leaves look pale, dreading the winter's near.

116

Let me not to the marriage of true minds
Admit impediments. Love is not love
Which alters when it alteration finds,
Or bends with the remover to remove.
O no, it is an ever fixèd mark
That looks on tempests and is never shaken;
It is the star to every wand'ring barque,
Whose worth's unknown although his height be taken.
Love's not time's fool, though rosy lips and cheeks
Within his bending sickle's compass come;
Love alters not with his brief hours and weeks,
But bears it out even to the edge of doom.
   If this be error and upon me proved,
   I never writ, nor no man ever loved.

129

Th'expense of spirit in a waste of shame
Is lust in action; and till action, lust

Is perjured, murd'rous, bloody, full of blame,
Savage, extreme, rude, cruel, not to trust,
Enjoyed no sooner but despisèd straight,
Past reason hunted, and no sooner had
Past reason hated as a swallowed bait
On purpose laid to make the taker mad;
Mad in pursuit and in possession so,
Had, having, and in quest to have, extreme;
A bliss in proof and proved, a very woe;
Before, a joy proposed; behind, a dream.
    All this the world well knows, yet none knows well
    To shun the heaven that leads men to this hell.

144

Two loves I have, of comfort and despair,
Which like two spirits do suggest me still.
The better angel is a man right fair,
The worser spirit a woman coloured ill.
To win me soon to hell my female evil
Tempteth my better angel from my side,
And would corrupt my saint to be a devil,
Wooing his purity with her foul pride;
And whether that my angel be turned fiend
Suspect I may, yet not directly tell;
But being both from me, both to each friend,
I guess one angel in another's hell.
    Yet this shall I ne'er know, but live in doubt
    Till my bad angel fire my good one out.

151

Love is too young to know what conscience is,
Yet who knows not conscience is born of love?
Then, gentle cheater, urge not my amiss,
Lest guilty of my faults thy sweet self prove.
For, thou betraying me, I do betray

My nobler part to my gross body's treason.
My soul doth tell my body that he may
Triumph in love; flesh stays no farther reason,
But rising at thy name doth point out thee
As his triumphant prize. Proud of this pride,
He is contented thy poor drudge to be,
To stand in thy affairs, fall by thy side.
   No want of conscience hold it that I call
   Her 'love' for whose dear love I rise and fall.

A Hate-Song

A Hater he came and sat by a ditch,
   And he took an old cracked lute;
And he sang a song which was more of a screech
   'Gainst a woman that was a brute.

To ——

Music, when soft voices die,
Vibrates in the memory –
Odours, when sweet violets sicken,
Live within the sense they quicken.

Rose leaves, when the rose is dead,
Are heaped for the belovèd's bed;
And so thy thoughts, when thou art gone,
Love itself shall slumber on.

To ——

I

One word is too often profaned
   For me to profane it,
One feeling too falsely disdained
   For thee to disdain it;
One hope is too like despair
   For prudence to smother,
And pity from thee more dear
   Than that from another.

I can give not what men call love,
But wilt thou accept not
The worship the heart lifts above
And the Heavens reject not, –
The desire of the moth for the star,
Of the night for the morrow,
The devotion to something afar
From the sphere of our sorrow?

Song and Chorus

Here's to the maiden of Bashful fifteen
　　Here's to the Widow of Fifty
Here's to the flaunting, Extravagant Quean,
　　And here's to the House Wife that's thrifty.

　　　CHORUS
　　　Let the toast pass –
　　　Drink to the Lass –
I'll warrant She'll prove an Excuse for the Glass!

Here's to the Charmer whose Dimples we Prize!
　　Now to the Maid who has none Sir;
Here's to the Girl with a pair of blue Eyes,
　　And Here's to the Nymph with but one Sir!

　　　CHORUS
　　　Let the Toast pass etc.

Here's to the Maid with a Bosom of Snow,
　　Now to her that's as brown as a berry:
Here's to the Wife with a face full of Woe,
And now for the Damsel that's Merry.

　　　CHORUS
　　　Let the Toast pass etc.

For let 'Em be Clumsy or let 'Em be Slim
　　Young or Ancient, I care not a Feather:
– So fill a Pint Bumper Quite up to the Brim
　　– And let us E'en toast 'Em together!

　　　CHORUS
　　　Let the Toast pass etc.

ALL　Bravo. Bravo!

JAMES SHIRLEY 1596–1666

Good-night

Bid me no more good-night; because
   'Tis dark, must I away?
Love doth acknowledge no such laws,
   And Love 'tis I obey,
Which, blind, doth all your light despise,
     And hath no need of eyes
       When day is fled;
Besides, the sun, which you
Complain is gone, 'tis true,
      Is gone to bed:
    Oh, let us do so too.

'My true Love hath my heart, and I have his'

My true Love hath my heart, and I have his,
By just exchange one for the other given:
I hold his dear, and mine he cannot miss;
There never was a better bargain driven.
His heart in me keeps me and him in one,
My heart in him his thoughts and senses guides:
He loves my heart, for once it was his own;
I cherish his because in me it bides.
His heart his wound receivèd from my sight,
My heart was wounded with his wounded heart;
For as from me, on him his hurt did light,
So still methought in me his hurt did smart.
    Both, equal hurt, in this change sought our bliss:
    My true Love hath my heart, and I have his.

'Sleep, baby mine, desire; nurse beauty singeth'
To the tune of Basciami vita mia

Sleep, baby mine, desire; nurse beauty singeth;
Thy cries, O baby, set mine head on aching:
The babe cries: 'Way, thy love doth keep me waking.'

Lully, lully, my babe; hope cradle bringeth,
Unto my children alway good rest taking:
The babe cries: 'Way, thy love doth keep me waking.'

Since, baby mine, from me thy watching springeth;
Sleep then a little, pap content is making:
The babe cries: 'Nay, for that abide I waking.'

'Ring out your bells, let mourning shows be spread'

Ring out your bells, let mourning shows be spread,
    For love is dead:
        All love is dead, infected
        With plague of deep disdain,
        Worth as naught worth rejected,
        And faith fair scorn doth gain.
            From so ungrateful fancy,
            From such a female franzy,
            From them that use men thus:
            Good lord, deliver us.

Weep, neighbours, weep: do you not hear it said
    That love is dead?
        His death-bed peacock's folly,
        His winding-sheet is shame,
        His will false-seeming holy,
        His sole executor blame.
            From so ungrateful fancy,
            From such a female franzy,
            From them that use men thus:
            Good lord, deliver us.

Let dirge be sung, and trentals rightly read,
    For love is dead.
        Sir wrong his tomb ordaineth,
        My mistress' marble heart,
        Which epitaph containeth:
        'Her eyes were once his dart.'
            From so ungrateful fancy,
            From such a female franzy,
            From them that use men thus:
            Good lord, deliver us.

Alas, I lie: rage hath this error bred;
  Love is not dead.
    Love is not dead, but sleepeth
    In her unmatched mind,
    Where she his counsel keepeth
    Till due desert she find.
      Therefore from so vile fancy,
      To call such wit a franzy
      Who love can temper thus:
      Good lord, deliver us.

'Fly, fly, my friends, I have my death wound, fly'

Fly, fly, my friends, I have my death wound, fly;
See there that boy, that murth'ring boy I say,
Who like a thief hid in dark bush doth lie,
Till bloody bullet get him wrongful prey.
  So tyrant he no fitter place could spy,
Nor so fair level in so secret stay
As that sweet black which veils the heavn'ly eye;
There himself with his shot he close doth lay.
  Poor passenger, pass now thereby I did,
And stayed, pleased with the prospect of the place,
While that black hue from me the bad guest hid:
But straight I saw motions of lightning grace,
And then descried the glist'ring of his dart:
But ere I could fly thence, it pierced my heart.

W. D. SNODGRASS 1926–

Partial Eclipse

Last night's eclipse, 99 percent complete, seemed at times to be total because of light mists and low-hanging clouds.

RADIO NEWS REPORT

Once we'd packed up your clothes
   It was something to talk about:
The full moon, how it rose
   Red, went pale, then went out

As that slow shadow crossed –
   The way Time might erase
Its blackboard: one cheek lost,
   The eyes, most of the face

Hovering dim as a ghost,
   Or the dark print of some light
That seared the eyes, almost,
   Yet lives in the lids, clenched tight.

But still one brilliant sliver
   Stayed, worrying the eye,
Till even that would shiver,
   Go sick and the whole sky –

We wished it all blank, bereft.
   But no; the mists drifted on;
Something, one glint was left.
   Next morning you had gone.

A Friend

I walk into your house, a friend.
Your kids swarm up my steep hillsides
Or swing in my branches. Your boy rides
Me for his horsie; we pretend
Some troll threatens our lady fair.
I swing him squealing through the air
And down. Just what could I defend?

I tuck them in, sometimes, at night.
That's one secret we never tell.
Giggling in their dark room, they yell
They love me. Their father, home tonight,
Sees your girl curled up on my knee
And tells her 'git' – she's bothering me.
I nod; she'd better think he's right.

Once they're in bed, he calls you 'dear.'
The boob-tube shows some hokum on
Adultery and loss; we yawn
Over a stale joke book and beer
Till it's your bedtime. I must leave.
I watch that squat toad pluck your sleeve.
As always, you stand shining near

Your window. I stand, Prince of Lies
Who's seen bliss; now I can drive back
Home past wreck and car lot, past shack
Slum and steelmill reddening the skies,
Past drive-ins, the hot pits where our teens
Fingerfuck and that huge screen's
Images fill their vacant eyes.

Leaving the Motel

Outside, the last kids holler
Near the pool: they'll stay the night.
Pick up the towels; fold your collar
Out of sight.

Check: is the second bed
Unrumpled, as agreed?
Landlords have to think ahead
In case of need,

Too. Keep things straight: don't take
The matches, the wrong keyrings –
We've nowhere we could keep a keepsake –
Ashtrays, combs, things

That sooner or later others
Would accidentally find.
Check: take nothing of one another's
And leave behind

Your license number only,
Which they won't care to trace;
We've paid. Still, should such things get lonely,
Leave in their vase

An aspirin to preserve
Our lilacs, the wayside flowers
We've gathered and must leave to serve
A few more hours;

That's all. We can't tell when
We'll come back, can't press claims;
We would no doubt have other rooms then,
Or other names.

The Last Time

Three years ago, one last time, you forgot
Yourself and let your hand, all gentleness,
Move to my hair, then slip down to caress
My cheek, my neck. My breath failed me; I thought

It might all come back yet, believed you might
Turn back. You turned, then, once more to your own
Talk with that tall young man in whom you'd shown,
In front of all our friends, such clear delight

All afternoon. You recalled, then, the long
Love you had held for me was changed. You threw
Both arms around him, kissed him, and then you
Said you were ready and we went along.

Old Jewelry

This Gypsy bodice of old coins
    From seven countries, woven fast
So that a silver braidwork joins
    The years and places their tribe passed;

This crown-shaped belt, cast in Souflí –
    Jeweled, enameling on silver-gilt –
A trothplight, then that surety
    On which a family would be built;

This Roman fibula, intact
    From the fourth century though bent;
This Berber fibula, once blacked
    With layers of thick tar to prevent

Theft but that, scoured and polished, shone
    As luminous as it ever was;
This lapis, Persian, the unfading stone
    Gold-flecked and implicate with flaws;

Brass arm bands, rings, pins, bracelets, earrings –
  Something from nearly every place
We'd been. Once more to see these dear things
  Laid out for buyers in a glass showcase.

I'd known them, each one – weighed in hand,
  Rubbed, bargained, and then with my love,
Pinned each one on for her, to stand
  In fickle times for emblems of

What lasts – just as they must have once
  For someone long dead. Love that dies
Can still be wrung out for quick funds;
  No doubt someone would pay the price.

A Valediction

  Since his sharp sight has taught you
To think your own thoughts and to see
What cramped horizons my arms brought you,
  Turn then and go free,

  Unlimited, your own
Forever. Let your vision be
In your own interests; you've outgrown
  All need for tyranny.

  May his clear views save you
From those shrewd, undermining powers
That hold you close just to enslave you
  In some such love as ours.

  May this new love leave you
Your own being; may your bright rebirth
Prove treacherous, change then and deceive you
  Never on this earth.

Now that you've seen how mindless
Our long ties were, I pray you never
Find, all your life through, such a blindness
    As we two shared together.

My dark design's exposed
Since his tongue opened up your eyelids;
May no one ever lip them closed
    So cunningly as I did.

WILLIAM SOUTAR 1898–1943

The Tryst

O luely, luely, cam she in
And luely she lay doun:
I kent her be her caller lips
And her breists sae sma' and roun'.

A' thru the nicht we spak nae word
Nor sinder'd bane frae bane:
A' thru the nicht I heard her hert
Gang soundin' wi' my ain.

It was about the waukrife hour
When cocks begin to craw
That she smool'd saftly thru the mirk
Afore the day wud daw.

Sae luely, luely, cam she in
Sae luely was she gaen;
And wi' her a' my simmer days
Like they had never been.

Gray Room

Although you sit in a room that is gray,
Except for the silver
Of the straw-paper,
And pick
At your pale white gown;
Or lift one of the green beads
Of your necklace,
To let it fall;
Or gaze at your green fan
Printed with the red branches of a red willow;
Or, with one finger,
Move the leaf in the bowl –
The leaf that has fallen from the branches of the forsythia
Beside you . . .
What is all this?
I know how furiously your heart is beating.

Love's World

1

In each mans heart that doth begin
To Love, there's ever fram'd within
A little world, for so I found,
When first my passion reason drown'd.

2

Instead of *Earth* unto this frame,
I had a faith was still the same,
For to be right it doth behoove
It be as that, fixt and not move;

3

Yet as the Earth may sometime shake
(For winds shut up will cause a quake)
So, often jealousie, and fear,
Stolne into mine, cause tremblings there.

4

My *Flora* was my *Sun*, for as
One *Sun*, so but one *Flora* was:
All other faces borrowed hence
Their light and grace, as stars do thence.

5

My hopes I call my *Moon*; for they
Inconstant still, were at no stay;
But as my Sun inclin'd to me,
Or more or lesse were sure to be:

6

Sometimes it would be full, and then
Oh! too too soon decrease agen;
Eclip'st sometimes, that 't would so fall
There would appear no hope at all.

7

My thoughts 'cause infinite they be
Must be those many *Stars* we see;
Of which some wandred at their will,
But most on her were *fixed* still.

8

My burning flame and hot desire
Must be the *Element of Fire*,
Which hath as yet so secret been
That it as that was never seen:

9

No Kitching fire, nor eating flame,
But innocent, hot but in name;
A fire that's starv'd when fed, and gone
When too much fewel is laid on.

10

But as it plainly doth appear,
That fire subsists by being near
The Moons bright Orbe, so I beleeve
Ours doth, for hope keeps love alive.

11

My fancy was the *Ayre*, most free
And full of mutability,

Big with Chimera's, vapours here
Innumerable hatcht as there.

12

The *Sea*'s my mind, which calm would be
Were it from winds (my passions) free;
But out alas! no *Sea* I find
Is troubled like a Lovers mind.

13

Within it Rocks and Shallows be,
Despair and fond credulity.

14

But in this World it were good reason
We did distinguish Time and Season;
Her presence then did make the *Day*,
And *Night* shall come when shee's away.

15

Long absence in far distant place
Creates the *Winter*, and the space
She tarryed with me; well I might
Call it my *Summer* of delight.

16

Diversity of weather came
From what she did, and thence had name;
Sometimes sh'would smile, that made it fair;
And when she laught, the Sun shin'd clear.

17

Sometimes sh'would frown, and sometimes weep,
So Clouds and Rain their turns do keep;

Sometimes again sh'would be all ice,
Extreamly cold, extreamly nice.

18

But soft my Muse, the world is wide,
And all at once was not describe:
It may fall out some honest Lover
The rest hereafter will discover.

A Song to a Lute

Hast thou seen the Doun ith' air
    when wanton blasts have tost it;
Or the Ship on the Sea,
    when ruder winds have crost it?
Hast thou markt the Crocodiles weeping,
    or the Foxes sleeping?
Or hast view'd the Peacock in his pride,
    or the Dove by his Bride,
      when he courts for his leachery?
Oh so fickle, oh so vain, oh so false, so false is she!

The Miracle

If thou bee'st Ice, I do admire
How thou couldst set my heart on fire;
Or how thy fire could kindle me,
Thou being Ice, and not melt thee;
But even my flames, light at thy own,
Have hardned thee into a stone!
Wonder of Love, that canst fulfill,
Inverting nature thus, thy will;
Making ice another burn,
Whilst it self doth harder turn!

Against Fruition [I]

1

Stay here fond youth and ask no more, be wise,
Knowing too much long since lost Paradise;
The vertuous joyes thou hast, thou would'st should still
Last in their pride; and would'st not take it ill
If rudely from sweet dreams (and for a toy)
Th'wert wak't? he wakes himself that does enjoy.

2

Fruition adds no new wealth, but destroyes,
And while it pleases much the palate, cloyes;
Who thinks he shall be happyer for that,
As reasonably might hope he should grow fat
By eating to a Surfet: this once past,
What relishes? even kisses loose their tast.

3

Urge not 'tis necessary, alas! we know
The homeliest thing which mankind does is so;
The World is of a vast extent we see,
And must be peopled; Children then must be;
So must bread too; but since there are enough
Born to the drudgery, what need we plough?

4

Women enjoy'd (what s'ere before th'ave been)
Are like Romances read, or sights once seen:
Fruition's dull, and spoils the Play much more
Than if one read or knew the plot before;
'Tis expectation makes a blessing dear:
It were not heaven, if we knew what it were.

5

And as in Prospects we are there pleas'd most
Where somthing keeps the eye from being lost,
And leaves us room to guesse, so here restraint
Holds up delight, that with excess would faint.
They who know all the wealth they have, are poor,
Hee's onely rich that cannot tell his store.

Against Fruition [II]

Fye upon hearts that burn with mutual fire;
I hate two minds that breath but one desire;
Were I to curse th'unhallow'd sort of men,
I'de wish them to love, and be lov'd agen.
Love's a *Camelion*, that lives on meer ayre,
And surfets when it comes to grosser fare:
'Tis petty Jealousies, and little fears,
Hopes joyn'd with doubts, and joyes with *April* tears,
That crowns our Love with pleasures: these are gone
When once we come to full *Fruition*;
Like waking in a morning, when all night
Our fancy hath been fed with true delight.
Oh! what a stroke 'twould be! Sure I should die,
Should I but hear my mistresse once say, I.
That monster Expectation feeds too high
For any Woman e're to satisfie:
And no brave Spirit ever car'd for that
Which in Down-beds with ease he could come at.
Shee's but an honest whore that yeelds, although
She be as cold as ice, as pure as snow:
He that enjoys her hath no more to say
But keep us Fasting if you'l have us pray.
Then fairest Mistresse, hold the power you have,
By still denying what we still do crave:
In keeping us in hopes strange things to see
That never were, nor are, nor e're shall be.

Sonnet I

1

Do'st see how unregarded now
   that piece of beauty passes?
There was a time when I did vow
     to that alone;
   but mark the fate of faces:
That red and white works now no more on me
Then if it could not charm or I not see.

2

And yet the face continues good,
   and I have still desires,
Am still the self same flesh and blood,
     as apt to melt
   and suffer from those fires;
Oh! some kind power unriddle where it lies,
Whether my heart be faulty, or her eyes?

3

She every day her Man doth kill,
   and I as often die;
Neither her power then, nor my will
     can question'd be,
   what is the mystery?
Sure Beauties Empires, like to greater States
Have certain periods set, and hidden fates.

Sonnet II

1

Of thee (kind boy) I ask no red and white
    to make up my delight,
     no odd becomming graces,
Black eyes, or little know-not-whats, in faces;
Make me but mad enough, give me good store
Of Love, for her I Court,
               I ask no more,
'Tis love in love that makes the sport.

2

There's no such thing as that we beauty call,
    it is meer cousenage all;
     for though some long ago
Like't certain colours mingled so and so,
That doth not tie me now from chusing new;
If I a fancy take
          To black and blue,
That fancy doth it beauty make.

3

'Tis not the meat, but 'tis the appetite
    makes eating a delight,
     and if I like one dish
More then another, that a Pheasant is;
What in our watches, that in us is found,
So to the height and nick
          We up be wound,
No matter by what hand or trick.

3

Proceeded on with no lesse Art,
  My Tongue was Engineer:
I thought to undermine the heart
  By whispering in the ear.

4

When this did nothing, I brought down
  Great Canon-oaths, and shot
A thousand thousand to the Town,
  And still it yeelded not.

5

I then resolv'd to starve the place
  By cutting off all kisses,
Praysing and gazing on her face,
  And all such little blisses.

6

To draw her out, and from her strength,
  I drew all batteries in:
And brought my self to lie at length
  As if no siege had been.

7

When I had done what man could do,
  And thought the place mine owne,
The Enemy lay quiet too,
  And smil'd at all was done.

8

I sent to know from whence, and where,
  These hopes, and this relief?

A Spie inform'd, Honour was there,
   And did command in chief.

9

March, march, (quoth I) the word straight give,
   Lets lose no time, but leave her:
That Giant upon ayre will live,
   And hold it out for ever.

10

To such a place our Camp remove
   As will no siege abide;
I hate a fool that starves her Love
   Onely to feed her pride.

Farewell to Love

1

Well shadow'd Landskip, fare-ye-well:
How I have lov'd you, none can tell,
   At least so well
 As he that now hates more
 Then e're he lov'd before.

2

But my dear nothings, take your leave,
No longer must you me deceive,
   Since I perceive
 All the deceit, and know
 Whence the mistake did grow.

3

As he whose quicker eye doth trace
A false star shot to a mark't place,

Do's run apace,
And thinking it to catch,
A gelly up do's snatch:

4

So our dull souls, tasting delight
Far off, by sence, and appetite,
　　Think that is right
　And real good; when yet
　'Tis but the Counterfeit.

5

Oh! how I glory now! that I
Have made this new discovery!
　　Each wanton eye
　Enflam'd before: no more
　Will I encrease that score.

6

If I gaze now, 'tis but to see
What manner of deaths-head 'twill be,
　　When it is free
　From that fresh upper skin,
　The gazers Joy, and sin.

7

The Gum and glist'ning which with art
And studi'd method in each part
　　Hangs down the heart,
　Looks (just) as if, that day
　Snails there had crawl'd the *Hay*.

8

The Locks, that curl'd o're each eare be,
Hang like two Master-worms to me,

    That (as we see)
  Have tasted to the rest
  Two holes, where they lik't best.

9

A quick corse me-thinks I spy
In ev'ry woman; and mine eye,
    At passing by,
  Checks, and is troubled, just
  As if it rose from Dust.

10

They mortifie, not heighten me:
These of my sins the Glasses be:
    And here I see
  How I have lov'd before.
  And so I love no more.

In Brennoralt

Thy love is chaste, they tell thee so,
    But how young Souldier shalt thou know?
    Do by her,
    As by thy Sword,
    Take no friends word,
    But try her;
'Twill raise her Honor one step higher
Fame has her tryal at Loves bar,
    Deify'd *Venus* from a Star,
    Shoots her lustre;
    She had never been Goddess't,
    If *Mars* had been modest:
    Try and trust her.

Circumstance

Two children in two neighbour villages
Playing mad pranks along the heathy leas;
Two strangers meeting at a festival;
Two lovers whispering by an orchard wall;
Two lives bound fast in one with golden ease;
Two graves grass-green beside a gray church-tower,
Washed with still rains and daisy blossomèd;
Two children in one hamlet born and bred;
So runs the round of life from hour to hour.

'Break, break, break'

Break, break, break,
    On thy cold gray stones, O Sea!
And I would that my tongue could utter
    The thoughts that arise in me.

O well for the fisherman's boy,
    That he shouts with his sister at play!
O well for the sailor lad,
    That he sings in his boat on the bay!

And the stately ships go on
    To their haven under the hill;
But O for the touch of a vanished hand,
    And the sound of a voice that is still!

Break, break, break,
    At the foot of thy crags, O Sea!
But the tender grace of a day that is dead
    Will never come back to me.

'Come not, when I am dead'

Come not, when I am dead,
　To drop thy foolish tears upon my grave,
To trample round my fallen head,
　And vex the unhappy dust thou wouldst not save.
There let the wind sweep and the plover cry;
　　　But thou, go by.

Child, if it were thine error or thy crime
　I care no longer, being all unblest:
Wed whom thou wilt, but I am sick of Time,
　And I desire to rest.
Pass on, weak heart, and leave me where I lie:
　　　Go by, go by.

from The Princess

IV

'Tears, idle tears, I know not what they mean,
Tears from the depth of some divine despair
Rise in the heart, and gather to the eyes,
In looking on the happy Autumn-fields,
And thinking of the days that are no more.

'Fresh as the first beam glittering on a sail,
That brings our friends up from the underworld,
Sad as the last which reddens over one
That sinks with all we love below the verge;
So sad, so fresh, the days that are no more.

'Ah, sad and strange as in dark summer dawns
The earliest pipe of half-awakened birds
To dying ears, when unto dying eyes
The casement slowly grows a glimmering square;
So sad, so strange, the days that are no more.

'Dear as remembered kisses after death,
And sweet as those by hopeless fancy feigned
On lips that are for others; deep as love,
Deep as first love, and wild with all regret;
O Death in Life, the days that are no more.'

[VI/VII]

Ask me no more: the moon may draw the sea;
   The cloud may stoop from heaven and take the
     shape
   With fold to fold, of mountain or of cape;
But O too fond, when have I answered thee?
               Ask me no more.

Ask me no more: what answer should I give?
   I love not hollow cheek or faded eye:
   Yet, O my friend, I will not have thee die!
Ask me no more, lest I should bid thee live;
               Ask me no more.

Ask me no more: thy fate and mine are sealed:
   I strove against the stream and all in vain:
   Let the great river take me to the main:
No more, dear love, for at a touch I yield;
               Ask me no more.

VII

   Now sleeps the crimson petal, now the white;
Nor waves the cypress in the palace walk;
Nor winks the gold fin in the porphyry font:
The fire-fly wakens: waken thou with me.

   Now droops the milkwhite peacock like a ghost,
And like a ghost she glimmers on to me.
   Now lies the Earth all Danaë to the stars,
And all thy heart lies open unto me.

Now slides the silent meteor on, and leaves
A shining furrow, as thy thoughts in me.

Now folds the lily all her sweetness up,
And slips into the bosom of the lake:
So fold thyself, my dearest, thou, and slip
Into my bosom and be lost in me.

from In Memoriam A. H. H.

VII

Dark house, by which once more I stand
   Here in the long unlovely street,
   Doors, where my heart was used to beat
So quickly, waiting for a hand,

A hand that can be clasped no more –
   Behold me, for I cannot sleep,
   And like a guilty thing I creep
At earliest morning to the door.

He is not here; but far away
   The noise of life begins again,
   And ghastly through the drizzling rain
On the bald street breaks the blank day.

IX

Fair ship, that from the Italian shore
   Sailest the placid ocean-plains
   With my lost Arthur's loved remains,
Spread thy full wings, and waft him o'er.

So draw him home to those that mourn
   In vain; a favourable speed
   Ruffle thy mirrored mast, and lead
Through prosperous floods his holy urn.

All night no ruder air perplex
    Thy sliding keel, till Phosphor, bright
    As our pure love, through early light
Shall glimmer on the dewy decks.

Sphere all your lights around, above;
    Sleep, gentle heavens, before the prow;
    Sleep, gentle winds, as he sleeps now,
My friend, the brother of my love;

My Arthur, whom I shall not see
    Till all my widowed race be run;
    Dear as the mother to the son,
More than my brothers are to me.

x

I hear the noise about thy keel;
    I hear the bell struck in the night:
    I see the cabin-window bright;
I see the sailor at the wheel.

Thou bring'st the sailor to his wife,
    And travelled men from foreign lands;
    And letters unto trembling hands;
And, thy dark freight, a vanished life.

So bring him: we have idle dreams:
    This look of quiet flatters thus
    Our home-bred fancies: O to us,
The fools of habit, sweeter seems

To rest beneath the clover sod,
    That takes the sunshine and the rains,
    Or where the kneeling hamlet drains
The chalice of the grapes of God;

Than if with thee the roaring wells
    Should gulf him fathom-deep in brine;

And hands so often clasped in mine,
Should toss with tangle and with shells.

XI

Calm is the morn without a sound,
   Calm as to suit a calmer grief,
   And only through the faded leaf
The chestnut pattering to the ground;

Calm and deep peace on this high wold,
   And on these dews that drench the furze,
   And all the silvery gossamers
That twinkle into green and gold:

Calm and still light on yon great plain
   That sweeps with all its autumn bowers,
   And crowded farms and lessening towers,
To mingle with the bounding main:

Calm and deep peace in this wide air,
   These leaves that redden to the fall;
   And in my heart, if calm at all,
If any calm, a calm despair:

Calm on the seas, and silver sleep,
   And waves that sway themselves in rest,
   And dead calm in that noble breast
Which heaves but with the heaving deep.

XCV

By night we lingered on the lawn,
   For underfoot the herb was dry;
   And genial warmth; and o'er the sky
The silvery haze of summer drawn;

And calm that let the tapers burn
   Unwavering: not a cricket chirred:

The brook alone far-off was heard,
And on the board the fluttering urn:

And bats went round in fragrant skies,
    And wheeled or lit the filmy shapes
    That haunt the dusk, with ermine capes
And woolly breasts and beaded eyes;

While now we sang old songs that pealed
    From knoll to knoll, where, couched at ease,
    The white kine glimmered, and the trees
Laid their dark arms about the field.

But when those others, one by one,
    Withdrew themselves from me and night,
    And in the house light after light
Went out, and I was all alone,

A hunger seized my heart; I read
    Of that glad year which once had been,
    In those fallen leaves which kept their green,
The noble letters of the dead:

And strangely on the silence broke
    The silent-speaking words, and strange
    Was love's dumb cry defying change
To test his worth; and strangely spoke

The faith, the vigour, bold to dwell
    On doubts that drive the coward back,
    And keen through wordy snares to track
Suggestion to her inmost cell.

So word by word, and line by line,
    The dead man touched me from the past,
    And all at once it seemed at last
The living soul was flashed on mine,

And mine in this was wound, and whirled
    About empyreal heights of thought,

And came on that which is, and caught
The deep pulsations of the world,

Æonian music measuring out
   The steps of Time – the shocks of Chance –
   The blows of Death. At length my trance
Was cancelled, stricken through with doubt.

Vague words! but ah, how hard to frame
   In matter-moulded forms of speech,
   Or even for intellect to reach
Through memory that which I became:

Till now the doubtful dusk revealed
   The knolls once more where, couched at ease,
   The white kine glimmered, and the trees
Laid their dark arms about the field:

And sucked from out the distant gloom
   A breeze began to tremble o'er
   The large leaves of the sycamore,
And fluctuate all the still perfume,

And gathering freshlier overhead,
   Rocked the full-foliaged elms, and swung
   The heavy-folded rose, and flung
The lilies to and fro, and said

'The dawn, the dawn,' and died away;
   And East and West, without a breath,
   Mixt their dim lights, like life and death,
To broaden into boundless day.

from Maud

V

A voice by the cedar tree
In the meadow under the Hall!

She is singing an air that is known to me,
A passionate ballad gallant and gay,
A martial song like a trumpet's call!
Singing alone in the morning of life,
In the happy morning of life and of May,
Singing of men that in battle array,
Ready in heart and ready in hand,
March with banner and bugle and fife
To the death, for their native land.

Maud with her exquisite face,
And wild voice pealing up to the sunny sky,
And feet like sunny gems on an English green,
Maud in the light of her youth and her grace,
Singing of Death, and of Honour that cannot die,
Till I well could weep for a time so sordid and mean,
And myself so languid and base.

Silence, beautiful voice!
Be still, for you only trouble the mind
With a joy in which I cannot rejoice,
A glory I shall not find.
Still! I will hear you no more,
For your sweetness hardly leaves me a choice
But to move to the meadow and fall before
Her feet on the meadow grass, and adore,
Not her, who is neither courtly nor kind,
Not her, not her, but a voice.

VIII

She came to the village church,
And sat by a pillar alone;
An angel watching an urn
Wept over her, carved in stone;
And once, but once, she lifted her eyes,
And suddenly, sweetly, strangely blushed
To find they were met by my own;

And suddenly, sweetly, my heart beat stronger
And thicker, until I heard no longer
The snowy-banded, dilettante,
Delicate-handed priest intone;
And thought, is it pride, and mused and sighed
'No surely, now it cannot be pride.'

XXII

Come into the garden, Maud,
　For the black bat, night, has flown,
Come into the garden, Maud,
　I am here at the gate alone;
And the woodbine spices are wafted abroad,
　And the musk of the rose is blown.

For a breeze of morning moves,
　And the planet of Love is on high,
Beginning to faint in the light that she loves
　On a bed of daffodil sky,
To faint in the light of the sun she loves,
　To faint in his light, and to die.

All night have the roses heard
　The flute, violin, bassoon;
All night has the casement jessamine stirred
　To the dancers dancing in tune;
Till a silence fell with the waking bird,
　And a hush with the setting moon.

I said to the lily, 'There is but one
　With whom she has heart to be gay.
When will the dancers leave her alone?
　She is weary of dance and play.'
Now half to the setting moon are gone,
　And half to the rising day;
Low on the sand and loud on the stone
　The last wheel echoes away.

I said to the rose, 'The brief night goes
  In babble and revel and wine.
O young lord-lover, what sighs are those,
  For one that will never be thine?
But mine, but mine,' so I sware to the rose,
  'For ever and ever, mine.'

And the soul of the rose went into my blood,
  As the music clashed in the hall;
And long by the garden lake I stood,
  For I heard your rivulet fall
From the lake to the meadow and on to the wood,
  Our wood, that is dearer than all;

From the meadow your walks have left so sweet
  That whenever a March-wind sighs
He sets the jewel-print of your feet
  In violets blue as your eyes,
To the woody hollows in which we meet
  And the valleys of Paradise.

The slender acacia would not shake
  One long milk-bloom on the tree;
The white lake-blossom fell into the lake
  As the pimpernel dozed on the lea;
But the rose was awake all night for your sake,
  Knowing your promise to me;
The lilies and roses were all awake,
  They sighed for the dawn and thee.

Queen rose of the rosebud garden of girls,
  Come hither, the dances are done,
In gloss of satin and glimmer of pearls,
  Queen lily and rose in one;
Shine out, little head, sunning over with curls,
  To the flowers, and be their sun.

There has fallen a splendid tear
  From the passion-flower at the gate.
She is coming, my dove, my dear;
  She is coming, my life, my fate;
The red rose cries, 'She is near, she is near;'
  And the white rose weeps, 'She is late;'
The larkspur listens, 'I hear, I hear;'
  And the lily whispers, 'I wait.'

She is coming, my own, my sweet;
  Were it ever so airy a tread,
My heart would hear her and beat,
  Were it earth in an earthy bed;
My dust would hear her and beat,
  Had I lain for a century dead;
Would start and tremble under her feet,
  And blossom in purple and red.

EDWARD THOMAS 1878–1917

Lovers

The two men in the road were taken aback.
The lovers came out shading their eyes from the sun,
And never was white so white, or black so black,
As her cheeks and hair. 'There are more things than one
A man might turn into a wood for, Jack,'
Said George; Jack whispered: 'He has not got a gun.
It's a bit too much of a good thing, I say.
They are going the other road, look. And see her run.' –
She ran – 'What a thing it is, this picking may.'

'Go Now'

Like the touch of rain she was
On a man's flesh and hair and eyes
When the joy of walking thus
Has taken him by surprise:

With the love of the storm he burns,
He sings, he laughs, well I know how,
But forgets when he returns
As I shall not forget her 'Go now'.

Those two words shut a door
Between me and the blessed rain
That was never shut before
And will not open again.

The Execration

Enslaved by passions, swelled with pride,
In love with one whom all deride;
A carcase well, yet mind in pain,
Reduced to beg, but beg in vain;
To live reserved and free from blame,
And yet incur an evil fame:
Let this! this be the wretched fate
Of Rosalinda, whom I hate.

A New Litany, Occasioned by an Invitation to a Wedding

From marrying in haste, and repenting at leisure;
Not liking the person, yet liking his treasure:

Libera nos.

From a mind so disturbed that each look does reveal it;
From abhorring one's choice, and not sense to conceal it:

Libera nos.

From a husband to govern, and buy him his wit;
From a sullen, ill-natured and whimsical cit:

Libera nos.

ANTHONY THWAITE 1930–

Simple Poem

I shall make it simple so you understand.
Making it simple will make it clear for me.
When you have read it, take me by the hand
As children do, loving simplicity.

This is the simple poem I have made.
Tell me you understand. But when you do
Don't ask me in return if I have said
All that I meant, or whether it is true.

Romance

When I was but thirteen or so
  I went into a golden land,
Chimborazo, Cotopaxi
  Took me by the hand.

My father died, my brother too,
  They passed like fleeting dreams,
I stood where Popocatapetl
  In the sunlight gleams.

I dimly heard the master's voice
  And boys' far-off at play,
Chimborazo, Cotopaxi
  Had stolen me away.

I walked in a great golden dream
  To and fro from school –
Shining Popocatapetl
  The dusty streets did rule.

I walked home with a gold dark boy
  And never a word I'd say
Chimborazo, Cotopaxi
  Had taken my speech away:

I gazed entranced upon his face
  Fairer than any flower –
O shining Popocatapetl
  It was thy magic hour:

The houses, people, traffic seemed
  Thin fading dreams by day,
Chimborazo, Cotopaxi
  They had stolen my soul away.

Giraffe and Tree

Upon a dark ball spun in Time
   Stands a Giraffe beside a Tree:
Of what immortal stuff can that
   The fading picture be?

So, thought I, standing by my love
   Whose hair, a small black flag,
Broke on the universal air
   With proud and lovely brag:

It waved among the silent hills,
   A wind of shining ebony
In Time's bright glass, where mirrored clear
   Stood the Giraffe beside a Tree.

On a Girdle

That which her slender waist confined
Shall now my joyful temples bind;
No monarch but would give his crown,
His arms might do what this has done.

It was my heaven's extremest sphere,
The pale which held that lovely deer;
My joy, my grief, my hope, my love,
Did all within this circle move!

A narrow compass! and yet there
Dwelt all that's good, and all that's fair;
Give me but what this ribbon bound,
Take all the rest the sun goes round.

Song

Go, lovely rose!
Tell her that wastes her time and me
That now she knows,
When I resemble her to thee,
How sweet and fair she seems to be.

Tell her that's young,
And shuns to have her graces spied,
That hadst thou sprung
In deserts where no men abide,
Thou must have uncommended died.

Small is the worth
Of beauty from the light retired;
Bid her come forth,

Suffer herself to be desired,
    And not blush so to be admired.

    Then die, that she
The common fate of all things rare
    May read in thee;
How small a part of time they share,
    That are so wondrous sweet and fair!

SYLVIA TOWNSEND WARNER 1893–1978

'Drawing You, Heavy with Sleep . . .'

Drawing you, heavy with sleep to lie closer,
Staying your poppy head upon my shoulder,
It was as though I pulled the glide
Of a full river to my side.

Heavy with sleep and with sleep pliable
You rolled at a touch towards me. Your arm fell
Across me as a river throws
An arm of flood across meadows.

And as the careless water its mirroring sanction
Grants to him at the river's brim long stationed,
Long drowned in thought, that yet he lives
Since in that mirroring tide he moves,

Your body lying by mine to mine responded:
Your hair stirred on my mouth, my image was dandled
Deep in your sleep that flowed unstained
On from the image entertained.

Terminus

Wonderful was the long secret night you gave me, my Lover,
Palm to palm, breast to breast in the gloom. The faint red
lamp
Flushing with magical shadows the common-place room of
the inn,
With its dull impersonal furniture, kindled a mystic flame
In the heart of the swinging mirror, the glass that has seen
Faces innumerous and vague of the endless travelling
automata
Whirled down the ways of the world like dust-eddies swept
through a street,
Faces indifferent or weary, frowns of impatience or pain,
Smiles (if such there were ever) like your smile and mine
when they met
Here, in this self-same glass, while you helped me to loosen
my dress,
And the shadow-mouths melted to one, like sea-birds that
meet in a wave –
Such smiles, yes, such smiles the mirror perhaps has reflected;
And the low wide bed, as rutted and worn as a high-road,
The bed with its soot-sodden chintz, the grime of its brasses,
That has born the weight of fagged bodies, dust-stained,
averted in sleep,
The hurried, the restless, the aimless – perchance it has also
thrilled
With the pressure of bodies ecstatic, bodies like ours,
Seeking each other's souls in the depths of unfathomed
caresses,
And through the long windings of passion emerging again to
the stars . . .
Yes, all this through the room, the passive and featureless room,

Must have flowed with the rise and fall of the human
    unceasing current,
And lying there hushed in your arms, as the waves of rapture
    receded,
And far down the margin of being we heard the low beat of
    the soul,
I was glad as I thought of those others, the nameless, the
    many,
Who perhaps thus had lain and loved for an hour on the
    brink of the world,
Secret and fast in the heart of the whirlwind of travel,
The shaking and shrieking of trains, the night-long shudder
    of traffic;
Thus, like us they have lain and felt, breast to breast in the
    dark,
The fiery rain of possession descend on their limbs while
    outside
The black rain of midnight pelted the roof of the station;
And thus some woman like me waking alone before dawn,
While her lover slept, as I woke and heard the calm stir of
    your breathing,
Some woman has heard as I heard the farewell shriek of the
    trains
Crying good-bye to the city and staggering out into darkness,
And shaken at heart has thought: 'So must we forth in the
    darkness,
Sped down the fixed rail of habit by the hand of implacable
    fate –'
So shall we issue to life, and the rain, and the dull dark
    dawning;
You to the wide flair of cities, with windy garlands and
    shouting,
Carrying to populous places the freight of holiday throngs;
I, by waste land and stretches of low-skied marsh,
To a harbourless wind-bitten shore, where a dull town
    moulders and shrinks,

And its roofs fall in, and the sluggish feet of the hours
Are printed in grass in its streets; and between the featureless
    houses
Languid the town-folk glide to stare at the entering train,
The train from which no one descends; till one pale evening
    of winter,
When it halts on the edge of the town, see, the houses have
    turned into grave-stones,
The streets are the grassy paths between the low roofs of the
    dead;
And as the train glides in ghosts stand by the doors of the
    carriages;
And scarcely the difference is felt – yes, such is the life I
    return to . . . !
Thus may another have thought; thus, as I turned, may have
    turned
To the sleeping lips at her side, to drink, as I drank there,
    oblivion.

When I Heard at the Close of the Day

When I heard at the close of the day how my name had been
   receiv'd with plaudits in the capitol, still it was not a happy
   night for me that follow'd,
And else when I carous'd, or when my plans were
   accomplish'd, still I was not happy,
But the day when I rose at dawn from the bed of perfect
   health, refresh'd, singing, inhaling the ripe breath of
   autumn,
When I saw the full moon in the west grow pale and
   disappear in the morning light,
When I wander'd alone over the beach, and undressing
   bathed laughing with the cool waters, and saw the sun rise,
And when I thought how my dear friend my lover was on his
   way coming, O then I was happy,
O then each breath tasted sweeter, and all that day my food
   nourish'd me more, and the beautiful day pass'd well,
And the next came with equal joy, and with the next at
   evening came my friend,
And that night while all was still I heard the waters roll
   slowly continually up the shores,
I heard the hissing rustle of the liquid and sands as directed
   to me whispering to congratulate me,
For the one I love most lay sleeping by me under the same
   cover in the cool night,
In the stillness in the autumn moonbeams his face was
   inclined toward me,
And his arm lay lightly around my breast – and that night I
   was happy.

City of Orgies

City of orgies, walks and joys,
City whom that I have lived and sung in your midst will one
  day make you illustrous,
Not the pageants of you, not your shifting tableaus, your
  spectacles, repay me,
Not the interminable rows of your houses, nor the ships at
  the wharves,
Not the processions in the streets, nor the bright windows
  with goods in them,
Not to converse with learn'd persons, or bear my share in the
  soiree or feast;
Not those, but as I pass O Manhattan, your frequent and
  swift flash of eyes offering me love,
Offering response to my own – these repay me,
Lovers, continual lovers, only repay me.

Behold This Swarthy Face

Behold this swarthy face, these gray eyes,
This beard, the white wool unclipt upon my neck,
My brown hands and the silent manner of me without charm;
Yet comes one a Manhattanese and ever at parting kisses me
  lightly on the lips with robust love,
And I on the crossing of the street or on the ship's deck give a
  kiss in return,
We observe that salute of American comrades land and sea,
We are those two natural and nonchalant persons.

To a Stranger

Passing stranger! you do not know how longingly I look
  upon you,

You must be he I was seeking, or she I was seeking, (it comes
to me as of a dream,)
I have somewhere surely lived a life of joy with you,
All is recall'd as we flit by each other, fluid, affectionate,
chaste, matured,
You grew up with me, were a boy with me or a girl with
me,
I ate with you and slept with you, your body has become not
yours only nor left my body mine only,
You give me the pleasure of your eyes, face, flesh, as we pass,
you take of my beard, breast, hands, in return,
I am not to speak to you, I am to think of you when I sit
alone or wake at night alone,
I am to wait, I do not doubt I am to meet you again,
I am to see to it that I do not lose you.

We Two Boys Together Clinging

We two boys together clinging,
One the other never leaving,
Up and down the roads going, North and South excursions
making,
Power enjoying, elbows stretching, fingers clutching,
Arm'd and fearless, eating, drinking, sleeping, loving,
No law less than ourselves owning, sailing, soldiering,
thieving, threatening,
Misers, menials, priests alarming, air breathing, water
drinking, on the turf or the sea-beach dancing,
Cities wrenching, ease scorning, statutes mocking, feebleness
chasing,
Fulfilling our foray.

A Glimpse

A glimpse through an interstice caught,
Of a crowd of workmen and drivers in a bar-room around
  the stove late of a winter night, and I unremark'd seated in
  a corner,
Of a youth who loves me and whom I love, silently
  approaching and seating himself near, that he may hold me
  by the hand,
A long while amid the noises of coming and going, of
  drinking and oath and smutty jest,
There we two, content, happy in being together, speaking
  little, perhaps not a word.

Sometimes with One I Love

Sometimes with one I love I fill myself with rage for fear I
  effuse unreturn'd love,
But now I think there is no unreturn'd love, the pay is certain
  one way or another,
(I loved a certain person ardently and my love was not
  return'd,
Yet out of that I have written these songs.)

Among the Multitude

Among the men and women the multitude,
I perceive one picking me out by secret and divine signs,
Acknowledging none else, not parent, wife, husband, brother,
  child, any nearer than I am,
Some are baffled, but that one is not – that one knows me.

Ah lover and perfect equal,
I meant that you should discover me so by faint indirection,
And I when I meet you mean to discover you by the like in you.

O You Whom I Often and Silently Come

O you whom I often and silently come where you are that I
    may be with you,
As I walk by your side or sit near, or remain in the same
    room with you,
Little you know the subtle electric fire that for your sake is
    playing within me.

O Tan-Faced Prairie Boy

O tan-faced prairie-boy,
Before you came to camp came many a welcome gift,
Praises and presents came and nourishing food, till at last
    among the recruits,
You came, taciturn, with nothing to give – we but look'd on
    each other,
When lo! more than all the gifts of the world you gave me.

A Look

of 'How could you do this to me?'
was written all over her face,

which he knew very well would soon
be written all over his own.

Saturday Morning

Everyone who made love the night before
was walking around with flashing red lights
on top of their heads – a white-haired old gentleman,
a red-faced schoolboy, a pregnant woman
who smiled at me from across the street
and gave a little secret shrug,
as if the flashing red light on her head
was a small price to pay for what she knew.

Come On Up

I thought about you as crudely as possible,
till my hand reached for the phone
and I heard you laughing
on the other end of the line.

I'll never forget your rejection of my plan
to see a film at the weekend.
'I can't think that far ahead,' you explained.
'What are you doing right now?'

I wasn't doing anything of course.
I remember your voice on the entryphone:
'Come on up, Sunny Jim!'
I took the stairs two at a time.

Song

Love a woman? You're an ass!
    'Tis a most insipid passion
To choose out for your happiness
    The silliest part of God's creation.

Let the porter and the groom,
    Things designed for dirty slaves,
Drudge in fair Aurelia's womb
    To get supplies for age and graves.

Farewell, woman! I intend
    Henceforth every night to sit
With my lewd, well-natured friend,
    Drinking to engender wit.

Then give me health, wealth, mirth, and wine,
    And, if busy love entrenches,
There's a sweet, soft page of mine
    Does the trick worth forty wenches.

Against Constancy

Tell me no more of constancy,
    The frivolous pretense
Of cold age, narrow jealousy,
    Disease, and want of sense.

Let duller fools, on whom kind chance
    Some easy heart has thrown,
Despairing higher to advance,
    Be kind to one alone.

Old men and weak, whose idle flame
   Their own defects discovers,
Since changing can but spread their shame,
   Ought to be constant lovers.

But we, whose hearts do justly swell
   With no vainglorious pride,
Who know how we in love excel,
   Long to be often tried.

Then bring my bath, and strew my bed,
   As each kind night returns;
I'll change a mistress till I'm dead –
   And fate change me to worms.

The Disabled Debauchee

As some brave admiral, in former war
   Deprived of force, but pressed with courage still,
Two rival fleets appearing from afar,
   Crawls to the top of an adjacent hill;

From whence, with thoughts full of concern, he views
   The wise and daring conduct of the fight,
Whilst each bold action to his mind renews
   His present glory and his past delight;

From his fierce eyes flashes of fire he throws,
   As from black clouds when lightning breaks away;
Transported, thinks himself amidst the foes,
   And absent, yet enjoys the bloody day;

So, when my days of impotence approach,
   And I'm by pox and wine's unlucky chance
Forced from the pleasing billows of debauch
   On the dull shore of lazy temperance,

My pains at least some respite shall afford
　　While I behold the battles you maintain
When fleets of glasses sail about the board,
　　From whose broadsides volleys of wit shall rain.

Nor let the sight of honorable scars,
　　Which my too forward valor did procure,
Frighten new-listed soldiers from the wars:
　　Past joys have more than paid what I endure.

Should any youth (worth being drunk) prove nice,
　　And from his fair inviter meanly shrink,
'Twill please the ghost of my departed vice
　　If, at my counsel, he repent and drink.

Or should some cold-complexioned sot forbid,
　　With his dull morals, our bold night-alarms,
I'll fire his blood by telling what I did
　　When I was strong and able to bear arms.

I'll tell of whores attacked, their lords at home;
　　Bawds' quarters beaten up, and fortress won;
Windows demolished, watches overcome;
　　And handsome ills by my contrivance done.

Nor shall our love-fits, Chloris, be forgot,
　　When each the well-looked linkboy strove t' enjoy,
And the best kiss was the deciding lot
　　Whether the boy fucked you, or I the boy.

With tales like these I will such thoughts inspire
　　As to important mischief shall incline:
I'll make him long some ancient church to fire,
　　And fear no lewdness he's called to by wine.

Thus, statesmanlike, I'll saucily impose,
　　And safe from action, valiantly advise;
Sheltered in impotence, urge you to blows,
　　And being good for nothing else, be wise.

WILLIAM WORDSWORTH 1770–1850

'A slumber did my spirit seal'

A slumber did my spirit seal;
  I had no human fears:
She seemed a thing that could not feel
  The touch of earthly years.

No motion has she now, no force;
  She neither hears nor sees;
Rolled round in earth's diurnal course,
  With rocks, and stones, and trees.

'She dwelt among the untrodden ways'

She dwelt among the untrodden ways
  Beside the springs of Dove,
A Maid whom there were none to praise
  And very few to love:

A violet by a mossy stone
  Half hidden from the eye!
– Fair as a star, when only one
  Is shining in the sky.

She lived unknown, and few could know
  When Lucy ceased to be;
But she is in her grave, and, oh,
  The difference to me!

'Strange fits of passion have I known'

Strange fits of passion have I known:
And I will dare to tell,
But in the Lover's ear alone,
What once to me befell.

When she I loved looked every day
Fresh as a rose in June,
I to her cottage bent my way,
Beneath an evening moon.

Upon the moon I fixed my eye,
All over the wide lea;
With quickening pace my horse drew nigh
Those paths so dear to me.

And now we reached the orchard-plot;
And, as we climbed the hill,
The sinking moon to Lucy's cot
Came near, and nearer still.

In one of those sweet dreams I slept,
Kind Nature's gentlest boon!
And all the while my eyes I kept
On the descending moon.

My horse moved on; hoof after hoof
He raised, and never stopped:
When down behind the cottage roof,
At once, the bright moon dropped.

What fond and wayward thoughts will slide
Into a Lover's head!
'O mercy!' to myself I cried,
'If Lucy should be dead!'

'I travelled among unknown men'

I travelled among unknown men,
   In lands beyond the sea;
Nor, England! did I know till then
   What love I bore to thee.

'Tis past, that melancholy dream!
   Nor will I quit thy shore
A second time; for still I seem
   To love thee more and more.

Among thy mountains did I feel
   The joy of my desire;
And she I cherished turned her wheel
   Beside an English fire.

Thy mornings showed, thy nights concealed,
   The bowers where Lucy played;
And thine too is the last green field
   That Lucy's eyes surveyed.

Louisa

After Accompanying Her on a Mountain Excursion

I met Louisa in the shade,
And, having seen that lovely Maid,
Why should I fear to say
That, nymph-like, she is fleet and strong,
And down the rocks can leap along
Like rivulets in May?

And she hath smiles to earth unknown;
Smiles, that with motion of their own
Do spread, and sink, and rise;
That come and go with endless play,

And ever, as they pass away,
Are hidden in her eyes.

She loves her fire, her cottage-home;
Yet o'er the moorland will she roam
In weather rough and bleak;
And, when against the wind she strains,
Oh! might I kiss the mountain rains
That sparkle on her cheek.

Take all that's mine 'beneath the moon,'
If I with her but half a noon
May sit beneath the walls
Of some old cave, or mossy nook,
When up she winds along the brook
To hunt the waterfalls.

'Surprised by joy – impatient as the Wind'

Surprised by joy – impatient as the Wind
I turned to share the transport – Oh! with whom
But Thee, deep buried in the silent tomb,
That spot which no vicissitude can find?
Love, faithful love, recalled thee to my mind –
But how could I forget thee? Through what power,
Even for the least division of an hour,
Have I been so beguiled as to be blind
To my most grievous loss! – That thought's return
Was the worst pang that sorrow ever bore,
Save one, one only, when I stood forlorn,
Knowing my heart's best treasure was no more;
That neither present time, nor years unborn
Could to my sight that heavenly face restore.

'They flee from me that sometime did me seek'

They flee from me that sometime did me seek
With naked foot stalking in my chamber.
I have seen them gentle, tame, and meek
That now are wild and do not remember
That sometime they put themself in danger
To take bread at my hand; and now they range
Busily seeking with a continual change.

Thanked be fortune it hath been otherwise
Twenty times better, but once in special,
In thin array after a pleasant guise,
When her loose gown from her shoulders did fall
And she me caught in her arms long and small,
Therewithal sweetly did me kiss
And softly said, 'Dear heart, how like you this?'

It was no dream: I lay broad waking.
But all is turned thorough my gentleness
Into a strange fashion of forsaking.
And I have leave to go of her goodness
And she also to use newfangleness.
But since that I so kindly am served
I would fain know what she hath deserved.

'Blame not my lute for he must sound'

Blame not my lute for he must sound
Of this or that as liketh me.
For lack of wit the lute is bound
To give such tunes as pleaseth me.
Though my songs be somewhat strange

And speaks such words as touch thy change
   Blame not my lute.

My lute, alas, doth not offend
Though that perforce he must agree
To sound such tunes as I intend
To sing to them that heareth me.
Then though my songs be somewhat plain
And toucheth some that use to feign
   Blame not my lute.

My lute and strings may not deny
But as I strike they must obey.
Break not them then so wrongfully
But wreak thyself some wiser way.
And though the songs which I indite
Do quit thy change with rightful spite
   Blame not my lute.

Spite asketh spite and changing change
And falsed faith must needs be known.
The faults so great, the case so strange
Of right it must abroad be blown.
Then since that by thine own desert
My songs do tell how true thou art
   Blame not my lute.

Blame but thyself that hast misdone
And well deserved to have blame.
Change thou thy way so evil begun
And then my lute shall sound that same.
But if till then my fingers play
By thy desert their wonted way
   Blame not my lute.

Farewell, unknown, for though thou break
My strings in spite with great disdain
Yet have I found out for thy sake

Strings for to string my lute again.
And if perchance this foolish rhyme
Do make thee blush at any time
   Blame not my lute.

'My lute, awake! Perform the last'

My lute, awake! Perform the last
Labour that thou and I shall waste,
And end that I have now begun;
For when this song is sung and past,
My lute, be still for I have done.

As to be heard where ear is none,
As lead to grave in marble stone,
My song may pierce her heart as soon.
Should we then sigh or sing or moan?
No, no, my lute, for I have done.

The rocks do not so cruelly
Repulse the waves continually
As she my suit and affection,
So that I am past remedy,
Whereby my lute and I have done.

Proud of the spoil that thou hast got
Of simple hearts thorough Love's shot
By whom, unkind, thou hast them won,
Think not he hath his bow forgot
Although my lute and I have done.

Vengeance shall fall on thy disdain
That makest but game on earnest pain.
Think not alone under the sun
Unquit to cause thy lovers plain
Although my lute and I have done.

May chance thee lie withered and old
The winter nights that are so cold,
Plaining in vain unto the moon.
Thy wishes then dare not be told.
Care then who list for I have done.

And then may chance thee to repent
The time that thou hast lost and spent
To cause thy lovers sigh and swoon.
Then shalt thou know beauty but lent
And wish and want as I have done.

Now cease, my lute. This is the last
Labour that thou and I shall waste
And ended is that we begun.
Now is this song both sung and past.
My lute, be still, for I have done.

'Is it possible'

Is it possible
   That so high debate,
So sharp, so sore, and of such rate,
Should end so soon and was begun so late?
   Is it possible?

   Is it possible
   So cruel intent,
So hasty heat and so soon spent,
From love to hate and thence for to relent?
   Is it possible?

   Is it possible
   That any may find
Within one heart so diverse mind
   To change or turn as weather and wind?
   Is it possible?

Is it possible
To spy it in an eye
That turns as oft as chance on die?
The truth whereof can any try?
Is it possible?

It is possible
For to turn so oft,
To bring that lowest that was most aloft
And to fall highest yet to light soft.
It is possible.

All is possible
Whoso list believe.
Trust therefore first and after preve,
As men wed ladies by licence and leave,
All is possible.

To an Isle in the Water

Shy one, shy one,
Shy one of my heart,
She moves in the firelight
Pensively apart.

She carries in the dishes,
And lays them in a row.
To an isle in the water
With her would I go.

She carries in the candles,
And lights the curtained room,
Shy in the doorway
And shy in the gloom;

And shy as a rabbit,
Helpful and shy.
To an isle in the water
With her would I fly.

Down by the Salley Gardens

Down by the salley gardens my love and I did meet;
She passed the salley gardens with little snow-white feet.
She bid me take love easy, as the leaves grow on the tree;
But I, being young and foolish, with her would not agree.

In a field by the river my love and I did stand,
And on my leaning shoulder she laid her snow-white hand.
She bid me take life easy, as the grass grows on the weirs;
But I was young and foolish, and now am full of tears.

When You Are Old

When you are old and grey and full of sleep,
And nodding by the fire, take down this book,
And slowly read, and dream of the soft look
Your eyes had once, and of their shadows deep;

How many loved your moments of glad grace,
And loved your beauty with love false or true,
But one man loved the pilgrim soul in you,
And loved the sorrows of your changing face;

And bending down beside the glowing bars,
Murmur, a little sadly, how Love fled
And paced upon the mountains overhead
And hid his face amid a crowd of stars.

The Fish

Although you hide in the ebb and flow
Of the pale tide when the moon has set,
The people of coming days will know
About the casting out of my net,
And how you have leaped times out of mind
Over the little silver cords,
And think that you were hard and unkind,
And blame you with many bitter words.

The Song of Wandering Aengus

I went out to the hazel wood,
Because a fire was in my head,
And cut and peeled a hazel wand,
And hooked a berry to a thread;
And when white moths were on the wing,

And moth-like stars were flickering out,
I dropped the berry in a stream
And caught a little silver trout.

When I had laid it on the floor
I went to blow the fire aflame,
But something rustled on the floor,
And some one called me by my names
It had become a glimmering girl
With apple blossom in her hair
Who called me by my name and ran
And faded through the brightening air.

Though I am old with wandering
Through hollow lands and hilly lands,
I will find out where she has gone,
And kiss her lips and take her hands;
And walk among long dappled grass,
And pluck till time and times are done
The silver apples of the moon,
The golden apples of the sun.

The Heart of the Woman

O what to me the little room
That was brimmed up with prayer and rest;
He bade me out into the gloom,
And my breast lies upon his breast.

O what to me my mother's care,
The house where I was safe and warm;
The shadowy blossom of my hair
Will hide us from the bitter storm.

O hiding hair and dewy eyes,
I am no more with life and death,

My heart upon his warm heart lies,
My breath is mixed into his breath.

The Lover Mourns for the Loss of Love

Pale brows, still hands and dim hair,
I had a beautiful friend
And dreamed that the old despair
Would end in love in the end:
She looked in my heart one day
And saw your image was there;
She has gone weeping away.

He Wishes for the Cloths of Heaven

Had I the heavens' embroidered cloths,
Enwrought with golden and silver light,
The blue and the dim and the dark cloths
Of night and light and the half-light,
I would spread the cloths under your feet:
But I, being poor, have only my dreams;
I have spread my dreams under your feet;
Tread softly because you tread on my dreams.

O Do Not Love Too Long

Sweetheart, do not love too long:
I loved long and long,
And grew to be out of fashion
Like an old song.

All through the years of our youth
Neither could have known

Their own thought from the other's,
We were so much at one.

But O, in a minute she changed –
O do not love too long,
Or you will grow out of fashion
Like an old song.

A Woman Homer Sung

If any man drew near
When I was young,
I thought, 'He holds her dear,'
And shook with hate and fear.
But O! 'twas bitter wrong
If he could pass her by
With an indifferent eye.

Whereon I wrote and wrought,
And now, being grey,
I dream that I have brought
To such a pitch my thought
That coming time can say,
'He shadowed in a glass
What thing her body was.'

For she had fiery blood
When I was young,
And trod so sweetly proud
As 'twere upon a cloud.
A woman Homer sung,
That life and letters seem
But an heroic dream.

No Second Troy

Why should I blame her that she filled my days
With misery, or that she would of late
Have taught to ignorant men most violent ways,
Or hurled the little streets upon the great,
Had they but courage equal to desire?
What could have made her peaceful with a mind
That nobleness made simple as a fire,
With beauty like a tightened bow, a kind
That is not natural in an age like this,
Being high and solitary and most stern?
Why, what could she have done, being what she is?
Was there another Troy for her to burn?

A Drinking Song

Wine comes in at the mouth
And love comes in at the eye;
That's all we shall know for truth
Before we grow old and die.
I lift the glass to my mouth,
I look at you, and I sigh.

To a Young Girl

My dear, my dear, I know
More than another
What makes your heart beat so;
Not even your own mother
Can know it as I know,
Who broke my heart for her
When the wild thought,
That she denies

[428]

And has forgot,
Set all her blood astir
And glittered in her eyes.

After Long Silence

Speech after long silence; it is right,
All other lovers being estranged or dead,
Unfriendly lamplight hid under its shade,
The curtains drawn upon unfriendly night,
That we descant and yet again descant
Upon the supreme theme of Art and Song:
Bodily decrepitude is wisdom; young
We loved each other and were ignorant.

A Last Confession

What lively lad most pleasured me
Of all that with me lay?
I answer that I gave my soul
And loved in misery,
But had great pleasure with a lad
That I loved bodily.

Flinging from his arms I laughed
To think his passion such
He fancied that I gave a soul
Did but our bodies touch,
And laughed upon his breast to think
Beast gave beast as much.

I gave what other women gave
That stepped out of their clothes,
But when this soul, its body off,
Naked to naked goes,

He it has found shall find therein
What none other knows,

And give his own and take his own
And rule in his own right;
And though it loved in misery
Close and cling so tight,
There's not a bird of day that dare
Extinguish that delight.

The Lover's Song

Bird sighs for the air,
Thought for I know not where,
For the womb the seed sighs.
Now sinks the same rest
On mind, on nest,
On straining thighs.

Politics

'In our time the destiny of man presents its meaning in political terms.' THOMAS MANN

How can I, that girl standing there,
My attention fix
On Roman or on Russian
Or on Spanish politics?
Yet here's a travelled man that knows
What he talks about,
And there's a politician
That has read and thought,
And maybe what they say is true
Of war and war's alarms,
But O that I were young again
And held her in my arms!

ACKNOWLEDGEMENTS

The publishers gratefully acknowledge permission to reprint copyright material in this book as follows:

FLEUR ADCOCK: 'Coupling', 'Incident', 'Happy Ending', 'Accidental', 'Send-off', *Poems 1960-2000* (Bloodaxe Books, 2000). KINGSLEY AMIS: 'An Ever-Fixed Mark', *Collected Poems* (Penguin Books), reproduced by permission of Jonathan Clowes Ltd. SIMON ARMITAGE: 'Somewhere Along the Line', *Zoom!* (Bloodaxe Books, 1989). W. H. AUDEN: 'You were a great Cunarder, I', 'Seen when nights are silent', 'As I Walked Out One Evening', 'O lurcher-loving collier, black as night', 'Dear, though the night is gone', 'Underneath an abject willow', 'Stop all the clocks, cut off the telephone', 'Some say that love's a little boy', 'Lullaby', 'Heavy Date', 'Law Like Love', 'Lady Weeping at the Crossroads', 'The More Loving One', *Collected Poems* (Faber & Faber, 1976). HILAIRE BELLOC: 'Juliet', Harcourt Trade Publishers and Peters Fraser and Dunlop Group Ltd, from *Complete Verse*. JOHN BETJEMAN: 'Pot Pourri from a Surrey Garden', 'Myfanwy', 'A Subaltern's Love-Song', 'In a Bath Teashop', 'Indoor Games near Newbury', 'The Licorice Fields at Pontefract', © John Murray (Publishers). ELIZABETH BISHOP: *from* 'Songs for a Coloured Singer', 'Insomnia', 'Argument', 'The Shampoo', 'It is Marvellous', 'Close, Close All Night', 'Breakfast Song', © Farrar, Straus & Giroux. GEORGE MACKAY BROWN: 'Fiddler's Song', *The Collected Poems of George Mackay Brown*, John Murray (Publishers), 2005. PADRAIC COLUM: 'She Moved Through the Fair', *The Poet's Circus: The Collected Poems of Ireland* (Dolman Press/Oxford University Press, 1960). WENDY COPE: 'My Lover', *Making Cocoa for Kingsley Amis* (Faber & Faber, 1986), 'Flowers', 'Defining the Problem', 'The Aerial', 'The Orange', 'As Sweet, *Serious Concerns* (Faber & Faber, 1992). NOEL COWARD: 'I am No Good at Love', 'Any Little Fish', 'Mad About the Boy', 'Let's Do it', by permission of Alan Brodie Representation. CAROL ANN DUFFY: 'Oppenheimer's Cup and Saucer', © Anvil Press. DOUGLAS DUNN: 'Re-Reading Katherine Mansfield's *Bliss and Other Stories*', *Elegies* (Faber & Faber, 1985). T. S. ELIOT: 'The Love Song of J. Alfred Prufrock', 'Portrait of a Lady', 'La Figlia Che Piange', *Collected Poems 1909–1962* (Faber & Faber, 1963). JAMES FENTON: 'Out of

INDEX